THE EIGHTEENTH-CENTURY FRENCH NOVEL
TECHNIQUES OF ILLUSION

TO
PATIENCE WEBB

The Eighteenth-Century French Novel

TECHNIQUES OF ILLUSION

by

VIVIENNE MYLNE

CAMBRIDGE UNIVERSITY PRESS

Cambridge

London   New York   New Rochelle

Melbourne   Sydney

Published by the Press Syndicate of the University of Cambridge
The Pitt Building, Trumpington Street, Cambridge CB2 1RP
32 East 57th Street, New York, NY 10022, USA
296 Beaconsfield Parade, Middle Park, Melbourne 3206, Australia

First published by Manchester University Press
and Barnes & Noble 1965
Second edition published by the Cambridge University Press 1981

Printed in Great Britain at the University Press, Cambridge

Library of Congress catalogue card number: 81–3911

British Library Cataloguing in Publication Data
Mylne, Vivienne
The eighteenth-century French novel. – 2nd ed.
1. French literature – History and criticism – 18th century
I. Title
809.3′3   PQ261
ISBN 0 521 23864 1 hard covers
ISBN 0 521 28266 7 paperback

Contents

Preface

IN this book I have set out to consider the development of the novel in France during the course of the eighteenth century. I have concentrated not on the study of themes or subject-matter, or on trends of thought and feeling, but on the novelists' methods and literary techniques. This approach seems to me justifiable because a great deal of criticism has hitherto been concerned with the traits which distinguish the eighteenth-century novel from its predecessors, but relatively little attention has been paid to the precise ways in which these differences appeared and spread.

As its sub-title implies, this is chiefly a study of writers who were concerned with painting what purported to be a 'true' picture of life. Such a choice inevitably rules out certain types of eighteenth-century fiction, including fairy-tales, Oriental fantasies and the vast majority of *contes philosophiques*. This means that there will be no detailed discussion in these pages of works such as the fictional writings of Voltaire.

In preparing this work I have assumed that readers will already possess some knowledge of most of the novels dealt with. For this reason, descriptive accounts of plot and characters are provided only in the case of works which are now neglected or difficult to obtain. The standard novels are all available in the *Classiques Garnier* series, for the most part in recent editions with a useful critical apparatus. I have therefore used these editions for purposes of quotation and reference. (When quoting from other seventeenth- and eighteenth-century works I have modernized the spelling unless a modern critical edition is available; in this case I have observed the practice of the editor.)

Since the Garnier editions also contain bibliographies indicating the major critical works, I have not attempted to provide a complete bibliography of the subject. Instead I have listed only those works on which I have drawn directly. The field of study is a vast one, and I am of course deeply indebted to the many scholars and critics who have written on the various authors here chosen for discussion.

In the course of writing I have received invaluable help from a number of friends. These include my colleagues in the Department of French at the University College of Swansea, in particular Professor R. C. Knight, who read the script as it progressed; and also Mrs Janet Osborne, Mr George Watson and Mr David Welch. Such errors as remain are of course entirely my own.

My thanks are also due to the editors and publishers of two periodicals, *Renaissance and Modern Studies* and *French Studies*, for allowing me to use, in Chapters I and IV respectively, material which originally appeared in their pages.

V. M.

Swansea
1964

NOTE TO THE SECOND EDITION

In this edition the central argument of the book remains unaltered, since I still consider it to be valid; and I have not indulged in minor changes of style or phraseology – even though there are passages which I would now express differently. The alterations that have been made involve matters of fact, chiefly relating to statistics which have only recently become available, together with a few questions of detail on which I have changed my mind, such as Crébillon's literary style and the problems of the narrator's knowledge in *La Religieuse*. The Conclusion has also been amplified. The new 'Post-script' deals with developments in research during the past twenty years; and a Supplement to the Bibliography lists some of the recent major contributions to the subject.

V. M.

Canterbury
1980

I

Prolegomena, Theory and Background

Ut pictura poesis: there was a time when it was a common-place of literary theory that poetry, and literature in general, should 'paint' the world of human activities and feelings for the reader. The writer's work is nowadays more often discussed in terms of expression, imagination, import or symbolism, concepts which have to some extent replaced the simple notion of portrayal. However, there may still be something to gain from taking up the analogies and assumptions of earlier times, and studying the technique of representation in literature, just as art critics and historians have traced its progress in pictures.

Now a major aspect of the history of European painting from the fourteenth to the mid-nineteenth century is the constant struggle to achieve more accurate and convincing representations of the visible world, and to give the spectator the illusion that he is looking at a 'real' scene. Certain artists and certain discoveries are outstanding in this long campaign, to mention only the obvious example of Giotto, with his portrayal of figures in depth. Nowadays such interests are often considered as 'purely technical' or even 'merely technical'. But to those who judged pictures partly or largely on their supposed accuracy in representation, the working out of, for instance, the correct principles of perspective signified a real discovery in the visual arts. Such a discovery also meant that later artists could build on this foundation of acquired knowledge and aspire to produce even better works.

It is now recognized that representational accuracy may be an irrelevant criterion of judgment, especially in cases where the artist himself worked with other aims and assumptions. But where successive generations of artists have aimed—with a more or less explicit avowal of their purpose—at creating 'true'

pictures of the world, we are justified both in drawing conclusions as to their success, and in tracing the kinds of discovery
which stand out as advances in this type of effort.

My basic proposition, in the chapters that follow, is that the
history of the novel, like that of painting, was for a considerable
period linked with the notions of accurate representation and of
creating an illusion of reality. This fundamental tenet of the
aesthetic theory of the time will be discussed and elaborated in
later sections of this chapter. It seems to me equally true to say
that in this striving towards a faithful portrayal of real life, the
eighteenth century can be seen as a period of discoveries and
technical advances, and my chapters on individual authors will
be concerned chiefly, though not wholly, with this aspect of
their work. The book as a whole is therefore intended to show
what intrinsically valuable advances in the technique of the
novel came about through the efforts of eighteenth-century
authors to achieve an increasingly accurate representation of
life.[1]

If anyone should ask whether the term 'representation' is not
here merely a synonym for 'realism', my answer would be that
while the sense of the two words does to a certain extent over-
lap, 'realism' is not exactly what I want to discuss. Moreover,
as a term of literary criticism it has several disadvantages. It
may, for instance, lead to confusion in a discussion of French
novels, since French critics already use *le roman réaliste* to refer
to a certain kind of seventeenth-century novel, as well as to
another, very different, type of work in the nineteenth century.
Secondly, both 'realism' and *réalisme* tend to be applied to the
portrayal of the lower strata of society, and virtually exclude
scenes of upper-class life. Thirdly, the term is usually confined to
the description of the outward and material aspects of life—
clothes, surroundings, concrete objects, etc. And finally, the
concept of literary realism, with the fields of reference outlined
above, is a product of the nineteenth century. If one wishes to
discuss what eighteenth-century novelists thought they were
doing, the word 'realism' is therefore an anachronism, and by
virtue of its associations is likely to be misleading. Similarly, if
one is trying to assess the achievements of these novelists, one

[1] For the place of such eighteenth-century developments in the wider field
of European literature, see Erich Auerbach, *Mimesis*, Berne, 1946.

may require a term of less limited scope and implications. For these reasons, while not eschewing the use of 'realism' in appropriate contexts, I have framed my argument round the broader notion of 'representation'.

Although representation and its techniques will provide much of our subject-matter, these will not be used as the only or even as the chief measure of artistic excellence. This, after all, would be something like considering *trompe l'œil* effects to be the acme of pictorial achievement. The choice of books and authors to be discussed is in itself an implicit judgment of literary merit, made by wider standards than that of mere adequate portrayal of real life. Moreover, the kind of terms used so far in these opening remarks—'representation', 'real life', 'accuracy of portrayal'—do not conceal any assumption that human life is a storehouse from which some ideally observant and accomplished writer could extract the elements of the perfect representational novel. The 'Illusion' of our sub-title has many senses: it includes the fluid patterns of action and feeling which the novelist may set out to portray; the novelist's own belief that he is capturing or copying real human life; and the reader's 'belief', while he is reading, in the phantom world of the novel.

Having considered the general approach to our subject, viewed from a modern standpoint, we can now turn to the ideas held by people of the period under discussion.

From the writings of critics in the seventeenth and eighteenth centuries we can reconstruct a body of literary theory regarding contemporary practice in the novel.[1] Many of the component ideas were also applicable to poetry and the theatre, and had in fact been worked out primarily in relation to these genres. If we break this theory down into its basic assumptions and deductions, we find that it involves two main types of argument, which start from different points but converge to much the same conclusion. They could be called the 'Improvement' and the 'Enjoyment' arguments respectively.

[1] For further detail and documentation of this subject, see M. Magendie, *Le Roman français au XVIIe siècle*, Paris, 1932; M. Ratner, *Theory and Criticism of the Novel in France from L'Astrée to 1750*, New York, 1938; F. C. Green, 'The eighteenth-century critic and the contemporary novel', *Modern Language Review*, XXIII (1928), pp. 174–87; G. May, *Le Dilemme du roman au XVIIIe siècle*, Paris, 1963; and H. Coulet, *Le Roman jusqu'à la Révolution*, t. II (Anthologie), Paris, 1968.

The Improvement theory, which was much the more widely accepted of the two, assumed that the purpose of literature was to instruct and edify. Sometimes the didactic function was envisaged in relatively practical terms. Novels could provide a young man with models of behaviour in polite society; or they might furnish information about historical personages and incidents.[1] Far more widespread, however, was the notion that the novel should aim at the moral edification of the reader. He should lay down the book, just as the play-goer should leave the theatre, a better and wiser man.

In order to achieve this end, the moral implications of the novel or the play must of course be driven home. This will not happen, however, said the theorists, unless the reader's emotions are touched. Only by being moved is a man led to accept and inwardly digest the instruction which will benefit his everyday behaviour in the future. This touching of the heart, and the amended life which should ideally ensue, can be seen as a kind of secular parallel to the workings of Divine Grace, by which the heart is stirred and the soul purified for a better way of life. For some of the eighteenth-century writers who rejected Christianity, it is clear—to us, if not to them—that works of art had become a substitute for Grace, in that they could help to implement a secular code of morality. And in both cases, one might add, it was the 'true believer' who was most likely to benefit, for the upholders of the Improvement theory maintained that we are touched by a work of literature only if we believe in it. The novelist's business, therefore, if the reader is to be improved, is to win that reader's belief in the truth of the novel.

This theory, when reduced as here to its bare essentials, may seem naïve and untenable. There is however plenty of evidence that it was accepted, wholly or in part, by many novelists and critics of the seventeenth and eighteenth centuries.

The clearest proof that a novel was expected to be morally instructive is found in the frequent statements by authors that their novels do in fact provide such edifying lessons. This does not of course mean that we can accept the novelists' assurances

---

[1] Cf. Daniel Huet, *Traité de l'origine des romans* (1670), ed. A. Kok, Amsterdam, 1942, pp. 225–6; and Pierre François Guyot, Abbé Desfontaines, *Histoire de Dom Juan de Portugal*, Paris, 1724, *Préface*.

as valid (even supposing we were to agree with the initial assumption that a novel *can* improve the reader's morals). But the mere fact that a large number of writers took the trouble to announce the moral value of their work shows that such a standard was considered both relevant and desirable. What individual novelists really thought about their claim to moral usefulness may have been quite a different matter from what they wrote. One can imagine a wide range of varying sentiments, from a simple and sincere belief that some particular story might keep a few souls from sin, to the cynical use of the 'moral' label as a cover for pornography. However, examples can show clearly enough that the novelist accepted—in the letter if not always in the spirit—the idea that moral instruction was one of the proper functions of his work. Prévost says of *Manon Lescaut* and similar stories:

Chaque fait qu'on y rapporte est un degré de lumière, une instruction qui supplée à l'expérience; chaque aventure est un modèle, d'après lequel on peut se former; il n'y manque que d'être ajusté aux circonstances où l'on se trouve. L'ouvrage entier est un traité de morale, réduit agréablement en exercice.[1]

Mme de Beaumont prefaces the second edition of her *Lettres du Marquis de Roselle* (1764) with the following remarks:

L'accueil que le public a bien voulu faire à cet ouvrage moral a rendu cette seconde édition nécessaire plus tôt qu'on ne l'aurait pensé. L'auteur s'est fait un devoir de répondre à cet empressement en y faisant quelques changements et quelques corrections qui lui ont paru plus propres à remplir le double objet d'instruction et d'agrément qu'on s'est proposé.

And Laclos justifies the usefulness of *Les Liaisons dangereuses* by this argument:

Il me semble au moins que c'est rendre un service aux mœurs, que de dévoiler les moyens qu'emploient ceux qui en ont de mauvaises pour corrompre ceux qui en ont de bonnes, et je crois que ces lettres peuvent concourir efficacement à ce but.[2]

Prévost not only states that works such as *Manon Lescaut* are

---

[1] Prévost, *Manon Lescaut*, Garnier, 1969, *Avis*, p. 6.

[2] Laclos, *Les Liaisons dangereuses*, ed. Yves Le Hir, Paris, Garnier, 1952, *Préface du rédacteur*, p. 5.

morally instructive, but also discusses the way this instruction becomes effective. Moral precepts are general, abstract and vague. One way of making them a more useful and practical guide to conduct is to embody them in the events of a specific story: 'Mettons la chose dans un exemple'. This justifies the existence of the novel, as a cautionary or exemplary tale, and is halfway along the road to the second stage of our general theory: a work must stir the reader's emotions if its moral lesson is to be effective. Prévost does not bring out this notion explicitly, but he has admitted that mere discussion of moral precepts, in the abstract, may be ineffective.

Other writers indicate more clearly that it is the emotional impact of the novel which drives home the moral lesson. Diderot's handling of the idea in the *Eloge de Richardson* is doubtless the best-known expression of this point of view:

Une maxime est une règle abstraite et générale de conduite dont on nous laisse l'application à faire. Elle n'imprime par elle-même aucune image sensible dans notre esprit: mais celui qui agit, on le voit, on se met à sa place ou à ses côtes, on se passionne pour ou contre lui; on s'unit à son rôle, s'il est vertueux; on s'en écarte avec indignation, s'il est injuste et vicieux.

S'il importe aux hommes d'être persuadés qu'indépendamment de toute considération ultérieure à cette vie, nous n'avons rien de mieux à faire pour être heureux que d'être vertueux, quel service Richardson n'a-t-il pas rendu à l'espèce humaine? Il n'a point démontré cette vérité; mais il l'a fait sentir.[1]

This idea, which makes the moral effectiveness of a novel dependent on the arousing of emotions, is closely linked to critical theories already current in the seventeenth century concerning, for instance, the cathartic effects of tragedy. The further step, making the emotion in its turn dependent on belief, is also met with in the seventeenth century. Chapelain resumes the whole chain of reasoning when, discussing the epic, he comes to the subject of

la foi, ou la créance que l'on peut donner au sujet; point important sur tous autres pour ce qu'ils disent qu'où la créance manque, l'attention ou l'affection manque aussi; mais où l'affection n'est

[1] Diderot, *Œuvres esthétiques*, Paris, Garnier, 1959, pp. 29–30, 32.

point, il n'y peut avoir d'émotion et par conséquent d'amendement ès mœurs des hommes, qui est le but de la poésie.[1]

Before he can be moved, and improved, by a work, therefore, the reader must believe in it.

The Enjoyment theory is simpler. It presupposes that the purpose of novels is merely to please and entertain; such works do no more than provide what Huet calls 'un agréable amusement des honnêtes paresseux'.[2] On this assumption, any novel which interests the reader can be said to fulfil its function. But some writers maintained that our enjoyment of a story is increased if we think it to be true. Others went so far as to say that we cannot enjoy or appreciate a story once we realize that its people, places or events are purely imaginary:

Comment serai-je touché des infortunes de la reine de Guindaye, et du roi d'Astrobacie, puisque je sais que leurs royaumes mêmes ne sont point en la carte universelle, ou pour mieux dire, en l'être des choses?[3]

The same notion was expressed by many eighteenth-century writers, as in this comment by Baculard d'Arnaud:

La fiction ne se pardonne qu'autant qu'elle n'est point aperçue. Dès que le mensonge se trahit, il perd sa séduction; l'intérêt qu'il avait excité s'évanouit, et la raison, rendue à toute la sévérité de son jugement, critique et prononce en quelque sorte contre le plaisir du sentiment.[4]

For the supporters of this point of view, it followed that the novelist must create a complete illusion of truth and persuade his readers to believe in the story. As we have already seen, the same requirement was fundamental in the Improvement theory too.

Most modern critics would accept the notion that the reader will be moved by, or emotionally involved in, a novel only if he believes in it. But the similarity of wording here conceals an

[1] Jean Chapelain, 'Préface de l'*Adone* de Marin', *Opuscules critiques*, ed. A. C. Hunter, Paris, 1936, p. 85.

[2] Huet, *Traité des romans*, p. 113.

[3] Madeleine de Scudéry, *Ibrahim*, Paris, 1641, *Préface*. (According to some critics, this preface was written by Georges de Scudéry, Madeleine's brother.)

[4] Baculard d'Arnaud, *Nouvelles historiques*, Paris, 1774, *Préface*, p. i.

important difference of thought. We now make a distinction between 'believing in' a work of literature and 'believing in', say,
the events of an historical narrative. These two aspects of the
activity may be called, for the sake of convenience, 'imaginative belief' and 'literal belief' respectively. In the seventeenth
and eighteenth centuries most critics made no such distinction.
Belief was for them a single activity, one that admitted no differences of kind or of degree. Thus the audience at a tragedy, if
convinced by the theatrical illusion, would believe to the extent
of taking the world of the stage to be the real world. The man
looking at a picture should be under the illusion that what he
sees inside the frame, as though through a window, is a scene
behind and beyond the picture-surface. And the reader of the
novel should believe what he is reading as though it were a true
account of events, conversations, etc. which have in fact taken
place.

   This point of view may seem strange to the modern reader,
accustomed to applying to plays and novels the general concept
expressed in Coleridge's phrase: 'the willing suspension of dis-
belief'. Coleridge was not of course the first to point out that
the 'illusion' of a work of art does not mean that the reader or
spectator is completely and continuously deceived. Godeau,
writing to Chapelain, suggested that the audience may envisage the play as a pretence (a notion Chapelain would not
accept).[1] And among English critics, Dryden clearly foreshadows Coleridge when he says that in the theatre our
imagination

can prescribe to the reason, during the time of the representation,
somewhat like a weak belief of what it sees and hears; and reason
suffers itself to be so hoodwinked that it may better enjoy the
pleasures of the fiction.[2]

But this distinction between different types of belief, which now
seems a matter of common-sense, was quite exceptional in the
seventeenth century, and gained ground only spasmodically in
the eighteenth.

---

[1] See Chapelain, 'Lettre sur la règle des vingt-quatre heures', *Opuscules
critiques*, p. 121.
[2] Dryden, *Of Dramatic Poesy and Other Critical Essays*, ed. G. Watson,
London, 1962, 2 vols., I, 126.

Now one of the most striking characteristics of imaginative belief is its intermittent quality. At one moment we are 'under the spell' of a novel or a play; at the next, the spell may be broken, and we cease to 'believe in' the characters and their actions. This kind of belief can flicker off and on. The same could not be said, presumably, for our reactions while reading a history book, if we accept the authority of the historian.

This last proviso, however, brings in a new and important element, the question of the reader's expectations or 'mental set'. The steadiness or fluctuation of our belief depends ultimately on the attitude of mind we bring to a book. When we are convinced that the contents are historical or factual, we are predisposed to accept without query, and to maintain a steady attitude of literal belief. This attitude will be altered only if we meet, in our reading, some statement which from our previous knowledge we judge to be untrue. Thus a remark that fire-arms were used at the Battle of Hastings would bring most readers to a halt, and effectively stop their passive acceptance of the narrative as factual. It might indeed set up a disposition of doubt or uncertainty about other statements in the book which the reader had not previously met as facts.

The mental set for a work approached as fiction entails a different type of response. Here the reader is probably willing to 'believe'—otherwise he would scarcely have started the book —but his attitude is less passive. At any moment he may withdraw his acceptance. The causes of such a withdrawal may vary, but the most important ones in the present context are elements which offend the reader's standards of possibility and probability: what can happen and what may happen. The obstacles to literal belief, it will be remembered, arise from factual knowledge of what did happen or what does happen. In either case, the reader's reaction depends upon his own experience, using that word to cover all that he has ever learnt. The difference, with fiction, is that judgments as to probability and possibility must be made by inference. We cannot *know*, in all certainty, the whole range of possible or likely events and actions. Our decisions, therefore, are not based on single specific items of information, but deduced from the sum of what we have heard and read and lived through.

Allowing for these uncertain standards, which vary from

individual to individual, and for our lightning ability to stop being passively receptive and become actively critical, the novelist may well think that he has, in some ways, a more difficult task than the historian. Balzac, for one, recognized this difficulty:

> L'historien des mœurs [i.e. the novelist] obéit à des lois plus dures que l'historien des faits; il doit rendre tout probable, même le vrai, tandis que dans le domaine de l'histoire proprement dite, l'impossible est justifié par la raison même qu'il est advenu.[1]

No writer of the seventeenth or eighteenth centuries, to my knowledge, expressed the novelist's predicament as succinctly as this.[2] But many of them did realize that since 'belief' is desirable or even necessary, the novelist must take special steps to achieve and maintain it.

Two methods are open to him. One is deliberately to set about convincing the reader that he is dealing with a factual account, that the story is literally true. This, if it can be managed, is the most effective way of inducing acceptance of the whole work, since the reader is then in a generally acquiescent frame of mind. When this method is successful, the reader of a novel is indeed 'under an illusion'. The alternative is so to write the novel that no incident, no character, no action, will startle the reader out of his imaginative belief by flouting his standards of possibility and probability.[3] The first method is obviously cruder, and usually involves an explanatory introduction intended to establish the 'authenticity' of the whole work and induce the desired attitude. The second calls for the kinds of skill in plausible narration which we now expect from a competent novelist. And the development of the novel through the eighteenth century is, in its general lines, the story of a swing from the first method to the second. From novels which

---

[1] Balzac, *Les Paysans*, Paris, Pléiade, 1937, VIII, 154.

[2] But see the discussion by d'Argens of the novelist's freedom and its limitations in his 'Discours sur les Nouvelles', *Lectures amusantes*, La Haye, 1739, 2 vols., I, 33–8.

[3] Dryden illustrates this idea, for dramatic illusion, by an ingenious analogy with the 'first law of nature' in Cartesian physics: 'What the philosophers say of motion, that when it is once begun it continues of itself, and will do so to eternity without some stop being put to it, is clearly true on this occasion;' etc. (*Dramatic Poesy*, I, 52).

claim to be literally true (and are often wildly implausible), there is a trend towards works laying less emphasis on their supposedly factual origin, and displaying instead more concern for everyday standards of probability and possibility.

We may seem, in all this, to have moved rather far from the questions of representation and illusion. But we have only worked round to rejoin them: the business of not offending the reader's notions about what can and may happen is, in essence, the problem of convincing representation, of maintaining for the reader the illusion that he is dealing with 'real life'. As successive writers discover and learn to exploit effective ways of portraying real life, the novel becomes more plausible, that is, more capable of sustaining the illusion of truth and commanding the reader's imaginative belief.

So far we have concentrated on the positive aspect of early theories about the proper aims and functions of the novel. Much of the current discussion of the genre, however, was in negative terms, dealing with the novelists' failure, in practice, to fulfil such aims. Hostile criticisms of this kind undoubtedly exerted a considerable influence on the way in which a novelist set about his work. Professor May goes so far as to say, referring to these attacks on fiction, 'Ce sont . . . les conditions défavorables qui seules peuvent expliquer les aspects particuliers que prirent les romans du temps.'[1]

The criticism was frequently based on moral grounds, and such objections can be classed under two general headings. One line of attack was to claim that novels were not merely powerless to improve the reader's morals, but actively pernicious and a source of corruption. Varying degrees of severity are shown on this matter. Sometimes novel-reading is blamed as a frivolous and futile pastime. Prévost makes the Dean of Coleraine express this point of view when discussing the education of his young sister:

Elle prit du goût pour la lecture; mais elle recevait ses livres de Georges, et le hasard me fit un jour découvrir qu'il ne lui prêtait que des romans. Je leur en fis des reproches à l'un et à l'autre. Elle me promit d'abandonner cette frivole occupation.[2]

[1] Georges May, *Le Dilemme du roman*, p. 7.
[2] Prévost, *Le Doyen de Killerine* (1735-40), 1784, I, 49.

There were other, minor, accusations regarding the undesirable effects of novel-reading. It was said, for instance, that these works glorified the un-Christian idea of honour, and therefore lent their support to duelling. But the major complaint was the novelists' handling of the subject of love. This, said the critics, was portrayed as an attractive passion, and discussed in ways which were liable to mislead and inflame the thoughts of readers, particularly the young and inexperienced. One writer in the Jesuit periodical *Le Journal de Trévoux* goes so far as to say that the reading of novels should be forbidden

non seulement aux personnes soigneuses de leur salut, mais à tous ceux qui craignent avec raison les suites toujours criminelles et toujours funestes d'un engagement; le soin qu'on y prend d'ôter à l'amour tout ce qui le ferait paraître une passion honteuse et grossière, le rend plus propre à s'insinuer dans les âmes bien élevées. La morale corrompue dont ces livres sont pleins . . . laisse une impression de tendresse, un penchant pour la galanterie, un goût pour l'intrigue, qui dans les jeunes personnes étouffe tout sentiment de piété et de pudeur austère.[1]

The second main accusation on moral grounds is based on a confusion between fiction and falsehood which harks back to our previous discussion of the current ideas about belief. Logically enough, a system which did not allow for imaginative belief had no special category for the type of work which evokes or requires imaginative belief. A story was held to be either true or, inevitably, false. Thus the novelist could be charged with trying to trick the public with lies; the 'illusion' of an imaginary tale was envisaged as a deliberate deception, a *trompe-l'esprit*. It was usually the critics, often churchmen, who objected to fiction on these grounds, but the novelists themselves do not in general seem to have been any more clear-sighted about the nature of fiction. They too equate it with falsehood. Sorel, discussing the insidious attractions of fiction, says, 'Ce n'est pas d'aujourd'hui que le mensonge se fait écouter dans le monde.'[2] Marivaux imagines his critics saying, 'Mais après tout, . . . ce roman n'est qu'un roman; tout ce qu'on y peint est faux', and he frames his

---

[1] *Le Journal de Trévoux*, février, 1703, Article XXVI.
[2] Charles Sorel, *De la Connoissance des bons livres*, Paris, 1671, p. 85.

answer to justify this 'falsehood'.[1] Duclos describes early historical novels as 'une espèce d'hommage que le mensonge rendit à la vérité'.[2]

As a consequence of this approach to fiction, many novelists accepted the idea that their work involved tricking the reader. This aspect of their theory is often concealed from modern readers by the terms in which it is presented. The words *vraisemblable*, *vraisemblance* nowadays convey concepts of probability and plausibility, qualities required for the maintenance of imaginative belief. But fully to understand seventeenth-century comments, one may need to interpret these terms in a sense much closer to their etymology: 'true-seeming', 'calculated to give an impression of truth'—that is, the literal truth of history. Novelists therefore admit that their work may entail persuading the reader, by means of *vraisemblance*, to accept 'lies' as truths:

> Si cette charmante trompeuse [la vraisemblance] ne déçoit l'esprit dans les romans, cette espèce de lecture le dégoûte au lieu de le divertir. J'ai donc essayé de ne m'en éloigner jamais, . . . et pour donner plus de vraisemblance aux choses, j'ai voulu que les fondements de mon ouvrage fussent historiques, mes principaux personnages marqués dans l'histoire véritable comme personnes illustres, et les guerres effectives. . . . Car lorsque le mensonge et la vérité sont confondus par une main adroite, l'esprit a peine à les démêler, et ne se porte pas aisément à détruire ce qui lui plaît.[3]

Obviously, when fiction was held to be on a par with falsehood, and when *vraisemblance* might involve wholesale deception, there were critics to blame the novel as undesirable or even roundly condemn it as sinful. In England, Defoe expressed the argument in all its primitive force:

> The Sister would have it be, that it was not fit that novels should be read at all; nay, that it was a sin; and that, as the making and writing them was criminal in itself, being, as she explained, what the

---

[1] Marivaux, *Les Aventures de* ***, *ou les Effets surprenants de la sympathie*, Paris, 1713, *Avis au lecteur*.

[2] Duclos, *Lettre à l'Auteur de Madame de Luz*, La Haye, 1741, p. 15. (Duclos, himself the author of *Madame de Luz*, is presumed to have written this article.)

[3] Scudéry, *Ibrahim*, *Préface*.

Scripture meant by *making a lie*, so no pretended use that might be made of it could justify the action.[1]

The same attitude was current among many French critics:

La vérité est, à proprement parler, la nourriture de l'entendement; il est dangereux de s'accoûtumer à aimer la fausseté, et on s'y accoûtume par la lecture des romans.[2]

This criticism, concerning the very nature of fiction, was fundamental. People who condemned novels on these grounds held that the genre as such was indefensible. They were therefore not likely to suggest improvements or reforms. The writer's only resource was to abjure the novel and, if he must narrate stories, cling to the truth.

A plea for the whole truth also came from another quarter. Although, or perhaps because, historians of the period took certain liberties which by modern standards seem reprehensible, a desire for strict factual accuracy was gaining ground. This meant that some critics objected to the mixture of fact and fiction in the novelists' 'histoires embellies de quelque invention'. Generally speaking, such critics do not condemn fiction *per se*. They merely protest that the juxtaposition of true and imagined elements in a single narrative may confuse and mislead the reader. Bayle makes frequent complaints on this score, e.g.

Il est fâcheux que Mademoiselle des Jardins ait ouvert la porte à une licence dont on abuse tous les jours de plus en plus; c'est celle de prêter ses inventions, et ses intrigues galantes, aux plus grands hommes des derniers siècles, et de les mêler avec des faits qui ont quelque fondement dans l'histoire. Ce mélange de la vérité et de la fable se répand dans une infinité de livres nouveaux, perd le goût des jeunes gens, et fait que l'on n'ose croire ce qui au fond est croyable.[3]

---

[1] Defoe, *A New Family Instructor*, 1727, pp. 51–2 (quoted in A. D. McKillop, *The Early Masters of English Fiction*, Lawrence, 1956, pp. 6–7).

[2] J.-B. Morvan, Abbé de Bellegarde, *Lettres curieuses de littérature et de morale*, Paris, 1702, pp. 106–7. Cf. also: 'Je n'ai jamais pu me persuader, Madame, qu'il fût nécessaire de tromper l'esprit pour instruire le cœur' (Jacquin, *Entretiens sur les romans*, Paris, 1755, p. 153).

[3] Pierre Bayle, *Dictionnaire historique et critique*, 1697, Article '*Jardins*'. (Marie-Catherine Desjardins is also known as Mme de Villedieu.)

Eighteenth-century critics such as Desfontaines and Fréron repeat this objection to the adulteration of historical truth by
fiction.

As if these various kinds of moral denigration were not
enough, the novel was also attacked on literary and aesthetic
grounds. Anyone familiar with the hierarchy of literary forms
in the seventeenth century will know that the novel occupied a
most humble place on this scale. While epic and tragedy stood
firmly aloft, the novel was insecurely perched on the bottom
rung of the ladder. As a consequence, both the reading and the
writing of novels were held to be pastimes of little inherent
worth or importance. Jane Austen was expressing the view of
generations of novel-readers before her time when she summed
up the conventional attitude in *Northanger Abbey* (written in
1798):

> 'And what are you reading, Miss ——?'
> 'Oh! it is only a novel!' replies the young lady, while she lays
> down her book with affected indifference or momentary shame
> (ch. 5).

Similarly, while a writer might say with pride that he was
working on a poem, a play or a history, he would be less likely
to expect admiration or respect if his current production was
'only a novel'. This attitude is borne out by the high proportion
of novels which were published anonymously. Of the 1050 or
so new French works of fiction published in the seventeenth
century, the title-page or the dedicatory epistle provides the
author's real name only in about 450 cases.[1] During the period
1700–1750, even fewer novelists revealed their identity: Jones
remarks that out of a total of 946 works, only 134 indicate the
author on the title-page.[2] As we shall see, the habit of taking
refuge in anonymity had special causes during this period, but
even allowing for these, one may justifiably deduce that novel-
writing was not generally held to enhance one's reputation.

Besides suffering in this general way from lack of official
prestige, the novel also came in for more specific criticism on

[1] These figures, which do not include translations, are compiled from
M. Lever, *La Fiction narrative en prose au XVIIe siècle*, Paris, 1976.

[2] S. Paul Jones, *A List of French Prose Fiction from 1700 to 1750*, New York,
1939, p. xiii. For data on the period 1751–1800, see below, p. 275.

literary grounds. There was occasional unfavourable comment on the structure of novels, with their rambling plots and inter-calated stories. Even more frequent were accusations of exag-geration and *invraisemblance*, in characters and especially in events. Sorel, in his *De la Connoissance des bons livres*, produced a thorough-going indictment of the common literary weaknesses of the novel. Such criticisms applied chiefly to the so-called 'heroic' novels, which began to lose favour towards the end of the century, but for many years to come the very word *roman* was to be associated, unfavourably, with rambling and ex-travagant stories about unlikely people.

Those who disliked the novel, therefore, could condemn it on moral grounds as a corrupting influence and a deceitful con-coction of lies; or they could disparage it as lacking in literary dignity and merit.

How was the novelist to rebut or evade such censure?

Defenders of the novel were usually concerned more with the moral objections to the genre than with its literary weaknesses.[1] In particular, the notion that novels were merely 'lies' called for rebuttal, since this undermined the status of fiction itself. There were three current lines of defence: to attempt a justifica-tion of fiction as such; to maintain that fiction could improve factual narratives; and—in the case of practising novelists—to claim that their works were not fiction at all but true stories.

The arguments in favour of fiction are ingenious rather than convincing. Sorel starts from the metaphors and tropes used by the orator, inventions which have become acceptable although they are not literally true. He goes on to ask:

> Pourquoi ne sera-t-il pas permis à la poésie et aux romans de se servir du même art? Ils en ont d'autant plus de droit, qu'ils ne sont faits que pour feindre, et que les histoires, qu'on dit être les images de la vérité, sont réduites en beaucoup d'occasions à chercher de semblables secours.[2]

---

[1] For an analysis of the various ideas utilized in the argument that novels *can* be morally improving, see Georges May, *Le dilemme du roman*, ch. IV, pp. 106–38. Professor May holds, however, that it was from aesthetic con-siderations, largely in response to the plea for *vraisemblance*, that novelists took to making their works more realistic. This interpretation does not, in my view, adequately explain why novelists should so frequently have claimed that their works were 'true'.

[2] Sorel, *De la Connoissance*, p. 146.

Desmarets de Saint-Sorlin had used the same argument in the preface to *Rosanne* (1639). These and other writers clearly felt that prose fiction needed the support of more respectable genres such as poetry and history. They seem not to have envisaged the possibility that a good story might be its own justification.

The starting-point for the second argument was the suggestion that unadorned historical truth tends to be boring and unattractive. Fiction is here seen as a saving grace.

L'histoire sans fictions est souvent sèche et peu intéressante; si on raconte les choses précisément comme elles se sont passées, on ennuye presque toutes les femmes, et on dégoûte aussi beaucoup d'hommes, qui par rapport aux livres sont femmes et se mettent peu en peine de la science. Ces personnes ont besoin de quelque attrait pour suivre une lecture.[1]

The end which justifies fiction in this case is the acquisition by the reader of historical information. A few writers went further, and claimed that fiction might have advantages over truth as a source of moral instruction:

Il va m'échapper une espèce de blasphème littéraire: ne vaudrait-il pas mieux pour notre instruction qu'on nous fît lire des romans où la vertu serait offerte dans tous ses charmes, au lieu de ces histoires qui nous présentent presque toujours de prétendus héros fameux par leurs excès criminels, . . . les oppresseurs du faible et de l'innocent, les fléaux du monde entier?[2]

Many novelists, however, tried to evade the attack on fiction by claiming that their books were true, and not novels at all. This solution of the problem became widespread in the eighteenth century. The seventeenth-century novelist had tended to say that his work was basically true as to its historical data, and that he had merely supplied further incidents and details. Later on, authors came to reject the implication that they had invented any part of their narrative. One thus meets 'historical' novels like the Abbé Terrasson's *Sethos* (1731), described on its title-page as: 'Histoire ou Vie tirée des monuments anecdotes de l'ancienne Egypte, traduite d'un manuscrit grec'.[3]

---

[1] Desfontaines, *Dom Juan, Préface*.
[2] Baculard d'Arnaud, *Nouvelles historiques*, pp. vi–vii.
[3] It should be remembered that *anecdote*, for the French reader of the time, meant a hitherto unpublished true story; eighteenth-century editions of the

And stories of contemporary French life are frequently preceded by assurances that 'Ceci n'est pas un roman'. Partly because fiction itself was in disrepute, the novelists try to persuade the public that they are producing something different.[1] (The irony of this situation is that in making such claims, the novelists really were telling the 'lies' of which some critics accused them.)

From all this discussion of seventeenth- and eighteenth-century ideas, it can be seen that both the aesthetic theories and the moral attitudes of the period were liable to push the novelist in the same direction, towards claiming that his work was morally improving, and true. The question of moral usefulness will be discussed in due course in relation to some of the individual novels. The claim to truth is itself a development of the historical pretensions of the heroic novel; in the next chapter we shall therefore proceed to a brief outline of the relations between history and the novel.

This general survey of the ideas which form a background to the eighteenth-century novel cannot be closed without some cautions and reservations. The argument of this chapter has been in general terms, and has dealt with only the main trends of the seventeenth and the early eighteenth centuries. There were other theories and other types of fiction. We have not, for instance, touched on the seventeenth-century works which are variously described as satiric novels, or *romans réalistes*, or in some cases as *anti-romans*. While these were supposed, like the heroic novel, to have a moral function, they were thought to be based on a different kind of 'truth', which will require separate discussion.

Secondly, there has been no mention of those rare authors who adopted a more clear-sighted attitude towards their own fictions. Madame de la Fayette in the preface to *La Princesse de Montpensier*, Boursault in *Le Prince de Condé*, warned their readers *not* to expect historical truth. Mme de Villedieu, after first claiming that her *Journal amoureux* (1669) was based on an

---

Dictionnaire de l'Académie define the word as: 'Particularité secrète d'histoire'. It could also be used adjectivally, as here.

[1] Cf. A. J. Tieje, 'A peculiar phase of the theory of realism in pre-Richardsonian fiction', *Publications of the Modern Language Association*, 28 (1913), pp. 213–52. (While agreeing with Tieje's main argument, I would query his over-precise dating of literary trends.)

authentic manuscript, changed her mind for later editions and described the work as 'un petit roman'.[1] Exceptional as such cases may be, they should not pass unnoticed.

Finally, we have ignored, as being beyond the scope of this argument, the whole range of fantasy-fiction, which put forward no claims to truth or historicity. One reason for this omission is that many of these fantasy-tales are too short to qualify as *romans*. This applies, for instance, to the *contes de fées* of Perrault and his successors, and to most of the Oriental and pseudo-Oriental tales which were in vogue during the early eighteenth century. However, the later writers who produced philosophic tales, and in particular Voltaire, extended the scope of these stories so that their works can occasionally be seen as borderline cases between the *conte* and the *roman*. Eighteenth-century usage of these two terms was by no means clear and fixed, and there seems little point in trying to establish a rigid distinction between their respective fields of reference. What matters at this stage is that philosophic tales relied for the most part on fantasy and unrealistic narratives, rather than on *vraisemblance* and historical pretensions. Works like these should help us to keep in mind that novels aspiring to 'truth' were only a part, though an extremely important part, of eighteenth-century activities in the realm of fiction.

[1] These examples are taken from the article by Georges May, 'L'Histoire a-t-elle engendré le roman?', *Revue d'histoire littéraire de la France*, LV (1955), pp. 155–76.

II

Fiction, History and Truth

CONNECTIONS between history and fiction can be traced back to the earliest known forms of European literature, and in particular to the epic.[1] However, for our immediate purpose the seventeenth century will serve as a starting-point. During this period, the novel tended increasingly to lay claim to some of the credit and privileges of history. Since the two genres are nowadays so distinct and separate, the problem for the modern reader is to discover why and how fiction could take on the guise of history.

A first point to notice is that, unlike the novel, history was a prosperous and relatively important genre. It had respectable classical antecedents, some glorious names in its family tree, and a high moral tone. What more natural, then, than that practitioners of the more lowly novel should aspire to the condition of history?

A second fact, which favoured novelists in this kind of literary trespass, was that the novel itself had no clear and well-defined limits. This was a consequence of its inferior status and humble background. Because it was a genre which had not achieved greatness in Greek or Latin literature, the novel clearly could not merit the kind of serious theoretical discussion which was accorded to tragedy, the epic or the ode. And because it was not taken seriously by major critics and theorists, it acquired no body of explicit rules to define its essence and its form. Admittedly, a fair quantity of comment and theory was published, much of it in prefaces to the novels themselves. And there were attempts to supply the novel with rules, for instance by classifying it as a prose epic. But the would-be legislators did not manage to impose their authority, and a novelist could happily ignore the advice of a Huet or a Lenglet du Fresnoy. The great advantage of this lack of accepted rules was that

[1] See A. Chassang, *L'Histoire du roman et de ses rapports avec l'histoire dans l'antiquité grecque et latine*, Paris, 1862.

novelists could experiment and make or break conventions in a way which was impossible for writers in more strictly-governed genres. There were no guardians of the novel to lay down its limits and see that it remained within them, and only a few voices to protest when it strayed into the purlieus of history.

A third factor which encouraged such incursions was that most historians of the period were more consciously literary than their modern counterparts. An elegant style, a dignified handling of events, a talent for drafting impressive speeches for great occasions, all these were requirements at least as important for most historians as the ability to sift the true from the legendary.

Il vaut mieux employer son temps à la composition, et à arranger les faits de l'histoire, qu'à les rechercher; il vaut mieux aussi songer à la beauté, à la force, à la netteté et à la brièveté du style, qu'à paraître infaillible dans tout ce qu'on écrit.[1]

Thus, while the style of heroic novels might seem to us quite inappropriate for works of history, the contemporary reader would not always find so striking a difference between the novels and the histories at his disposal.

The ability to invent speeches has been mentioned as a qualification for the historian, and this brings us to the question of narrative technique. Respectable and respected seventeenth-century historians considered that they had the right, and sometimes even a duty, to supplement or elaborate the known facts with details of 'what must have been'. If the results of a conversation between two kings are known, one can reconstruct the conversation; if the rebellious citizens were calmed by a harangue from a bishop, the gist of his speech can be deduced. But the heroic novel regularly took the form of a narrative by a well-informed chronicler who could likewise supply from reason what was lacking in facts. Scarron, in *Le Roman comique*, frequently makes fun of such authors' pretensions to know, for instance, what their heroes were doing at every hour of the day, showing that in his view the conventions of quasi-historical narrative were sometimes overstepped.

History and the novel even came together over their potential

[1] Cordemoy, quoted in P. Hazard, *La Crise de la conscience européenne* (*1680–1715*), Paris, 1935, 3 vols., I, 40.

effects on the reader, for history, it was often argued, could be morally instructive. As well as being a source-book of practical psychology—how men *do* behave—it also provided examples and warnings—how men should or should not behave. We have already seen that novelists assumed the same responsibility.

At the risk of being over-obvious, I should point out, finally, that in the matter of 'imitating nature' and pretending to be true, the novelist has a head-start on artists in other fields. He is working in exactly the same medium and materials as what he counterfeits. Most pictures are patently two-dimensional, even if they seek to convey depth; the drums in a 'musical storm' are clearly not thunder; the stage-set of a forest is not likely to convince us that we are looking at the real thing. But the words of the historian are the words of the novelist too, and as we riffle through the pages of a narrative, the sentences bear no evident stamp of their nature, true or false. Appearances alone will not reveal whether we are dealing with history or invention.

The traits so far described all go to show that novelists could take advantage of the similarities between the two genres, and it is a matter of literary history that they did so. D'Urfé, Segrais, La Calprenède, Mlle de Scudéry and many others advanced explicit claims to be historical writers. D'Urfé, for instance, provided accurate descriptions of Druid ceremonies. Some authors, like Gerzan and Segrais, incorporated passages translated from Livy or Tacitus into their own narratives.[1] And frequently the novelist chose a well-known historical figure as his hero, and claimed that his book supplied incidents and motives which had not been revealed by earlier 'historians'. The prefaces of such works usually stress their historical aspect and defend the method. La Calprenède says of such novels, including his own *Cassandre* and *Cléopâtre*, that

au lieu de les appeler des romans, comme les *Amadis* et autres semblables, dans lequel il n'y a ni vérité ni vraisemblance, ni charte, ni chronologie, on les pourrait regarder comme des histoires embellies de quelque invention, et qui par ces ornements ne perdent peut-être rien de leur beauté. En effet, je peux dire avec raison que dans la *Cassandre* ni dans la *Cléopâtre* non seulement il n'y a rien contre la vérité, mais il n'y a aucun endroit dans lequel on me

---

[1] Cf. Magendie, *Le Roman français au XVIIe siècle*, pp. 32, 201.

puisse convaincre de mensonge, et que par toutes les circonstances de l'histoire je ne puisse soutenir pour véritable quand il me plaira.[1]

The long series of heroic novels, of which only a handful are remembered today, and remembered only by name, drew to a close in the 1660's with the rising vogue of another form of fiction, the *nouvelle*. This was originally a short story, published either as one of a collection of such stories or as part of a full-length *roman*, two uses that we shall discuss at a later stage.[2] For the moment we are concerned with the kind of *nouvelle* which appeared as an isolated and independent work, like Mme de la Fayette's *La Princesse de Montpensier* (1662). From 1660 onwards there appeared more and more *nouvelles* which were long enough to be published alone.[3] In subject-matter and treatment these stories extend and exploit the resources of the earlier short *nouvelles*. Admittedly, it was not unknown for the longer independent works to borrow from the *roman* certain devices such as the interpolated story; *La Princesse de Clèves* shows this process at work. But even allowing for such borrowings, the general picture is of the old form of the *roman* dying out in 1670, with the last volume of *Faramond*, and leaving the field clear for the development of the *nouvelle* and other types of fiction.[4] (The older novels continued to be reprinted during the eighteenth century, so that the change in public taste was not as rapid as this outline might suggest.) A work like *La Princesse de*

---

[1] La Calprenède, *Faramond*, Paris, 1661–70, *Avis au lecteur*. (The novel was completed by Vaumorière after La Calprenède's death in 1661.)

[2] See below, pp. 57–8.

[3] See R. Godenne, *Histoire de la nouvelle française*, Genève, 1970, pp. 250–69. Godenne lists only three collections and three isolated *nouvelles* between 1620 and 1660; for the period 1661–1700 he gives some 30 publications containing more than one story, and about 220 *nouvelles* which appeared as separate works.

[4] For details of this change, see Antoine Adam, *Histoire de la littérature française au XVIIe siècle*, Paris, 5 vols., 1949–56, IV, 171–214; D. F. Dallas, *Le Roman français de 1660 à 1680*, Paris, 1932, pp. 141–67; and F. Deloffre, 'Le Problème de l'illusion romanesque et le renouvellement des techniques narratives entre 1700 et 1715', *La Littérature narrative d'imagination*, Paris, 1961, pp. 115–29. In England a similar change, led by Mrs Aphra Behn, took place only a few years later than in France. This has left its mark on the language in the substitution of the word 'novel' for the earlier 'romance' as a generic name for a long prose fiction.

Clèves is not, therefore, a lineal descendant of the mid-seventeenth-century *roman*, but the product of a parallel and separate form of fiction.

These independent *nouvelles* covered a wide range of mood and tone, from the romantic to the cynical, from the chaste to the scabrous. What they had in common, put in negative terms, is that they did not deal with classical antiquity, nor did they narrate the kind of fabulous or extravagantly heroic exploits hitherto found in the *roman*. The essential difference between the fantasy of the *roman* and the more realistic atmosphere of the *nouvelle* is indicated by Segrais when he makes Aurélie say that the *roman* describes the world

comme la bienséance le veut, et à la manière du poète; mais que la nouvelle doit un peu davantage tenir de l'histoire et s'attacher plutôt à donner les images des choses comme d'ordinaire nous les voyons arriver, que comme notre imagination se les figure.[1]

Segrais, it will be noticed, connects the *nouvelle* with history. Not all writers of *nouvelles* took this line, but in some cases the authors were as firm in maintaining the historical nature of their works as had been the *romanciers* of the mid-century.[2] Moreover, while it had never been very likely that readers would accept a Scudéry or a La Calprenède novel as a literal historical narrative, the *nouvelle historique* sometimes had a specious air of historical good faith which could mislead the unwary. Dulong sees in Saint-Réal's *Conjuration de Venise* (1672) the culmination of this confusion between history and fiction:

L'histoire n'a cessé de prétendre aux séductions du roman. Le roman n'a cessé d'aspirer aux prérogatives de l'histoire. Il était nécessaire qu'on en vînt à ne plus savoir distinguer véritablement l'un de l'autre. La *Conjuration* marque, dans notre histoire littéraire, le moment précis où fut possible cette aberration totale.[3]

This work was based on actual events, but Saint-Réal interpreted and elaborated them from his imagination rather than from historical sources. Moreover, while he had published a previous work, *Don Carlos*, under the heading of a *nouvelle*

---

[1] Segrais, *Nouvelles françoises*, 1656, I, 167–8.

[2] Cf. Adam, *Histoire de la littérature française au XVIIe siècle*, IV, 176.

[3] Gustave Dulong, *L'Abbé de Saint-Réal. Etude sur les rapports de l'histoire et du roman au XVIIe siècle*, Paris, 1921, 2 vols., I, 211–12.

historique, the *Conjuration de Venise* at first bore no such label and was accepted as straightforward history by many readers in the seventeenth and eighteenth centuries. Dulong deplores the deception of the *Conjuration*:

> Au moment même où il donnait au roman historique une forme intéressante et nouvelle, il lui manqua soit la conscience nette de ce qu'il faisait, soit la franchise de le dire. Ce malentendu pèse lourdement, aujourd'hui encore, sur sa réputation (p. 217).

In the light of our previous discussion about novelists trying to escape into history, Saint-Réal can be seen both as less guilty than he at first appears to modern eyes, and as a triumphant example of how to win belief for fictions by passing them off as historical facts.

Yet in the matter of winning belief, it would seem that the authors of *nouvelles historiques* had made things more difficult for themselves. In the field of recent history, for instance, major events in the lives of famous people were likely to be common knowledge, and therefore did not allow much scope for invention. On the other hand, one could scarcely expect to gain historical belief for supposedly important events and influential people who were purely imaginary. This drawback was pointed out by Segrais:

> Si l'on nous racontait quelque chose de ce temps ici qui fût un peu mémorable, il y aurait à craindre que personne n'en voulût rien croire; parce que si l'on décrivait des héros comme des gens que nous voyons dans le monde, on s'étonnerait de n'en avoir point ouï parler.[1]

However, the *nouvelle historique* was itself a specialized development. Traditionally, from Boccaccio onwards, the *nouvelle* in general could take as its heroes not only kings and nobles, but humbler folk as well. While the serious novel was concerned with 'private life', in the special sense of love and the pursuit of the beloved, the *nouvelle* regularly dealt with private individuals as well as monarchs and public figures.

This trend towards recent and private events was reflected in two other forms of fiction whose development can also be dated from the years around 1670. In 1669 came the publication of the

---

[1] Segrais, *Nouvelles françoises*, I, 22–3.

Lettres d'une religieuse portugaise, by Guilleragues, which gave
fresh impetus to the letter-novel. And in 1672 there appeared
Mme de Villedieu's *Mémoires de la Vie de Henriette-Sylvie de
Molière*, an early and important example of fictional autobiography. These works, by their very nature, offered further
examples of contemporary settings and of people not previously
known to the public. The early stages of the letter-novel and of
fictional memoirs will be discussed in more detail when we deal
with specific instances of these forms. At this stage we can
appreciate their significance in that they contributed to the
vogue for stories set in the near-past and dealing largely with
private individuals.[1] One cannot generalize too widely about
later developments: Prévost and others continued to use
'public' history in their novels. But in the eighteenth century
the centre of interest in a novel is usually the private citizen,
who may happen to become involved in recorded public
events, rather than the historical personage whose love-life is
supposedly being revealed for the first time.

The letter-novel and the memoir-novel introduced an
innovation of a different order and of no less importance: the
first-person narrator. The *nouvelle*, the *histoire secrète*, the *conte*
continued for the most part to utilize the quasi-historical
method of narration which had been established in the heroic
novel. Letters and memoirs presented the speaking voice of the
witness who had himself lived through the events of the story.
Obviously this makes for a different approach. In such works
the thoughts and feelings of the narrator tend to take on a new
importance, and the way is being prepared for the subjective
tone of much Romantic literature. This tendency is only latent
in the early memoir-novels: *Gil Blas*, for instance, while giving
a first-hand view of the narrator's life, is far from being an
intimate personal record. However, what is noteworthy in all
these changes is that many novelists, instead of pretending to

---

[1] An immediate consequence of this trend was a change in the type of
name given to characters in fiction. Subligny, in the preface of *La fausse
Clélie* (1671), draws attention to this 'nouvelle façon d'écrire': 'Il est à
craindre que quelques esprits romanesques, voyant un nom de *Marquis de
Riberville, Mirestain, de Franlieu*, et autres, au lieu de celui d'un *Tiridate* ou
d'un *Cléante*, ne fassent d'abord le procès à mon livre.' Concerning the same
development in English fiction, see Ian Watt, *The Rise of the Novel*, London,
1957, pp. 18–20.

provide history itself, have turned to writing what might be considered as the raw material of history, the private source-books rather than the official compilations.

In one respect it might be claimed that the shift from the long-distant past and its historical personages did not involve a real change: the ideas and manners of the characters in heroic novels had in any case been largely a reflection of seventeenth-century upper-class standards. But such novels, with their noble protagonists and extraordinary events all seen in a remote time-setting, could show ideal standards of behaviour being observed to the last iota. Common-sense and experience made seventeenth-century writers and readers aware that such ideals were scarcely ever put fully into practice in the Europe of their day. Stories in the recent past, therefore, could and did show lapses from the lofty code of the heroic novel, and this entailed a general modification in the outlook and tone of the genre as a whole.

To set these changes of time and class and tone in their proper perspective, we must end by noting that, as developments in the novel, they are only part of a wider movement of ideas which was becoming manifest in many other fields. In the realm of literature, the novel was carrying out its own revolution of Moderns against Ancients before the quarrel got into its stride over poetry and plays. And in relation to the larger domain of speculative thought, the changes in the novel reflect current interest in the particular, the individual, the observable aspects of human nature, as against the more general, universal and idealistic theories which had earlier prevailed. Fiction was caught up, in the trail of religion, philosophy and science, in 'la crisè de la conscience européenne'.

We have seen why and how the serious seventeenth-century novel established its claim to be historical. For the eighteenth century the claim is usually that of 'truth', and we must now consider what was meant at this period by the group of terms *vérité, vrai, véritable*.

The change from *histoire* to *vérité* was itself largely a matter of linguistic usage arising from the shift in subject-matter towards more recent and private stories. English usage follows the same pattern: an 'historical' incident or character is assumed to be further back in time, and perhaps better-known, than a 'true story' or a 'real person'.

One cannot, however, accept this new terminology without further question. There are marked differences between eighteenth-century and twentieth-century ideas as to what constitutes 'truth' in a narrative. In particular, many eighteenth-century novelists maintained, as their predecessors had done of history, that one may justifiably embroider the truth and still call the resulting mixture 'true'. Baculard d'Arnaud takes this line: 'Embellissons la vérité, mais qu'elle ne disparaisse point sous les ornements'; and he refers scornfully to 'ces esprits superstitieux dont l'espèce de fanatisme pour la vérité s'effarouche au moindre trait qu'on lui prête'.[1] For some people at least, therefore, truth was a foundation on which one could build without altering its nature. Thus, when an author said that his narrative was 'vrai', he might be implying no more than that the crucial incidents in it did take place. We shall find Bernardin de Saint-Pierre involved in precisely this kind of claim, on the strength of a 'real' shipwreck which he utilized as the climax of Paul et Virginie. And nearly half-a-century later Balzac manifests much the same attitude when he says of Le Père Goriot, 'All is true'. To realize the difference between this and the modern point of view, one has only to think of what is implied by a descriptive phrase such as 'a true spy-story'. Here we expect every episode and every detail to be factual. Invention is inadmissible. If any part of the narrative is based on inference or conjecture, the reader should be warned.[2] Clearly, if we apply these standards to the eighteenth-century writers' claims, we may judge them more severely than they deserve, and certainly more strictly than did most of their early readers. When an eighteenth-century novelist says that his story is 'true', we should in many cases be prepared to substitute the modern equivalent, 'based on fact'.

---

[1] Baculard d'Arnaud, *Nouvelles historiques*, pp. vi, vii. Cf. also Desfontaines' commendation of *romans historiques* 'dont le fond est exactement vrai, et est seulement embelli dans les circonstances' (*Dom Juan, Préface*).

[2] This attitude is exemplified in the slightly superior and reproving tone adopted by Ewen Montagu in *The Man who Never Was* (1953) towards the fictionalized version of the same incident in Duff Cooper's *Operation Heartbreak* (1950).

There are some types of work, however, in which it would seem that the claim to truth allows of no such mitigation. Invention or embellishment should not, one assumes, creep into books which set up to be authentic autobiographies or collected letters. But a fair number of memoir-novels and letter-novels were supposedly 'edited' or 'translated' by another hand. And in the presentation of documents we find a parallel to the current attitudes towards truth in narrative; the authentic text was by no means the inviolable object we have now made it. Both editors and translators assumed that they had the right to improve the texts they worked on. Their freedom of action might depend to some extent on the prestige of the original writer and his conformity to the accepted canons of good taste. Thus Desfontaines lays down the principle of absolute fidelity in translation, but adds that in his own versions of Swift (*Gulliver's Travels*) and Echard,

> La réputation de ces auteurs n'était pas assez grande pour m'asservir à leurs pensées. J'ai donc supprimé librement tout ce qu'il y avait d'ennuyeux, de bizarre ou de puéril dans le premier, et je l'ai remplacé par d'autres choses que mon imagination sut me dicter en ce temps-là.[1]

Desfontaines' justification for his own additions to the original is that they replaced unsuitable elements which he felt obliged to omit. In this he was following current practice, for most writers not only embellished the truth if they felt so inclined, but also made such cuts as they saw fit, while continuing to claim that their story or manuscript remained a faithful version of the truth. These deletions were generally justified by respect for *les bienséances*, which covered both the vocabulary and also the moral and social standards of the subject-matter.[2] The practice of making such emendations and expurgations had already become established in the seventeenth century, in translations from the classics and in the editing of works such as Pascal's *Pensées*. Protests against 'improvements' of this kind were relatively rare. Editors and translators obviously thought they had gone as far as could reasonably be expected when they

---

[1] Desfontaines, *Observations sur les écrits modernes*, III (1735), p. 246.
[2] Cf. F. H. Wilcox, *Prévost's Translations of Richardson's Novels*, Berkeley, Univ. of California Press, 1927.

had admitted making such alterations. As in the case of 'true' stories, therefore, we must be prepared to attenuate the sense of phrases like 'traduit de l'anglais' or 'd'après les véritables lettres des personnages'.

There remains one further use of the word *vrai* which requires comment. This is its application to characters or manners, usually in the sense of a faithful or accurate portrayal: 'une peinture vraie'. Here the word expresses a general notion, referring to commonly observed traits of feeling and behaviour rather than to specific events or people. The same idea is conveyed in English by phrases such as 'true to life', 'true to nature' or 'artistic truth'. Among early theorists of the novel one often finds the recommendation that while the events of the plot should be *vraisemblables*, the characters' manners and emotional reactions should be *vrais*.

It was this kind of *vérité* which the authors of seventeenth-century comic and satirical novels claimed as their chief merit: with the help of a fictitious story, they provided a true picture of society. And by showing up the ridiculous aspect of human affectations and vanities, they would cure men of such weaknesses. (The nature, purpose and methods of the satirical novel are thus on a par with those of comedy, while the historical claims and the more serious approach of the heroic novel make it theoretically comparable to tragedy.)

This 'general truth' continues, in the eighteenth century, to be the aim and justification of satiric novels. Lesage says that his intention in *Gil Blas* is 'de représenter la vie des hommes telle qu'elle est'. But because he is making fun of contemporary foibles and follies, and might be suspected of caricature or personal attacks, he has to go a step further and affirm that he is *not* telling specific true stories about real people: 'A Dieu ne plaise que j'aie eu dessein de désigner quelqu'un en particulier!' The satirical novelist was therefore obliged to forego the specific truth claimed for more serious stories, and had to content himself with the plea that his work was 'true to nature'.

In the seventeenth and early eighteenth centuries, this kind of truth, belonging to a humbler sort of novel, was apparently held in less esteem than the so-called history and literal truth of more ambitious works. But as insistence on the authenticity of characters and plots gradually declined, 'truth to nature' came into its own. A 'true picture of life' was adopted by many novelists as an aim, and by many critics as a criterion of merit.

We are now in a position to sum up the ideas and practices which helped to produce the kind of novel which was popular during much of the eighteenth century.[1]

The authors of long novels up to about 1670 tended to claim affiliations with history. In practice, they distorted their historical material, presented characters who were exaggeratedly heroic or refined, and filled their stories with improbable events. Their methods depended, in part at least, on a desire to dignify the genre, but they came finally to discredit it. As a result of changing ideas and critical standards, serious novelists took to writing about their own period or the immediate past, and about unknown people instead of the historical personages of more remote periods. They thus began to offer increasingly realistic portrayals of contemporary society and manners. The reader's belief was usually solicited by claims that the novel was in some way 'true'. It is from these claims, as much as from any other signs, that we can deduce the continued lack of confidence, among writers and readers alike, in the intrinsic worth of fiction. The time had not yet come when the novel as a genre could be accepted unashamedly on its own terms.

[1] From these remarks, and my later discussion of the memoir-novel, it will be clear that I do not accept the initial assumptions made by Ian Watt in *The Rise of the Novel*. The twin notions that the eighteenth-century novel was 'a new literary form', and that it was 'begun by Defoe, Richardson and Fielding' (p. 9), seem to me equally fallacious.

III

Memoirs and Pseudo-Memoirs

O F the eighteenth-century French novels which are still widely read nowadays, whether for pleasure or for duty, nearly all belong to one or another of two forms: the fictional autobiography—*Gil Blas, Le Paysan parvenu*—which was in vogue up to about 1750; and the letter-novel—*La Nouvelle Héloïse, Les Liaisons dangereuses*—which had its heyday in the second half of the century. Was there any reason why these two forms should flourish at this particular period? The answer follows logically enough from the early novelists' claims to be presenting first 'historical' and then 'true' accounts of events. Before 1670, seeking to share the honour and prestige of history, the novel had utilized the methods of historical narrative. With the shift towards recent 'true' stories, it adopted two of the forms in which authentic records of private lives appear: memoirs and letters. The forms themselves are an outward sign of the novelist's desire to impose his work as literally true. The memoir-novel cannot be distinguished, in its manner of presentation, from an authentic autobiography; the letter-novel looks exactly like a collection of genuine letters.

Of the two types of narrative, memoirs may seem the more natural way of telling a story. The situation of a man recounting the events of his own life is commonplace enough, while it is on the whole less likely that a series of letters should reveal a complete story. One might therefore argue that the more artificial letter-novel came into favour only because the convention of a first-person record had already been established by memoirs, authentic and fictional. Be that as it may, it was certainly the memoir-novel which popularized first-person narrative in fiction. In this chapter we shall consider first the general problems of authenticity which a supposedly autobiographical narrative can pose, and then the various kinds of work which contributed to the development of fictional memoirs.

The whole question of the authenticity of autobiographical

memoirs is alive with difficulties.[1] To begin with, there are of course two possible standards by which to judge: are the facts and events reported accurately and without conscious falsification? And is the given work truly an autobiography, written by the 'I' who narrates the story?

Two instances from seventeenth-century literature will show the complications that may arise concerning both these aspects of authenticity. In 1643 there appeared a work by Tristan l'Hermite entitled *Le Page disgracié*. It does not seem to have had much success at the time, but a second edition was brought out in 1667, after Tristan's death. In the remarks of *Le Libraire au lecteur* in this edition, the work is described as a *roman*:

Entre ses œuvres, je n'ai pas estimé que le Roman de sa vie fust des moins achevez, puisqu'en cet Ouvrage il s'est voulu peindre soy-mesme et representer avec la vivacité de son esprit, la facilité qu'il avoit à s'énoncer, les avantages de sa naissance et les mal-heurs de sa fortune.

This qualification of the book is repeated in the *Privilège*, which speaks of 'un roman intitulé Le page disgracié'. Yet Tristan himself, in his first chapter, says that this is no mere fable or work of the imagination:

La Verité s'y presentera seulement si mal-habillée qu'on pourra dire qu'elle est toute nue. On ne verra point icy une peinture qui soit flattée, c'est une fidele copie d'un lamentable Original; c'est comme une reflexion de miroir.

And in the introduction to his critical edition of the work, Dietrich could write:

Le *Page disgracié*, que Sorel range parmi 'les Romans divertissans', l'Abbé Jacquin parmi 'les romans badins et satyriques', que Lenglet-Dufresnoy nomme 'un roman comique agréable', . . . est avant tout, il convient d'y insister, une autobiographie véritable et sincère.[2]

Novel or authentic memoirs? The answer does credit to the literary honesty of Tristan's publisher. The main outlines of the

---

[1] The term *mémoires* is sometimes used for third-person narrative as well as for autobiography. Unless otherwise stated, *mémoires* and 'memoirs' will here be used to refer only to first-person narrative.

[2] *Le Page disgracié*, ed. Auguste Dietrich, Paris, Bibliothèque Elzévirienne, 1898, p. xxxv. Cf. also N.-M. Bernardin, *Un précurseur de Racine: Tristan l'Hermite*, Paris, 1895, p. 45.

life-story are true as to events and chronology, but Tristan includes some romantic episodes which are either invented or highly embroidered, and it is presumably because of these that the work was described as a *roman*. There has never been any suggestion, however, that anyone besides Tristan had a hand in its composition.

By contrast, the *Mémoires du Sieur de Pontis* (1676) were certainly not written by de Pontis. This professional soldier ended his days as a *solitaire* at Port-Royal, and according to the *Avertissement* of his memoirs, it was there that a younger friend and admirer, Pierre Thomas du Fossé, recorded his conversational reminiscences.[1] After drafting them into a third-person narrative, 'rapportant comme un historien tous les événements qui y sont', the biographer subsequently recast the story in the first person, to make it easier reading and more effective. Obviously the results of such a procedure, in which de Pontis himself took no part, must inspire some distrust.

However, both Tristan l'Hermite and the author-editor of de Pontis's memoirs have this in common, that they do not seek to impose upon the public. The writer of pseudo-memoirs, on the other hand, publishes either the 'autobiography' of a real person, with no warning that the actual writer is someone else; or the memoirs of an imaginary character whose historical existence is vouched for on the title-page or in the preface. Apart from these two types of fraud, there is the more straightforward approach of the novelist who uses the autobiographical form for the life-story of an imaginary character, but who lets his own name appear on the title-page and makes no claims to be telling the truth. In the eighteenth-century we can find examples of all these three uses of the form of memoirs. Before we discuss specific works, however, it may be as well to consider what had so far been available to the French reader in the way of memoirs, and what expectations this title would usually arouse.

Although Villehardouin and Joinville could by some stan-

---

[1] Further proof of this authorship comes from du Fossé's own memoirs: 'C'étoit vers ce même temps [1657], et depuis encore, que je travaillay à recueillir les Mémoires du Sieur de Pontis' (*Mémoires de Pierre Thomas, sieur du Fossé*, ed. F. Bouquet, Rouen, 1876-9, 4 vols., II, 5).

dards be called memorialists, it is not until the fifteenth century, with Olivier de la Marche and Philippe de Commines, that we find the first important examples of writings which the authors themselves called *mémoires*. La Marche, whose memoirs are largely concerned with military matters, pointed out in his *Prologue* that they did not, as they stood, constitute a chronicle or a history, but that they might be of use to later historians. The same might be said of the memoirs of de Commines, which are chiefly political. Of these two kinds of subject-matter it was the military memoirs which became more popular, and the sixteenth century produced a crop of soldier-writers. The most famous of these is Blaise de Monluc, whose *Commentaires* were dubbed by Henri IV 'the soldier's Bible'. This work, according to Major, set a new standard for writings in this form:

> Monluc's presentation of himself in his memoirs had an important influence upon the nature of seventeenth-century memoirs, for from his time on the increasingly important place given to the actions and thoughts of the memorialist definitely colored the whole genre, distinguishing it, at once, from the old chronicle and from the seventeenth-century historical narrative like that of de Thou.[1]

This is a point of some significance for its effects upon fiction as well as upon other authentic memoirs. One may justifiably suppose that the personal note and self-description of Montaigne's *Essais* also encouraged this trend: Tristan l'Hermite cites Montaigne's example in the opening paragraph of *Le Page disgracié*.

The number of authentic memoirs began to increase from about 1660 onwards.[2] What might a seventeenth-century reader expect to find when he took up one of these works?

The author would practically always belong to the nobility, if only of petty gentry standard. He would have been involved in public affairs, sometimes in a political or administrative capacity, more often as an officer in the army. And his book generally dealt with three chief kinds of subject-matter: military campaigns or political events which were already common knowledge; hitherto unrevealed sidelights on these

---

[1] John C. Major, *The Role of Personal Memoirs in English Biography and Novel*, Philadelphia, 1935, p. 20.

[2] See the check-list provided by R. Démoris, *Le Roman à la première personne, Du classicisme aux Lumières*, Paris, 1975, pp. 463–77.

same military or state affairs; and some account of the writer's private life, his ambitions, successes and failures.

We may note, in passing, that each of these three elements found a place in the short works which replaced the heroic novel. The re-telling of known events appeared in some of the *contes* and *nouvelles historiques*; the now-it-can-be-told approach produced the numerous *histoires secrètes* and *anecdotes*; and the hero's private life, particularly his love-life, was portrayed in the *histoire galante*. Meanwhile pseudo-memoirs were gradually becoming established in their own right and continued to combine all three elements, though with varying emphasis on one or another of these aspects.

There are two key-figures in the opening stages of fictional autobiography: Mme de Villedieu and Courtilz de Sandras.[1] The former is a direct literary precursor of Prévost, Marivaux and the other memoir-novelists whose central character is a purely imaginary figure.

Mme de Villedieu was a literary personage of some importance in her day. She wrote three plays, one of which was staged by Molière's company at the Palais-Royal and later at Versailles. She also wrote a number of novels in the conventional third-person narrative form.[2] Bayle attributes to her the decline of the long novel, ousted by her shorter works.[3] Her writings continued in favour during the century after her death: between 1696 and 1741 there were seven editions of her complete works; and Mornet's analysis of the catalogues of private libraries between 1750 and 1780 shows her heading the list of seventeenth-century French novelists.[4]

This literary prestige, however, was initially of no help to the

---

[1] An interesting case of a first-person novel with a bourgeois hero occurs in César Oudin de Préfontaine's *L'Orphelin infortuné ou le portrait du bon frère* (1660). The author claims to be offering an authentic autobiography, but he says that the story is disguised and 'habillé à la Romanesque'. In tone and manner this work, which had no immediate successors in the seventeenth century, seems to lie somewhere between the comic novels of the period and the other pseudo-memoirs.

[2] See B. A. Morrissette, *The Life and Works of Marie-Catherine Desjardins* (*Mme de Villedieu*), Saint Louis, 1947.

[3] Bayle, *Dictionnaire historique*, Article *Jardins*.

[4] D. Mornet, 'Les enseignements des bibliothèques privées, 1750–1780', *Revue d'histoire littéraire de la France*, XVII (1910), p. 473.

Mémoires de la Vie de Henriette-Sylvie de Molière (1672), since the work was published as an authentic autobiography, with no indication that it was the work of Mme de Villedieu. Knowledge of its authorship, possibly shared at first by a limited number of readers, was not likely to become widespread until the novel appeared among her collected works. Morrissette has shown that the book is in no sense an account of Mme de Villedieu's own life, though a previous biographer, Emile Magne, thought it to be a romanced version of her career and drew on it for evidence.[1] (This provides yet another example of the problems which may be set by pseudo-memoirs.)

Magne's acceptance of the work as partly factual seems all the more surprising when we consider the nature of the story. It deals chiefly with the highly improbable complications of the heroine's love-affairs, and though real people and places are mentioned, the main plot seems pure fantasy. Henriette's parents are not known, and she acquires her family name only by being substituted, when still a baby, for the dead daughter of the financier Molière. As a young woman, her misfortunes begin when Molière tries to seduce her and she, being an adept with a pistol, shoots him and takes refuge in the house of Mme de Molière's lover. Later on, when she has found a protectress in Mme d'Englesac, the young Englesac, another would-be suitor, sets the family château on fire so as to obtain a few moments' tête-à-tête with Henriette in the general confusion. She is subsequently abducted by another suitor, and adopted by a capricious Marquise. She assumes male attire while fleeing from some enemies, and is then challenged to a duel by another woman also disguised as a man. These are only a few of the incidents which might make a modern reader sceptical as to the book's authenticity. There are however some episodes and small touches which seem fresh and lifelike by comparison with other works of the period, and one can understand contemporary enjoyment of these innovations. The mere fact that the heroine's story started with the beginning of her life would make it less like a conventional novel for the seventeenth-century reader, since the heroic novel, like the epic, regularly began by plunging *in medias res*.[2]

[1] E. Magne, *Mme de Villedieu*, Paris, 1907.
[2] Cf. Ratner, *Theory and Criticism*, pp. 14–15.

Mme de Villedieu produced no other memoir-novels, and it was left to Courtilz de Sandras (c. 1644–1712) to exploit the resources of the form in a slightly different way. His writings provide an extraordinarily clear illustration, first of the progress from biography to pseudo-memoirs in a single author's work, and secondly of a shift in these memoirs from predominantly public and military subject-matter to more private and intimate affairs.

One side of Courtilz's career as a story-teller can be seen in three collections probably modelled on or suggested by Bussy-Rabutin's *Histoire amoureuse des Gaules* (1665) and similar works. The titles are self-explanatory: *Conquêtes amoureuses du grand Alcandre*—i.e. Henri IV (1684); *Intrigues amoureuses de la cour de France* (1685); and *Les dames dans leur naturel* (1686). But Courtilz was also a political journalist and pamphleteer, well informed about current affairs and interested in public figures. In 1685 he published a biography of Turenne, who had died ten years previously (leaving, incidentally, some *Mémoires* of his own). This *Vie du Vicomte de Turenne* was offered to the public as the work of a certain Capitaine du Boisson; the manuscript, it was claimed, had been found among his papers after his death. (Courtilz de Sandras scarcely ever published under his own name.) The narrative is in the normal third-person style of biography, and the apocryphal du Boisson does not claim to have any special or superior sources of information about his subject. A year later came the *Vie de l'Amiral de Coligny*, and in this case the author says that he belongs to 'une maison alliée à celle de Coligny', and has therefore had access to documents which were not available to other biographers. The next stage in the process is for Courtilz to claim not merely better sources of information than anyone else, but the best source of all: he steps into the shoes of the person portrayed, casts the whole narrative in the first person, and publishes the result as authentic memoirs. So in 1686 there appeared the *Mémoires de M. L. C. D. R.*, usually identified as M. le Comte de Rochefort. The subject-matter is chiefly political and military, with little space devoted to Rochefort's love-affairs or to his thoughts and feelings. In fact the book bears a strong general resemblance to the *Mémoires* of de Pontis, which may indeed have served as a model.

Courtilz utilized the technique of the *Mémoires de Rochefort* in several subsequent works, of which the most famous is of course the *Mémoires de M. d'Artagnan* (1700). Here the military and political element is still strong—d'Artagnan takes part in several major campaigns and also carries out various secret diplomatic missions—but the musketeer is also a ladies' man, and the winning and breaking of hearts takes up a good many pages of his story. With the *Mémoires de la Marquise de Fresne* (1701), love—or scandal—has really come into its own. The chief interest in this lady's life-story lies in her adventures while outwitting her husband, who tries various methods of getting rid of her, including selling her to an Italian corsair. Here again Courtilz drew his materials from real life, but he was by now obviously writing with an eye on the reader who preferred a love-interest to more serious topics. In so doing, he was making his works approximate more and more closely to the current idea of the novel, which was presumed to deal chiefly with love.

There is little point in discussing any of Courtilz de Sandras's pseudo-memoirs in detail, since they are now largely forgotten except for Dumas's borrowing from d'Artagnan in *Les Trois Mousquetaires*. But a few points deserve attention before we leave these works. The first is that although Courtilz's 'auto-biographies' were in some sense frauds, they were based on the lives and adventures of real people, known by many contemporary readers to have existed, and they did have a foundation of historical truth and accuracy. As Le Breton points out,

Sandras fait le portrait de gens qui ont existé, qui existaient hier; il a noté quelques-uns de leurs faits et gestes, de leurs défauts, de leurs qualités, de leurs goûts. A ces traits individuels il en joint d'autres qu'il emprunte à des hommes du même temps et du même métier.[1]

That is, he filled out the narrative with embellishments and anecdotes, some of which were true, though they had not necessarily happened to the person to whom they were attributed. Works like these therefore represent a halfway stage between authentic memoirs and the life-stories of purely imaginary characters such as Cleveland and Marianne.

[1] André Le Breton, *Le Roman français au XVIIIe siècle*, Paris, 1898, p. 24.

Secondly, Courtilz's various *Mémoires* were extremely popular:

Le témoignage de ses contemporains est unanime à constater son succès. Sallengre, par exemple, dit dans les *Mémoires de Littérature*: 'Jamais livre du temps n'a peut-être été mieux reçu que les Mémoires de Rochefort.'[1]

And thirdly, he was attacked by various critics, including Bayle, for his impudence and conceit in passing off his works as authentic memoirs and thus tricking the unwary reader. Voltaire, half-a-century later, also thought it necessary to warn his readers against 'faux mémoires', and added: 'Courtilz fut un des plus coupables écrivains de ce genre. Il inonda l'Europe de fictions sous le nom d'histoires.'[2] The accusation is somewhat exaggerated; owing to his habit of anonymous publication, Courtilz has occasionally been credited with works which he probably did not write. Nevertheless, we have here, as in the case of Saint-Réal, an author who could exploit for his own ends the no-man's-land between fiction and history, and could win the reader's belief by a device against which only the occasional critic raised a voice of protest.

Courtilz's particular type of fraud was not much pursued in the eighteenth century. Collections of letters were sometimes attributed to historical characters—Aspasia, Ninon de Lenclos and others—but the subjects of 'memoirs' were by now usually imaginary, even if the 'editor' claimed that they were real persons. Prévost's *Cleveland* and similar novels are therefore not a direct development of the 'memoirs' written by Courtilz de Sandras, but the latter's works, by their form and popularity, undoubtedly paved the way for the fictional autobiographies that followed.[3]

---

[1] B. M. Woodbridge, *Gatien de Courtilz, Sieur du Verger*, Baltimore and Paris 1925, p. 1.

[2] Voltaire, *Œuvres*, ed. Moland, Paris, 1877–85, XIV, p. 57.

[3] A work frequently mentioned in studies of French literature as a landmark in the history of the novel is Hamilton's *Mémoires du Comte de Gramont* (1713). These memoirs fall outside the scope of this chapter, as they are not in autobiographical form. Gramont was a real person, a friend of Hamilton's; and although some episodes may have been invented or 'touched up', much of the biographical material is undoubtedly authentic. The book is therefore a romanced biography, plus a number of stories of

While the authors so far mentioned all contributed to the adoption of memoirs as a form for the novel, another group of writers are a probable source of one specific element in some memoir-novels. These were the composers of imaginary journeys, a genre with a long and occasionally illustrious history.[1] Already in Rabelais (Book V) we find fantastic travels being described in the first person, though it is not Pantagruel himself who speaks. Later on, just as authentic memoirs led to more-or-less fictional autobiographies, true travellers' tales encouraged the production of imaginary journeys couched in the same form. A notable instance is Cyrano de Bergerac's *L'Autre Monde*, which is told throughout as personal reminiscence. (Godwin's *The Man in the Moone*, on which Cyrano drew in other respects, is also told in the first person.) More important as a possible influence on the novel are works such as Gabriel Foigny's *La Terre Australe connue* (1676), supposedly an account of the travels of Jacques Sadeur; and *L'Histoire des Sévarambes* (1677) by Denis Varaisse d'Alais, in which the narrator is 'one Captain Siden'.[2] Both books claim to be authentic records, and contain practical details presumably intended to convince the reader that the work is no mere fantasy. In *La Terre australe*, Jacques Sadeur also provides a brief account of his birth, childhood and education. These works therefore have something in common with autobiographical fiction, though in purpose and subject-matter they are more closely allied to the *conte philosophique* than to the *roman* as it was then defined. We must surely diagnose a general debt to books of this kind when we find, for instance, in Prévost's *Cleveland*, the description of an imaginary island-colony of religious refugees (Book III), or an account of a tribe of American Indians whom the hero converts to 'natural religion' (Book IV).

After considering the various kinds of works by French

intrigues and love-affairs at the court of Charles II. Apart from considerations of style, there seems to be little reason for suggesting that this work was influential in the development of the French novel.

[1] See G. Atkinson, *The Extraordinary Voyage in French Literature before 1700*, New York, 1920; and P. B. Gove, *The Imaginary Voyage in Prose Fiction* (1941), 2nd edition, London, 1961.

[2] Part I of *L'Histoire des Sévarambes* was published in English in 1675. This may have been done to bolster up its supposedly English origin; cf. the similar procedure with *Cleveland* mentioned on p. 75, n.1 below.

authors which led up to the memoir-novel, we must also take into account a foreign contribution, the Spanish picaresque novel. This too was usually autobiographical, with the *pícaro* relating his own exploits in his struggle for survival within a hostile society.

The use of the form of memoirs for fiction was established earlier in Spain than in France.[1] *Lazarillo de Tormes* is usually considered to be the first true picaresque novel. The authorship of its first part, published in 1554, is still uncertain. A second part, not picaresque in character, came out not long after, but in 1620 Juan de Luna published an alternative sequel more in keeping with the original story, and this is now generally preferred. The two other principal works of this early period of the picaresque novel are Aleman's *Guzman de Alfarache* (1599) and *Marcos de Obregon* (1618) by Espinel. The latter has been shown to contain a good deal of authentic autobiographical material, and is thus a predecessor to the romanced memoirs of Tristan l'Hermite.[2]

These and many other picaresque novels were translated into French not long after their publication, and new or revised versions continued to appear throughout the seventeenth and eighteenth centuries.[3] Lesage himself published, in 1732, his *Histoire de Guzman d'Alfarache, nouvellement traduite, et purgée des moralités superflues*, and two years later came his *Histoire d'Estebanille Gonzalès*, which purported to be a translation of *Estevanillo Gonzalez* (1646), but in reality contained a good deal of his own invention. A fair number of these Spanish stories were therefore available in France, and some of their distinctive traits would seem to have been adopted by French novelists.

Of these, the most outstanding is the choice of the hero, or anti-hero, from the lower classes. And a second characteristic might be the episodic rambling form of the story—a trait which is sometimes taken nowadays as the principal meaning of the

---

[1] The earliest French autobiographical novel known to me does date back to 1538: Hélisenne de Crenne's *Les Angoysses douloureuses qui procedent d'amours*. However, its use of the first person is in all probability borrowed from Boccaccio's *Fiammetta*, and it would seem to have led to no imitations or successors in the sixteenth century. (See Gustave Reynier, *Le Roman sentimental avant L'Astrée*, Paris, 1908, pp. 100–22.)

[2] A. A. Parker, *Literature and the Delinquent*, Edinburgh, 1967, p. 53.

[3] F. W. Chandler, *Romances of Roguery*, London, 1899, pp. 399–469.

word 'picaresque'. If we start, however, to attribute 'influences' in matters like these, it is difficult to decide what kinds of limit to set. For instance, the seventeenth-century comic and satirical novels had already brought lower-class characters into the limelight, as well as employing a loose and disconnected kind of plot; and Sorel's *Francion*, for example, came out as early as 1622. Apart from special cases such as Lesage, therefore, it will be safer not to attempt any precise assessment of the Spanish influence. All we can do is to take note of this tributary which joins the main stream of autobiographical fiction in France and helps to swell its volume.

As the memoir-novel itself became more widespread, there was a parallel change in the form of the novel's preface or introduction. Many seventeenth-century novelists, especially the writers of *romans héroïques*, had indulged in prefaces, often quite long ones. Here aims and methods were discussed, and occasionally there was a parade of historical sources. But such introductions amount to little more than literary essays.

With the memoir-novel, the introductory matter regularly becomes an imaginative exercise in itself. It explains how or why the autobiography came to be written. And if the text is supposedly edited by a second writer, we are usually provided also with some explanation of how the manuscript came into his possession and why it is being published. Interspersed among these 'facts', it is common to find some assurances as to the authenticity of the whole work, plus possibly a pointed reminder that truth is stranger than fiction. Thus the novelists were apparently trying to evoke literal rather than imaginative belief. (Just how seriously these attempts at deception were taken, by writers and readers, is a point we shall need to consider at a later stage.)

As a typical example, covering all the themes usually found in such introductions, we may take some crucial passages from the preface of the *Mémoires de M. L. C. D. R.*, Courtilz de Sandras's first essay in pseudo-memoirs:

Le C. D. R. a été un homme si connu, et qui est mort depuis si peu de temps, qu'il semble presque inutile de vouloir justifier ce qu'il rapporte dans ses Mémoires. Tous ceux qui ont été hommes de guerre, ou hommes de Cour, savent qu'il n'était pas capable de conter une fable pour une vérité, et encore moins de l'écrire pour abuser le public. . . . . Ainsi, si dès le commencement de ses Mémoires il rapporte une chose de son père qui paraît surprenante, il ne faut pas inférer de là qu'elle n'est pas véritable. Nous en voyons arriver tous les jours de si extraordinaires, que ceux qui connaissent bien Paris ne s'en étonneront pas. . . . . Je le trouve même de bonne foi de vouloir ainsi rapporter des choses de sa famille, que beaucoup d'autres à sa place auraient voulu taire. Quoi qu'il en soit, je dirai pour rendre témoignage à la vérité, que m'étant trouvé l'autre jour en compagnie avec Mr le Président de Bailleul, et ayant l'esprit tout rempli de ces Mémoires, je lui demandai s'il ne se ressouvenait point de ce procès, aussi bien que de certaines choses dont Mr L. C. D. R. fait mention en parlant de lui. Il me dit qu'il s'en ressouvenait tout de même que si la chose venait de se passer: après quoi, y a-t-il rien à dire? . . .

L'on trouve dans tout cela des leçons pour savoir se conduire, ce qui est la plus grande utilité que l'on puisse retirer de la lecture d'un livre. Je crois aussi que le principal motif qui a poussé Mr L. C. D. R. à écrire, n'a pas tant été le désir qu'il avait de faire voir qu'il avait été employé dans les affaires secrètes, que celui de rendre les autres sages par son exemple. . . . Cependant si ces Mémoires ne sont pas si utiles que je me l'imagine, toujours seront-ils fort curieux. L'on y voit des choses fort touchantes, et qui n'ont jamais été écrites ailleurs. Ils seront aussi fort divertissants et je ne crois pas que personne s'ennuie jamais à les lire. . . .

Cependant il faut que j'avoue une chose dont je ne sais si on me saura gré ou non; je donne ici ces Mémoires contre la dernière volonté de leur auteur, lequel n'ayant survécu qu'un mois ou deux à sa retraite, me dit de les supprimer. Je n'en sais pas bien la raison, si ce n'est qu'étant prêt de quitter le monde, il voulait épargner quelques gens, avec qui il avait eu des démêlés, et de qui il ne dit pas trop de bien. Mais cela ne m'a pas paru une raison suffisante, pour priver le public d'un ouvrage si curieux: quoi qu'il en soit, le voilà tel que je l'ai reçu, et je n'y ai rien augmenté, ni diminué.

The insistence on authenticity needs no comment. And there is nothing to surprise us in finding the motive for the auto-biographer's work cited as 'le désir . . . de rendre les autres plus sages par son exemple'. To this the 'editor' adds interest and entertainment as further reasons for publication. These were all to become standard justifications for the writing and publishing of fictional memoirs. Very occasionally an eighteenth-century novelist finds some more cogent or less commonplace reason. Mme de Villedieu had shown the way by offering an explanation arising from the life and circumstances of the heroine herself. Mlle de Molière, having led a life full of adventures and catastrophes, has acquired an undeserved reputation for scandalous and flighty behaviour. Her *Mémoires* are written to explain and justify her actions, and they are addressed in the first instance to a noble lady who has asked her to undertake the task.[1] Mme de Villedieu maintains this initial fiction consistently throughout the book: explanations and asides are offered to 'Madame' or 'Votre Altesse' at frequent intervals. Moreover the supposition that she is providing the true story behind the apparent scandal often allows her to give confidential details which might otherwise have seemed unsuitable for mention by a lady.

Mme de Villedieu has here invented a situation with obvious advantages for the story-teller, and a framework which is a natural extension of the 'Life' it guarantees. The only motive-for-writing of comparable ingenuity in the eighteenth-century novel is, I think, that of Suzanne in Diderot's *La Religieuse*. Here the causation is even more compelling. Because Suzanne is a fugitive, and hopes to win the sympathy and help of the Marquis de Croismare, she 'must' offer him some account of the events which forced her to run away from convent-life. Hence her story.

The type of framework-situation which the novelist provides is important not merely for its ingenuity or its connection with the main plot, but also because it tends to influence the tone of the narrative. This is, of course, one of the distinctive features of *La Vie de Marianne*, supposedly written not for the reading public but for the eye of an intimate friend. The kind of reasons-for-writing supplied in introductory remarks can therefore have a bearing on the mood and texture of the whole novel.

Most eighteenth-century novelists were content with the well-worn motives of *plaire et instruire*, though as the vogue for *sensibilité* increases we also find people who say that they have written their life-stories in order to recall and dwell upon their

---

[1] The same device was used, for an authentic autobiography, by the Cardinal de Retz. He addressed his *Mémoires* to an anonymous lady, thought by critics to be fictitious, who had supposedly asked him to write them. This technique may well have been an offshoot of the dedicatory epistles common at the time.

sufferings, like the hero of Mme de Tencin's *Comte de Comminge*. It is noticeable, however, that novelists of this period no longer see any necessity for excusing first-person narrative as such. Tristan l'Hermite was half-apologetic, and quoted the precedent of Montaigne to support his method. The Abbé Arnauld comments that de Pontis's memoirs were unfavourably received by some readers: 'Il ne parle que de lui, disaient-ils, Et qu'avons-nous affaire de savoir ce qui le regarde?'[1] But the eighteenth-century writer assumes that it is 'natural'— or at least not a matter requiring excuse—for someone to think that his own life, told in the first person, can be interesting and instructive.

With the pretence of authenticity to maintain, the writers of memoir-novels could scarcely lay much stress on the purely literary advantages of first-person narrative. The convention, after all, assumed that no other method of telling the story was open to them. But an interest in the specific qualities of the narrative 'I' had begun to arise in other quarters. The earliest discussion of the subject known to me occurs in the English translation of the *Mémoires de Henriette-Sylvie de Molière*, which appeared in the same year as the original, 1672. The anonymous translator of Part I of the novel has transposed Mme de Villedieu's first person into the third. In the appended notes he (or she?) justifies the procedure as follows:

. . . I hope you will find it as smooth every whit, to say *Silvia* did, *Silvia* said, as I did or I spoke thus. Some indeed will have it, that when you reade any thing that is very pleasant; as for example, the burning of the Castle, and *Silvia's* being carried in a swoon out of the House in the arms of *Birague*; her being in the Closet with *Englesac*: It is more pleasant still to have it in the first person, by reason of an application, and a certain interim [*sic*] that the Reader takes in it: But when the case is altered, and that *Silvia* is lockt up in another Closet with the Old Countess, or guarded in the Cloyster, or stript of the Prince of *Salmes* his clothes, as you shall see in the second part. Then, I believe, some had rather it were *She* than *I*. 'Tis sometimes your fear, and sometimes your pleasure that rules you; 'twere hard to serve them both at once.

Here the first-person narrative is seen, by a now-familiar

[1] *Mémoires de l'abbé Arnauld* (written 1677), Amsterdam, 1756, *Avertissement*, p. iv.

argument, as tending to involve the reader's sympathies more closely, and as leading to 'identification' with the 'I' of the story. (We have already seen the importance attached by some French theorists to the rousing of the reader's emotions.) It may be added that the translator of the remainder of the novel, Parts II–VI, ridiculed the arguments noted above and reverted to the first person.

The reasons given for the transposition of de Pontis's reminiscences back into the first person are rather different. The writer, we are told in the *Avertissement*,

> trouva que la répétition trop fréquente du *Sieur de Pontis*, qu'il fallait nommer une infinité de fois, rompait toute la suite de l'histoire. Il jugea d'ailleurs qu'elle aurait un tout autre poids étant dans la bouche même de celui qu'elle regardait et qui en faisait le principal sujet.

Here we are offered as justification, beside the minor advantage of avoiding awkward repetitions, the increased authority which seems to be inherent in a first-person narrative.

There are of course no grounds for assuming that first-person narrative will of itself lend conviction to any and every story. Indeed, as a narrative technique it has as many pitfalls as advantages to offer. Trollope thought it dangerous; Henry James called it 'the darkest abyss of romance'.[1] Nevertheless, for some readers the speaking 'I' does seem to lend an additional touch of authority and veracity to a tale. How many eighteenth-century novelists realized and traded upon the potential virtues of first-person narrative we can scarcely know, since the effect of the memoir-novel was not, in theory, based upon such merely literary factors. But the point made concerning de Pontis's 'memoirs' might well strike subsequent writers too. Prévost, for one, suggested that readers were more likely to be impressed and affected by the narrative methods of autobiography than by the third-person accounts of historians:

> La force qui règne ordinairement dans ces ouvrages, cette chaleur que le souvenir de ce qu'on a fait inspire toujours en l'écrivant, et surtout l'intime connaissance qu'on a du sujet, ... frappent le lecteur avec plus de force, et l'intéressent bien plus pour un héros qui s'offre à lui sous la double qualité d'acteur et d'écrivain, que ne

[1] Quoted in M. Allott's *Novelists on the Novel*, London, 1959, p. 260.

le peuvent jamais les relations moins animées d'un simple compila-teur.[1]

This view was borne out, he said, by the fact that 'les auteurs des meilleurs romans n'ont pas imaginé de plus puissantes méthodes pour plaire et pour attacher, que de mettre leur narration dans la bouche même du héros'. As the stream of memoirs—authentic and fictional—began to swell, considera-tions of this kind may have contributed to the increasing popularity, among novelists, of autobiography as a means of creating the desired illusion and inducing belief.

[1] Prévost, *Lettres de Mentor à un jeune seigneur*, in *Œuvres choisies*, Paris, 1784, Vol. 34, p. 52.

IV

Lesage and Conventions

L ESAGE states that in *Gil Blas* he intends to portray 'la vie des hommes telle qu'elle est' (I, 1).[1] To the reader of the period this announcement would indicate clearly enough that the book was of the kind known as a *roman comique* or *roman satirique*, that it would present a humorously critical view of various social types, and had no pretensions as to being 'historical'. The further admission, 'J'avoue que je n'ai pas toujours exactement suivi les mœurs espagnoles', would provide a hint, if any were needed, that Lesage had drawn his material from French society: for 'Madrid', read 'Paris'. Many of his readers would in any case be familiar with his previous book, *Le Diable boiteux* (1707), which had proved extremely popular. This work contains a number of satirical sketches set in a pseudo-Spanish milieu. The 'local colour' is however limited to superficial details with which most French readers would be familiar: duennas, guitar-playing and the like. In some cases the supposedly 'Spanish' personages are palpably modelled on French originals; the *inquisiteur malade* whose anxious female penitents compete to supply him with remedies is plainly less an Inquisitor than the kind of *Directeur* we shall meet again in *Le Paysan parvenu*. For Frenchmen, Lesage's 'Spain' was therefore no unfamiliar territory, and the reader of 1715, as he began *Gil Blas de Santillane*, might well expect to be offered the same kind of entertainment as he had already enjoyed.

The first pages of the novel itself would however show that Lesage was now following a different convention. In *Le Diable boiteux* he had borrowed, as a framework for his sketches, the fairy-tale device of a djinn or demon who has been imprisoned in a bottle.[2] When this Devil is released he entertains his

---

[1] Page-numbers refer to the two-volume Garnier edition, ed. Maurice Bardon, Paris, 1955.
[2] See I, 371, n. 391, and the *Dédicace* of *Le Diable boiteux*.

49

liberator, Don Cléophas, by showing him the secret life which goes on beneath the roofs of 'Madrid'. In contrast to this fantasy-framework, the opening paragraphs of *Gil Blas*, where the hero describes his upbringing and sets out on his travels, indicate that the book is cast in the mould of the picaresque novel. Even within the limits of the first chapter, however, the story has become picaresque-with-a-difference. Gil Blas's parents, though poor, are respectable; he has an uncle who is a canon of the Church; and the boy is given as good an education as the town of his birth can provide. This is already in contrast to the opening pages of most Spanish picaresque novels: these 'heroes' start their stories as ragged foundlings or as the children of rogues and swindlers, and are left to fend for themselves at an early age. (The life-story of Scipion, in *Gil Blas*, is typical in this respect.) For Gil Blas himself, Lesage has adapted the convention and lifted his narrator above the squalor and poverty, the brutality and coarseness of the traditional *picaro*:

> Ce n'est plus le même monde, ce ne sont plus ces gueux pouilleux, cette vermine repoussante, ces va-nu-pieds sans feu ni loi, ces ventres creux et affamés, ces aigrefins sans vergogne ni conscience. Si Gil Blas se souvient de son origine picaresque, le picaro du moins a été sérieusement décrassé.[1]

The same kind of conclusion emerges if, because of Lesage's opening promises, we compare *Gil Blas* with earlier French satirical novels. These too laid much emphasis on the sordid, on grotesque physical details and crude or scabrous incidents. (Such an approach was often part of a deliberate protest against the ridiculously over-refined attitudes of heroic novels.) By its general tone, therefore, *Gil Blas* marks a shift away from both the picaresque novel and the *roman comique*, towards a world which, without being idealized, does observe certain standards of polite society. This does not entirely preclude vulgar episodes and scatalogical details, but in the overall effect coarseness has become the exception rather than the rule.

If we look for precedents in the urbane presentation of a first-person story, then memoirs and memoir-novels are the obvious comparable form. These works, generally written—or

[1] Léo Claretie, *Essai sur Lesage romancier*, Paris, 1890, p. 182.

supposedly written—by persons of birth and breeding, usually kept within those limits of discretion and decency which a gentleman might be expected to observe.

Gil Blas can therefore be described as a fusion of at least three kinds of work: while covering much the same subject-matter as previous satiric novels, its plot begins along the lines of the traditional Spanish picaresque novel, and it has the tone of the more recent French development, fictional memoirs. Lesage's originality lies in his combination of these different elements.

The aspect of *Gil Blas* which readers remember most clearly is probably the general tone or 'feel' of the book, and we shall consider this first. The most important factor in this urbane atmosphere is the prose style which Lesage attributes to Gil Blas, as narrator. This style would have been inappropriate for a rough-and-tumble *pícaro*, since it is the mode of expression of an educated man with a neat turn of verbal wit. Gil Blas was eventually to owe his political power to a gift for clear, effective writing; the Duc de Lerme gave him a job largely on the strength of a written report which Gil Blas had prepared. It may not be safe to assume that Lesage foresaw this turn of the plot when he began writing, but whether by accident or design he made Gil Blas narrate his adventures in a style which is happily consistent with his education and his capabilities.

In vocabulary and grammar this style is 'neutral'. It avoids the pretentious inflated effects of some heroic novels, and also eschews low or vulgar terms. A more original and idiosyncratic aspect of Gil Blas's narrative manner is its peculiarly witty and astringent quality. This can be called 'ironic' in the general sense that many statements do not mean what they appear to say, but it is not always the simple irony of suggesting the opposite of the surface meaning. For instance, when the cook and the negro servant try to persuade Gil Blas that he is well off in the robbers' den, they use the very terms and arguments which could be used—and doubtless often were—to convince some reluctant postulant of the advantages of the monastic life:

Vous êtes jeune, et vous paraissez facile; vous vous seriez bientôt perdu dans le monde. Vous y auriez indubitablement rencontré des libertins qui vous auraient engagé dans toutes sortes de débauches, au lieu que votre innocence se trouve ici dans un port assuré. La dame Léonarde a raison, dit gravement à son tour le vieux nègre, et l'on peut ajouter a cela qu'il n'y a dans le monde que des peines. Rendez grâce au ciel, mon ami, d'être tout d'un coup délivré des périls, des embarras, et des afflictions de la vie (I, 23).[1]

This kind of wit-by-implication and various other forms of irony, usually employed for criticism, are frequent in Gil Blas's narrative, and one consequence of this trait is that the reader is, or should be, continually on the alert.

Such wit and irony are appropriate to the general attitude of Gil Blas towards his own adventures and the foibles of other people. Lesage has thus given an added piquancy to the cheerful if disillusioned outlook of the traditional *picaro*. But a consistently ironic style has its disadvantages. The coolness and detachment which generally characterize this manner may be out of place in sad or pathetic situations, and can become an obstacle to the adequate treatment of serious feeling.

Admittedly it is not often that Gil Blas is deeply touched, since his ebullient nature makes light of incidents which would be catastrophic for more impressionable characters. However, on the rare occasions when Lesage does deal with some moving experience in Gil Blas's life, the limitations of the ironic approach become evident. One may take as an instance the death of Gil Blas's first wife, Antonia. He refers to this as 'un événement que plus de vingt années n'ont pu me faire oublier, et qui sera toujours présente à ma pensée' (II, 269). He then describes his immediate reaction to Antonia's death:

Je tombai dans un accablement stupide; à force de sentir la perte que je faisais, j'y paraissais comme insensible. Je fus cinq ou six jours dans cet état; je ne voulais prendre aucune nourriture; et je crois que, sans Scipion, je me serais laissé mourir de faim, ou que la tête m'aurait tourné: mais cet adroit secrétaire sut tromper ma douleur en s'y conformant; il trouvait le secret de me faire avaler des bouillons en me les présentant d'un air si mortifié, qu'il semblait me les donner moins pour conserver ma vie que pour nourrir mon affliction.

There is surely something slightly comic about the mortified air of Scipion bringing in the soup; and the neat play on words in 'conserver ma vie' and 'nourrir mon affliction' is not particularly suggestive of a man still feeling the full bitterness of his

---

[1] Cf. Laure's echo of this situation and argument (II, 29).

loss. Furthermore, this and other emotional crises of Gil Blas's life are dealt with so briefly that such passages may make little impression on the reader. Thus the moments of stress lack the emphasis which can come from ample development as well as from stylistic differentiation. We must not however be led into concluding that Lesage was, in general, unwilling to portray the deeper emotions. He certainly tried to do so in *Gil Blas*, and he can even be said to have cultivated a different style for such subject-matter. The novel contains two tragic love-stories, *L'Histoire de doña Mencia* and *Le Mariage de vengeance*, as well as several other tales in which feelings run high. And it is obvious that Lesage adapts his manner to suit these narratives. The style in such episodes tends to be more elevated, and there is clearly some attempt to achieve effects of deep emotional stress and pathos. This attempt, we may feel, is not wholly successful. Lesage relies too much upon simple predictable reactions in his characters and a conventional expression of their feelings. For instance, the dialogue between Blanche and the young King in *Le Mariage de vengeance* (I, 224–5) is built on emotional as well as verbal clichés. As M. Bardon justifiably points out, when she protests that both her marriage-vows and her *gloire* forbid her listening to the King's pleas, 'Blanche parle ici comme une héroïne de Corneille' (I, 387, n.756). But Lesage has not established either the dramatic tension or the poetic context which could support such language.

One might also criticize Lesage for failing to differentiate between the speaking voices of the various aristocratic characters in their misfortunes. Doña Mencia's first husband says, as he resigns himself to leaving her, 'Je vous aime plus que moi-même; je respecte votre repos, et je vais, après cet entretien, achever loin de vous de tristes jours que je vous sacrifie' (I, 42). Don Alphonse, forced to leave Séraphine because he has killed her brother in a duel, strikes the same note: 'Je vais attendre avec impatience à Tolède le destin que vous me préparez; et, me livrant à vos poursuites, j'avancerai moi-même la fin de mes malheurs' (I, 272).[1] One reason for these similarities is that the

---

[1] In both these examples there are echoes, this time not of Corneille but of Racine: 'Ces jours malheureux que je vous sacrifie' (*Bérénice*, 1468); and 'Sa mort avancera la fin de mes ennuis' (*Andromaque*, 376).

noble characters in Lesage's serious stories rarely if ever go beyond the limits of their strict code of ethics and behaviour; they conform to type.

Not all the interpolated stories, however, are attributed to the nobility. We hear the adventures, as told by themselves, of the *garçon-barbier* and Don Raphaël (a 'Don' by courtesy only), of Laure and Scipion. And here again one's verdict must surely be that these characters share a common style rather than possessing any distinctive tone which might mark them off as individuals. It is, in essentials, the manner of Gil Blas himself, and a number of verbal echoes accentuate the family ressemblance. Gil Blas, arriving in the robbers' den, is told that he is to work under Léonarde. He says, 'La cuisinière (il faut que j'en fasse le portrait) était une personne de soixante et quelques années' (I, 14). Don Raphaël, taken prisoner by corsairs, becomes the servant of a Pacha, and observes, 'Ce pacha (il faut que j'en fasse le portrait) était un homme de quarante ans . . .' (I, 299). Apart from such repetitions, these lower-class narrators have the same turns of speech, the same bent for irony, and a general homogeneity of expression which tends to make the narrative manner of any one of them indistinguishable from that of the others, or indeed from that of Gil Blas himself.[1] Once again we are dealing with types rather than with unique individuals, and this is an aspect of Lesage's characterization which we shall need to consider more fully at a later stage. Here we can conclude that at a purely linguistic level, Lesage has two distinct narrative styles: the neutral manner of Gil Blas and his compeers, frequently spiced with irony and wit; and the rather more elevated mode of expression of the aristocracy, generally serious, and often verging on bombast when it aims at a high and tragic tone.

The doctrine of stylistic levels was of course a commonplace of literary theory in the seventeenth and eighteenth centuries. (Auerbach, in *Mimesis*, sees the breakdown of this hierarchy of styles as a crucial factor in the development of realism.) In practice, it was based on three interdependent factors: the social status of the characters involved; the nature of the subject-matter—tragic, serious or gay; and on the established

[1] For further examples, see N. Wagner, 'Quelques cadres d'études pour "Gil Blas" ', *L'Information littéraire*, VIII (1956), pp. 29-30.

hierarchy of literary genres. In *Gil Blas* the element of class would seem to predominate, for, as we have seen, Gil Blas and his equals are not made noticeably to change their normal style when they suffer some serious misfortune. Unlike the aristocrats, they have no heights of language which may help to express their feelings in moments of stress. Against this, however, one must set the contemporary notion that, by the very nature of things, the sufferings of kings and nobles are inherently more important, more deserving of our interest and sympathy, than any misfortunes of a person of lower social status. Beresford Cotton, for instance, suggests that de Pontis's *Mémoires*

may suffer in some people's esteem because the person whose life is described attained to no higher a post than that of a Captain in the Guards and Commissary-General of the Swiss troops.[1]

He then explicitly formulates, and accepts, the idea on which such criticisms were based:

I own that persons of the first quality are more entertaining subjects, as their virtues and their vices commonly bear proportion to their higher station. They have it most in their power to be eminently good or bad; and consequently such relations fill our minds with greater and more surprising ideas.

The unhappy incidents in the aristocratic stories in *Gil Blas* are therefore automatically more serious than any mishaps undergone by lesser men, and the language of the noble episodes is thus geared to the true gravity of events, as well as to the class of the narrator.

The third factor, the correlation between various levels of style and their appropriate literary genres, seems to break down in *Gil Blas*, since in this work the different styles are juxtaposed in successive chapters. Here, however, we are dealing with a consequence of the freedom which the comic novel enjoyed, largely because it was outside the dictates of serious literary theory. Writers of comic novels paid no allegiance to the concept of unity of style. They could and did bring passages of

---

[1] *Memoirs of the Sieur de Pontis*, translated by Charles Cotton, London, 1694, Publisher's preface (written by the translator's son).

For a detailed discussion of the same attitude among French critics of the early eighteenth century, see Georges May, *Le Dilemme du roman*, pp. 163–73.

lofty rhetoric into their more colloquial and vulgar narrative, for purposes of burlesque. Another procedure utilized in the comic novel, and apparently at odds with its general aims, was the use of an elevated style for episodes which were clearly meant to be taken seriously. Such episodes were often inserted stories of the type known as *nouvelles,* and were supposedly related by someone other than the principle narrator.

This device raises two problems of technique: a question of realism concerning the style of the secondary narrator; and the larger issue of plot-structure and interpolated stories.

In the picaresque novel and the memoir-novel we have, in theory, only one narrator. When other characters 'tell us' their stories, these tales are, in the fictional situation, merely passed on to us by the chief narrator himself. But supposing such stories are couched in a different and distinctive style? If we apply real-life standards, the question then arises whether anyone is likely to be able to repeat a whole story faithfully, in the exact terms of the original narration, without altering it according to his own habits of speech and thought. An author who shows some awareness of this problem is already utilizing, to however slight a degree, a criterion of realism: he is conscious of possible disparities between the postulated fictional situation and the corresponding situation in real life. As early as 1599, Aleman noticed the problem and attempted a solution. In *Guzman de Alfarache,* about one-third of Book I is taken up by the tale of Daraja and Osmin, related by one of the group of people with whom Guzman is travelling. After the story, Guzman makes an appreciative comment on how it had held their interest, and adds: 'Howbeit, it was somewhat more enlarged by the author, flourished over with finer phrases and a different soul to that which I have delivered unto you.'[1] But remarks on this subject are exceptional among the early writers of first-person novels. They tend to follow implicitly the literary convention that their narrator has a memory like a tape-recorder, and can play back a story exactly as it was told to him. Lesage took this line, and it is by this criterion that we can blame his failure to convey

---

[1] 'aunque más dilatada y con el alma diferente nos la dijo de lo que yo la he contado'. *Guzman de Alfarache,* ed. Samuel Gili y Gaya, Madrid, 1926, 5 vols., I, 245. The English is from the translation by Griffiths (London, 1622), p. 101.

individual differences within his two main narrative styles. Later novelists, more alive to questions of realism and plausibility, were to give the problem more attention. Reported stories and reported conversations, as we shall see, became the subject of comments and explanations by writers who were concerned with creating an effect of authenticity.

As for the larger question of how and why novelists made such a generous use of inserted stories, we are dealing here with the combined effects of several literary models and traditions.

On the one hand we have the *nouvelle*, a genre whose development in France was linked to its growth in Italy and Spain.[1] The early examples of such stories were usually grouped in collections, with a framework which described the occasion on which the tales were supposedly narrated. The *Decameron* and Marguerite de Navarre's *Heptameron* illustrate this pattern. The stories thus grouped together often had no connection with each other or with the framework situation. It was therefore a simple matter to lift them from their context and 'borrow' them for use in other settings or in another language. This ease of transfer probably contributed to the development of the *nouvelle* as an independent form. Thus a story from *Don Quixote, Novela del Curioso impertinente*, was translated into French and published separately in 1608, before the whole novel had appeared in French. As this example indicates, Spanish writers of comic or burlesque novels had begun to insert *novelas* into the body of their works. (The tale of Daraja and Osmin, in *Guzman de Alfarache*, shows the same process in the picaresque novel.) French authors, too, soon made a habit of introducing *nouvelles* in comic novels.

The method of presenting the interpolated *nouvelle* is simple, and somewhat reminiscent of the framework situation devised for collections of tales. In the novel, some reason is provided for a principal character to have a few hours on his hands, and at this juncture someone happens to be present who happens to know an interesting story, and proceeds to tell it. The story does not, as a rule, involve the person who recounts it. Occasionally this secondary narrator reappears at a later stage in the

[1] See George Hainsworth, *Les 'Novelas exemplares' de Cervantes en France au XVIIe siècle*, Paris, 1933, Bibliothèque de la Revue de litt. comparée, No. 95.

novel, but more often he or she drops out after telling the *nouvelle*, and is never seen again.

The narrator of an *histoire*, on the other hand, is generally a character who plays some part in the main action of the novel. Moreover, the *histoire* itself is often concerned with the narrator's own adventures. Theoretically, therefore, the *histoire* should be more closely linked to the whole work than is an interpolated *nouvelle*.[1] The link may nevertheless be slight or almost non-existent. When the barber has told his life-story to Gil Blas, the latter does go on to share in the festivities provided by the barber's uncle, and he even begins the next chapter: 'Je fis quelque séjour chez le jeune barbier' (I, 130). But this is the last we hear of the barber, and the whole episode could be deleted from the book without in any way affecting the course of Gil Blas's career. An *histoire* which is brought in like this has scarcely any more connection with the novel as a whole than the average *nouvelle*.

In contrast to this example, Doña Mencia's *histoire* does have some bearing on the main plot. It is to save her that Gil Blas devises his stratagem to escape from the robbers' den, and she later gives him some money which sets off his next adventure. Her story also explains how she came to be making the journey on which the robbers killed her husband and captured her. This kind of *histoire*, one might agree, has a legitimate function in the structure of the whole novel, while this particular example also possesses the merit, to our eyes, of being fairly short. More debatable are the *histoires* related by Don Raphaël, Laure and Scipion. Apparently Lesage himself realized that Don Raphaël's account had exceeded the appropriate limits: Gil Blas comments that 'le récit me parut un peu long' (I, 334). The *Histoire de Scipion* also takes up a good deal of space. As for their bearing on the plot, these three characters do all exert some influence,

---

[1] It is perhaps because of this convention that Robert Challe (or Chasles) preferred the term *histoire* for the interlinked stories which make up his *Illustres Françaises* (1713). This work is an outstanding early case of literary realism, but it can hardly be classified as a novel, and therefore falls outside the scope of the present study. See the relevant articles by F. Deloffre in *La Littérature narrative d'imagination*, Paris, 1961, pp. 115–29; and *Cahiers de l'Association Internationale des études françaises*, 11 (1959), pp. 9–32. See also the special number on Challe of the *Revue d'Histoire littéraire de la France*, nov.-déc. 1979.

in their varying ways, upon the course of Gil Blas's life. But one might still be tempted to query the relevance of much of the information they supply about their past lives.

A further refinement or complication of technique is the *histoire* which is split into two or more instalments. In the Tower of Segovia, Don Gaston de Cogollos relates the misfortunes which attended his love for Doña Helena (II, 151–65). Several years later, when he meets Gil Blas again, he is in a position to describe the incident which has brought his love-affair to a happy conclusion (II, 306–8). The trouble here is that as Don Gaston plays no appreciable rôle in the main plot, the reader has heard nothing of him for nearly thirty chapters, and may well have some difficulty in remembering the first part of his story when the sequel is presented.

All these types of interpolated *histoires*, and yet more complicated variants, had been current in the seventeenth century, not only in comic and satiric novels, but in serious fiction such as *L'Astrée* and the heroic novels of the mid-century. (In the more ambitious works, the *histoires* were of course of a prevalently refined tone.) It was this practice of inserting minor narratives into the main story-line which earned such novels the label of *romans à tiroir*. Since the use of interpolated stories like these is now quite foreign to our ideas of plot-structure and coherence, we shall understand it only if we discover the reasons which led to its adoption.

The most obvious reason is the existence of an early and respected model. The *Aethiopica*, a novel written in the third century A.D. by Heliodorus, was as near as the genre could get to a truly 'classical' precedent. A copy of this work was discovered after the sack of Budapest, and was published at Basle, in Greek, in 1534. Amyot's translation appeared in 1547, and Magendie lists seven re-impressions up to 1626, as well as other versions and adaptations of the novel.[1] More than any other single work, this story of the adventures of Theagenes and Charicleia helped to shape the seventeenth-century serious novel. Huet says of the work:

Tel qu'il est, il a servi de modèle à tous les faiseurs de Romans, qui

---

[1] Magendie, *Le Roman français au XVIIe siècle*, p. 16.

l'ont suivi, et on peut dire aussi veritablement qu'ils ont tous puisé à sa source que l'on dit que tous les Poètes ont puisé à celle d'Homere.[1]

This model consists of a main story, episodic in structure, which acts as a framework for other intercalated stories.

Some writers also defended *histoires* on the basis of supposed similarities between serious novels and the epic. The episodes of epic poems and the 'histories' in novels were classed together and described as 'plutôt des beautés que des défauts'.[2]

Apart from such appeals to respected literary antecedents, there were even some claims that the use of interpolated *histoires* presented positive literary advantages. Stories told by minor characters could add variety to the main plot by introducing new points of view. They could provide moments of respite and repose in the flow of the central narrative. They could create suspense by intervening to delay the outcome of some crucial incident. They could even contribute to *vraisemblance*, since it is 'natural' for two people meeting for the first time to tell each other something about their past life.

These arguments would not, I imagine, carry much weight with most modern critics. And already in the seventeenth century there were some writers who were prepared to attack the procedure:

> Outre que l'auteur en déduit lui-même l'histoire principale, il introduit plusieurs personnages qui en récitent d'autres, avec un langage qui est souvent trop affecté pour le temps et le lieu. . . . Et même pour embrouiller davantage le roman, ayant introduit un homme qui raconte quelque histoire, celui-là rapporte aussi celle qu'un autre a raconté, avec ses propres termes, faisant une histoire dans une autre histoire, ou le roman d'un roman; de sorte qu'on a peine à se ressouvenir qui c'est qui parle, de l'auteur, et du premier personnage, ou du second; et quelque attention qu'y donne le lecteur, il ne sait plus enfin où il est.[3]

Some sixty years later Lenglet du Fresnoy, looking back on the history of the genre, saw these complications as a cause of the decline of the long heroic novel:

> Les aventures des grands romans . . . étaient si coupées et si

---

[1] Huet, *Traité des romans*, p. 158. Cf. similar remarks by Sorel, Balzac, etc. cited by Magendie, *Le Roman français*, p. 17.

[2] Scudéry, *Ibrahim, Préface.* Cf. Magendie, op. cit., p. 126.

[3] Sorel, *De la Connoissance*, pp. 121-2.

embarrassées les unes avec les autres, que l'attention se partageait trop . . .

On s'est rebuté de tant d'embarras dans une lecture qui doit instruire sans fatiguer. Les petits romans ont suppléé à ce désagrément.[1]

Even if this diagnosis is true as regards the *grands romans*, the practice of inserting subsidiary stories lingered on until well into the eighteenth century. The last volume of *Gil Blas*, containing the *Histoire de Scipion*, came out in 1735. It was in 1742 that Marivaux published Parts IX, X, and XI of *La Vie de Marianne*, devoted to the life-story of Marianne's friend, the nun. And Prévost's unfinished *Le Monde moral* (1760) likewise shifts its centre of interest from the narrator's adventures to those of the Abbé Brenner.

Were there, perhaps, unavowed or unrecognized reasons for this widespread and persistent habit? One mundane practical consideration not likely to be mentioned by the novelists themselves, is that such intercalated stories helped to spin out the work. The ease with which they could be inserted spared the writer the effort of extending or elaborating his main plot, or of creating sub-plots. For an author like Lesage, not skilled in the structure of long stories, such a method was extremely useful in padding out his successive volumes.

A further and more specifically literary reason for the practice is that the chief interest of novels, at this time, lay in their story-line, in the adventures, in the element of what-happens-next. At this level, any story with lively events is a good thing; and the more stories a novel contains, the better it will be. This attitude would account for the apparently gratuitous inclusion of *nouvelles*, which seem to have even less artistic justification than *histoires*. And the relative importance attached to interpolated stories as such is shown, for instance, by the fact that the eighty or so *histoires* in *L'Astrée* are separately indexed in each volume, as though they were attractions to which the reader might want to return. Indeed, when the intercalations are on this scale, the novel seems to be moving towards the form of the collection of *nouvelles*, where the framework is no more than a pretext for assembling the stories.

[1] Lenglet du Fresnoy, *De l'Usage des romans*, Amsterdam, 1734, 2 vols., I, 200–1.

There is not much explicit evidence to support this suggestion that actions and events took pride of place in the novel.
Indeed, the occasional plea for greater subtlety and verisimilitude in characterization would seem to imply that some novelists
were aware of other potential sources of interest in the genre.[1]
Nevertheless, the multiplicity of separate tales, the speed of
events, the way that novelists press on to the next adventure, all
seem to bear out the notion that the story-line was the prime
object of interest for writer and reader alike.

This approach to the novel is a simple one, indeed it is little
more than the child's love of a 'good story'. But we should not
on that account adopt a condescending or dismissive attitude
towards it. A 'good story' has never ceased to be a merit in the
novel. However, it is obvious that the seventeenth-century taste
for a wealth of interwoven stories produced works which are, by
modern standards, confused as to structure and artistically un-
satisfying. We can scarcely recover the approach of those early
readers, who had learnt to suspend their interest in the hero so
as to follow up the adventures of some other character. But at
least we can realize that for such readers these interpolations
were not unexpected distractions, but an accepted element of
the novel as they knew it.

Apart from the stories, there is in *Gil Blas* another element
which can be seen as digression. This is the portrayal of people
who cross Gil Blas's path without affecting his career. A case in
point is the former actor, Carlos Alonso de la Ventoleria.
When he calls on the actress Arsénie, Gil Blas provides a brief
description of his appearance (I, 184). Curious as to the character of this *Señor cavallero*, he then turns for information to
Laure, who says: 'Je vais te le peindre au naturel', and proceeds
to sketch in the actor's past life and present habits. Gil Blas
rounds off the description with: 'Tel fut le portrait que ma
soubrette me fit de cet histrion honoraire.' The portrait is thus
made to stand out as something of a set-piece.

A page or two later comes another vignette, this time a playwright who is forced to accept the actresses' haughty treatment

---

[1] E.g.: 'Ce n'est point par les choses de dehors, ce n'est point par les
caprices du destin que je veux juger de lui [du personnage], c'est par les
mouvements de son âme et par les choses qu'il dit', Scudéry, *Ibrahim*,
Préface.

in order to get his play a reading. Here it is the situation, and especially the behaviour of the actresses, which is the point of the picture, and Lesage obtains his effect by showing the personages in action.

On other occasions we are given a whole group of portraits together. In the *salon* of the Marquise de Chaves, an obliging colleague sums up for Gil Blas the characters of the various *habitués* as they appear, providing illustrative anecdotes, and ending up with a sketch of the Marquise herself (I, 253–5).

In the mind of Lesage and his first readers, there was a distinction to be made among these portraits. Some were drawn from specific models, and readers in the know would recognize the actor Baron or a distinguished *salonnière* like Mme de Tencin. (It was to cover cases of this kind that Lesage included his assurance that he had *not* portrayed any particular person.) Others were based on familiar Parisian types like the *petit-maître*, and such descriptions would have been qualified at the time as *caractères*. Generally speaking, the *caractère* stresses some specific trait or tendency in its subject, such as the frivolity and fatuity of the *petits-maîtres*.

The individual *portrait*, after being a pastime in seventeenth-century *salons*, found its way into novels such as Mlle de Scudéry's *Clélie*, which were *romans à clef*. These portraits tended to be isolated set-pieces. We have seen how Lesage draws attention to his portrait of La Ventoleria-Baron, and we shall find Marivaux following the same method in *La Vie de Marianne*. The literary *salons* had also fostered the writing of *caractères*, a minor genre which might have faded into oblivion had it not found a master-hand in La Bruyère.

In *Gil Blas* the modern reader cannot always distinguish between these two kinds of character-sketch, unless there are editorial notes to supply the requisite information. However, the difference in origin is obviously of minimal importance nowadays. It is rather the literary merit of these sketches, whether specific or typical, which deserves our attention. Lesage would seem to have enjoyed creating them; they are usually well and wittily executed, with a neat and vivid touch; and they exhibit his special flair for highlighting motives of vanity.

Since the character-sketches in *Gil Blas* possess these real

merits, it is perhaps thankless to ask whether they should be
there at all. Yet the fact remains that they are, from a structural point of view, a defect rather than an asset. During the
histoires, Gil Blas is reduced to the rôle of a listener; for the kind
of portrait we have been discussing, he has become a passive
spectator. And in either case, his own story is temporarily
shelved. To be fair, one should notice that just as he *can* inte-
grate an *histoire* into the main plot, Lesage can also work his
social portraits into the stuff of Gil Blas's life. The group of
petits-maîtres and their valets who give Gil Blas his first notions
of the life of fashionable young aristocrats are just as much types
as the guests in the Marquise's *salon*. But Gil Blas learns from
the valets, so that the episode affects him and is a stage in his
development. The actor, the playwright, the guests of Mme de
Chaves, merely pass before his eyes, exert no influence on him,
and disappear after having halted the action yet once more.

The justification for these supernumerary portraits lies of
course in Lesage's undertaking to show us life as it is. And their
presence reveals his interest, an interest which overrides considerations of plot, in the various kinds of foolishness and self-
importance which flourished in the society of his day. We see
people not only as participants in unusual actions and adventures,
but carrying out their everyday rôle in society, as flatterers or
would-be intellectuals or quarrelsome men of letters. The whole
purpose of passages like these is to capture the essence of certain
social types.

This fondness of Lesage for the typical personage goes even
deeper, and underlies his whole approach to the portrayal of
character. The majority of his characters in *Gil Blas* are types:
we can fit them into categories, and their behaviour is always
predictable within the limits of that category. Among the remaining characters, many could be termed eccentrics, but even
those eccentrics whom Lesage chooses to portray follow a clear
pattern. The character simply carries to extremes one of the
traits which is in any case associated with his class or type.
Spaniards are by reputation dilatory and fond of idleness; Don
Bernard de Castil Blazo takes this to the point of arranging his
whole life so that he can avoid even the trouble of managing an
income. Many Church dignitaries are vain of their talents as
preachers, and the Archbishop of Grenada shows how far such

vanity can go. Doctors are ignorant, but each of them swears by his own system; Dr Sangrado's excesses are only an extension of this habit. What is lacking, in such cases, is the unexpected touch which lifts a character out of the rut and gives him individuality.

Since some critics have expressed doubts as to whether Gil Blas himself is a complete and convincing character, it is clear that even he, the hero of the book, may not convey to every reader that vivid sense of a unique personality which is created by masters of characterization. Gil Blas, it may be claimed, has no trait, no quirk of feeling or behaviour, which makes him absolutely distinct from other characters of his kind and class. On this particular and crucial case, opinions may differ; Gil Blas's own adventures do after all dominate the novel, and his reactions may seem variable enough, within their limited range, to evoke for some readers the image of a complete and credible personality. The fact remains, however, that Lesage's talents lie more in the portrayal of types and recurrent traits than of unique individuals.

From all this it would seem that Lesage, whatever his failings, did at least fulfil his initial promise to provide a general portrait of society. But as the novel progresses, we move from a timeless scene, with a transparent veneer of Spanish local colour, to a specific period, with Spanish historical events and personages dominating the action. From the middle of Book VIII onwards, *Gil Blas* becomes as much an 'historical novel' as some of the seventeenth-century works with their inflated claims to historicity. Since this development is scarcely foreshadowed in the earlier part of the novel, we need to consider how the historical element makes its appearance, what effects it produces on the work as a whole, and the possible reasons for its introduction.

The first chapters of Gil Blas's story are timeless. They are set in a vague past which is Gil Blas's youth, but have no precision as to a date or even a decade. If any reader were interested in pinning the story down to a definite period, he could find his first clue in the course of the barber's story. In the discussion of contemporary playwrights which the barber overhears (I, 104), two living authors are mentioned. The elder of these, Luis Velez de Guevara, died in 1644. Therefore, even allowing for the lapse of time in the barber's life since this incident, we might safely suppose this stage of Gil Blas's story to be happening before 1650. Actually, of course, it seems highly unlikely that the average reader of *Gil Blas* would have either the interest or the requisite factual knowledge to date the episode in this way. Nor can I believe that Lesage had any intention of fixing his story in time by a reference of this kind. The names of the two writers are thrown in partly as local colour, and partly to confirm the prestige of the barber's uncle, who is mentioned as having more talent than either of them.

The same approach is evident at a later stage, when Fabrice speaks of three contemporary writers, Lope de Vega, Cervantes and Gongora (II, 61). The point here is that Fabrice has chosen Gongora as his model in matters of style.

However, by this stage in the novel (Book VII), Lesage had at least become aware of the problem of period. In the first edition of Volume I, Gil Blas listened to Don Pompeyo telling the story of some recent events which were supposed to have taken place in Portugal before Philip II's conquest of that country in 1580. Unfortunately, this episode turned out to be an anachronism in relation to the events of Gil Blas's career in Volume III. It is here, only six or seven years after hearing Don Pompeyo's story, that Gil Blas begins to work for the Duc de Lerme, a minister of Philip III—and de Lerme's period in power ran from 1598 to 1618.

Having thus fixed the novel in time by references to the Duc de Lerme and Philip III, Lesage realized the discrepancy between this dating and that of the Don Pompeyo episode. In the preface of 1724 he offered the reader his excuses:

On a marqué dans ce troisième tome une époque qui ne s'accorde pas avec l'histoire de Pompeyo de Castro qu'on lit dans le premier volume. Il paraît là que Philippe II n'a pas encore fait la conquête du Portugal et l'on voit ici tout d'un coup ce royaume sous la domination de Philippe III sans que Gil Blas en soit beaucoup plus vieux. C'est une faute de chronologie dont l'auteur s'est aperçu trop tard, mais qu'il promet de corriger dans la suite avec quantité d'autres.

Lesage corrected this mistake by the simple expedient of transferring the story to a Polish setting, though without bothering to alter the references to things Portuguese, such as bull-fights.

As for the other mistakes, he did not succeed in eradicating them all, and a score or so of chronological inconsistencies remain in his final text.

We shall discuss more fully, in a later chapter, the whole problem of the novelist's accuracy in factual and practical details. For the moment it is enough to say that eighteenth-century authors attached far less importance to such details than do most modern writers. And in the case of *Gil Blas*, the chronological slips are not serious enough to distract the reader or be considered as major flaws in the work.

It is, then, by the introduction of the Duc de Lerme that Lesage takes the decisive step into history. Most of his early readers must have recognized de Lerme as a real person; he had, after all, been a famous statesman of a major European power, and had lived not much more than a century earlier. Much the same effect might be produced nowadays, for English readers, by bringing a person such as Talleyrand into a novel set in France. A majority of readers, though not possessing much detailed knowledge about him, would still be aware that this was an historical personage. This particular effect of the Duc de Lerme's appearance has now faded; unless there are editorial notes to help them, most readers will not appreciate the 'reality' of this character. And how many readers, when they come across mentions of two successive Kings of Spain, pay any heed to the authenticity of the events in which Gil Blas is involved? It seems likely that time, shifts of political power, and increasing literary sophistication have largely destroyed for us the effect of Lesage's incursion into history.

On the other hand, the move into real time produced an effect upon the plot of *Gil Blas* which is still perceptible. Having chosen to link his hero's career with the successive 'reigns' of the Duc de Lerme and the Comte d'Olivarès, Lesage found himself tied down to a precise chronology instead of a vague slipping past of the years.

In the first part of the novel there is little attempt to convey a realistic impression of the passing of time. We move from one event to the next, and the periods between events are briefly dismissed, often with a mere phrase such as, 'Après six mois', or 'Quelques semaines plus tard'. One might say that this is a picaresque handling of time. Just as the traditional *picaro* wanders freely from town to town, not bound by any ties of place, so his actions follow on each other's heels without any apparent relation to objective standards of time. This rambling method is quite suitable for Gil Blas's early days, but breaks down when his life has to obey the exigencies of history. In particular, Lesage does not manage to suggest the length of the period when the Comte d'Olivarès is in power. It comes as a distinct shock when, after a brief sequence of episodes taking up some sixty pages, the Count talks of his twenty years of service (II, 337), or when Gil Blas mentions the lapse of twenty-two years since Antonia's death (II, 348).

It would seem, from all this, that Lesage increased his own difficulties by choosing to combine Gil Blas's life with the events of a given historical period. Why did he make the choice?

One likely reason depends on his persistently derivative method of writing. Apart from the translations and adaptations which he published as such, Lesage always drew largely on other authors for anecdotes and situations, and Claretie has shown that he also plagiarized himself.[1] In 1734 Lesage published *Estebanille Gonzalès*, his adaptation of a quasi-picaresque work which purported to be the memoirs of a clown in the service of the Duke of Amalfi. Volume IV of *Gil Blas* appeared in 1735, and it is clear from the similarities between the two that much of the historical matter in this last part of *Gil Blas* was adapted from the 'Life' of Gonzalès. Since the historical episodes of Volume IV follow coherently and smoothly from those of Volume III, it seems more than likely that Lesage had already studied the Spanish 'memoirs' when he was writing the chapters which introduce the Duc de Lerme and the historical background. The shift into history may therefore be a development suggested merely by Lesage's other current occupations.

Apart from this external stimulus, it may be argued that there were artistic reasons for this development, since it fulfils certain logical requirements of the plot. One should not, I think, accept too easily the assertions of some critics that the novel has no coherent plot.[2] We have already noticed the various digressions and distractions which may blur the out-

---

[1] Claretie, *Lesage romancier*, pp. 182–3.

[2] See my article 'Structure and symbolism in *Gil Blas*', *French Studies*, XV (1961), pp. 134–45.

lines of the central story, but there *is* a main thread to be discerned: Gil Blas's gradual rise from helplessness and poverty to power and wealth. This rise is conducted on three levels. Gil Blas works in households of successively higher social status (the few weeks with Arsénie are the only backward step in this otherwise steady progress). Within these households he occupies positions of increasing trust and responsibility, from valet to steward to confidential secretary. And finally there is a parallel increase of self-assurance and sophistication in his own character and behaviour. This progress may be the simplest of linear plots, but it does provide a story which is more than a sequence of casually juxtaposed episodes.

In relation to this plot, Gil Blas's move into the realm of history can be seen as an artistic necessity. By the end of Book VI he is not merely the trusted employee of a rich noble, Don Alphonse, but even his friend. In Book VII he has a position of trust with the Comte Galiano which involves overseeing the whole household, including the *intendant*. After this, if he is to continue his gradual rise in status, the inevitable step is from service with a 'private' aristocrat to working for a grandee who is involved in public affairs, and who is thus known and 'historic'. This development can therefore be seen as logically consonant with the preceding stages of the plot of the novel, and even as a necessity.

In a sense, once Gil Blas has become confidential secretary to the Duc de Lerme, there are no more worlds for him to conquer. Lesage has given the story a new lease of life, however, by making him become corrupted by power, so that a fresh field for improvement is in fact open to him—the reform and mastery of his own vices. This conquest of character is adroitly fitted into the pattern of historical events. Gil Blas is disgraced for his part in the Prince's *affaire* with Catalina. This has the effect of separating his career from the Duc de Lerme's, and when the Prince comes to the throne and de Lerme falls from power, the way is open for Gil Blas to return to court. The interval in Gil Blas's life between his release from prison and his service with the Comte d'Olivarès is chiefly taken up with the idyllic interlude of his love-match with Antonia, which shows him in a new light. And when, after Antonia's death, he comes back to Madrid and regains his previous heights of influence, he shows that his change of heart in prison has taught him to resist the temptations of power. The period serving the Comte d'Olivarès is therefore a contrast to, and not a mere repetition of, the years with the Duc de Lerme. So it seems fair to say that Lesage has shown considerable skill in his dovetailing of Gil Blas's moral development into the successive 'reigns' of de Lerme and d'Olivarès.

It can safely be assumed that Lesage never had in mind any 'master-plan' of *Gil Blas*. With its linear plot, the story could grow indefinitely by the mere addition of fresh episodes showing the continuance of Gil Blas's progress. And Volume III carries on this trend, established in the first two volumes. Nevertheless, once he began drawing on his sources of Spanish history, Lesage must surely have realized that the novel was taking a fresh turn. His prefatory remarks, and especially the assurance that he had portrayed no particular persons, were clearly contradicted by the introduction of historic Kings and courtiers. Why, then, did Lesage not alter his *Déclaration* when he revised his first two volumes?

Various reasons, alone or in combination, may account for his letting this inconsistency remain. There is, first, the general insouciance about accuracy which has already been mentioned. Secondly, Lesage may have considered that the comic or satiric aspect of the novel was more important than the historic element, which did not merit any special mention. Thirdly, he may not even have fully appreciated the fact that his utilization of specific historic 'truths' might be inconsistent with the aim of offering general truths about society.

Lesage was indeed, as far as one can gather or deduce, the very reverse of a conscious artist. Steadily occupied with all kinds of writing, some of which amounted to little more than hack-work, he seems to have given little or no thought to the theory of his craft. What he did, in practice, was to draw freely on all the resources of prose fiction which were familiar to him, and to make his novels follow any convention of form or subject-matter that seemed to him convenient or likely to please the public. Where he accepted the conventions without query or modification, he is generally, by modern standards, at his weakest. This is most obvious in the *nouvelles* and *histoires*, the *portraits* and *caractères* with their effect of cumbering and confusing the plot. Where he adapts the traditional elements to his own ends, the change tends to be advantageous. His alterations to the picaresque convention, making the hero rise through society instead of remaining in the gutter, meant that he covered a far wider range of social strata and callings than any previous writer of satiric novels. *Roman de mœurs* is a phrase often used rather loosely; if it implies a work which provides an overall impression of a given society, then there is much to be said for calling *Gil Blas* the first true *roman de mœurs* in French. At the same time, Lesage's avoidance of the coarser elements hitherto associated with comic and satiric novels, showed that this type of work could be respectable by both social and literary standards.

On these two counts alone, it is clear that *Gil Blas* is important, a landmark in the development of the novel which cannot be neglected by anyone who is studying the history of the genre. This is not however to affirm that it can necessarily claim a place among world masterpieces, or even among French ones.[1] Apart from its unsatisfactory structure, a defect one may learn to ignore, this novel seems, by comparison with the works of comic masters such as Cervantès or Molière, both superficial and obvious. Lesage's penetration of emotions and motives is rarely more than skin-deep, and is totally lacking in subtlety. In successive episodes he illuminates the surface of his world, but throws scarcely any light into the depths of more complex feeling and behaviour. The human reactions he can effectively convey are limited both as to range and as to intensity.

What merits remain when we have made these reservations? Even if the work is episodic, many of the episodes are brilliantly handled. Gil Blas's first experience of being a valet—and a legatee—in the household of the cosseted canon; his sad lesson concerning the penalties of honesty with the Archbishop of Grenada; these and many another incident are concisely, wittily and vividly narrated, and linger in the memory. Even if we complain that the characters are types rather than individuals, and broadly sketched in rather than delineated with subtle detail, we still remember Laure and the rogue Don Raphaël,

---

[1] For an account of the high esteem in which *Gil Blas* was held during the first half of the nineteenth century, see Marguerite Iknayan, *The Idea of the Novel in France: the critical reaction, 1815–1848*, Paris, 1961, pp. 23–7.

Dr Sangrado and the grandee whose life revolved round his pet monkey. We remember, that is, those characters and those episodes which are fully in harmony with the novelist's most distinctive trait: that lucid, ironic style which is the voice not only of Gil Blas, but of Lesage himself.

V

Prévost

THE NEW 'REALISM'

WITH the novels of Prévost we come to the kind of memoir-novel which was to dominate French fiction during the first half of the eighteenth century. Lesage nowhere claims that Gil Blas's autobiography is a genuine 'Life'. Prévost, on the other hand, pretends that he is offering the public a series of authentic manuscripts. This pretence, as we shall find, was neither consistent nor wholly serious. It was a legacy from the writers of pseudo-memoirs, but in the hands of novelists like Prévost it developed along fresh lines.

If we look first at Prévost's claims for his 'manuscripts', we discover that in each case the original text was apparently by someone other than himself, and in each case he provides an explanation of how the work came to be published. In the *Mémoires d'un Homme de Qualité*, an *Avis de l'éditeur* tells how this text was obtained from the Man of Quality, then living in retirement in an abbey. The Man of Quality is referred to as the *auteur*, the style of the memoirs is described as being 'tel qu'on le doit attendre d'une personne de condition', and it is not even suggested that the manuscript required any revision to make it suitable for publication.

The title-page of Prévost's next novel ran as follows:

Le Philosophe anglois, ou Histoire de Monsieur Cleveland, fils naturel de Cromwell, ecrite par lui-mesme, et traduite de l'anglois par l'auteur des Memoires d'un homme de qualité.

We are told, in the preface, that the 'editor' of this work had happened to meet Cleveland's son in London:

Il avait lu mes mémoires, et ce fut la plus forte raison qui le porta à me parler de ceux de son père. . . . Il me permit de prendre une copie de son manuscrit, et, l'ayant apporté en France à mon retour, j'ai employé ce que des occupations plus importantes m'ont laissé de liberté, pour lui donner la forme sous laquelle elle peut paraître aujourd'hui.

Four years later, in 1735, Prévost published the first volume of *Le Doyen de Killerine*, again described as being edited 'Par l'auteur des Mémoires d'un homme de qualité'. And once more the preface contained an account of the circumstances of publication:

L'indulgence avec laquelle on a reçu de moi quelques ouvrages de la même espèce, a fait croire aux héritiers des illustres frères dont on va lire les aventures que je pouvais retoucher avantageusement leur manuscrit.

If all these indications could be taken at their face value, it would appear that the Man of Quality, after writing his own memoirs, then translated and edited the manuscripts left by Cleveland and the Dean of Coleraine. But Volume V of the *Mémoires d'un Homme de Qualité*, which appeared in 1731, contained a *Lettre de l'éditeur* which begins: 'La mort de M. le Marquis de . . ., l'illustre sujet de ces Mémoires, me procure la liberté d'en donner la dernière partie au Public.'[1] This letter was signed 'D'Exiles'. (Prévost was known as 'Prévost d'Exiles'.) Many readers of *Cleveland* and *Le Doyen* might therefore be expected to know that it was not the Man of Quality himself who had done the translating and editing of these texts. The phrase 'Par l'auteur des Mémoires d'un homme de qualité' was really equivalent to saying 'By Prévost'.

By using this phrase, Prévost let it be known that he had written, not merely published, the first of these *Lives*. And his readers could discover, from other remarks, that the other two were also his own work. In the *Avertissement* of *Le Doyen de Killerine*, for instance, he defends the probity of his intentions, and says that no work of this kind has come from his pen

qui n'ait été composé dans des vues aussi sérieuses que ce genre d'écrire peut les admettre. Le *Cleveland*, par exemple, dans lequel on m'a reproché fort injustement d'avoir donné quelque atteinte à la

---

[1] This letter is reproduced in the critical edition of Vol. V of the *Mémoires d'un Homme de Qualité* prepared by Mysie E. I. Robertson, Paris, 1927 (Bibliothèque de la Revue de littérature comparée, no. 38), *Appendice* I, pp. 201–2.

religion, était fait au contraire pour en montrer la nécessité, autant
du moins qu'un ouvrage d'imagination peut y servir.

'Un ouvrage d'imagination', indeed! And what has become of
Cleveland's son and the precious manuscript? How are we to
reconcile Prévost's apparent efforts to guarantee his works as
authentic memoirs with these implicit or overt admissions of his
own responsibility for the works?[1]

Contradictions of this kind are the outward signs of a complex
and unstable situation. Novelists of the sort we are discussing
had adopted the form of autobiography as a fictional device,
but were unwilling, it seems, to abandon the traditional claim
of the serious novelist that his work was 'historical' or based on
fact. The only way to maintain this claim for memoirs is, of
course, to insist that the life-story is an authentic autobiography.
This the novelist continued to do in his titles and prefaces. At
the same time, however, some writers reveal, as we have seen
Prévost doing, that the claim is not one they are prepared to
support consistently and in all seriousness.

This ambivalent attitude is, in part, a reaction to, or a consequence of, the growing public awareness of the fictional
nature of many works masquerading as *Mémoires*. Many French
readers had been put on their guard by Bayle; in England, Steele
was one of the first to warn his compatriots against

some merry gentlemen of the French nation, who have written very
advantageous histories of their exploits in war, love, and politics,
under the title of memoirs. ... The most immediate remedy I can
apply to prevent this growing evil, is, That I do hereby give notice
to all booksellers and translators whatsoever, that the word Memoir
is French for a *novel*; and to require of them that they sell and
translate it accordingly.[2]

We can see the outcome of increasing scepticism about memoirs
when we find a Jesuit historian maintaining that the *Mémoires
du Sieur de Pontis* is merely a novel; and Voltaire himself saying,

[1] It is even possible that Prévost arranged for the first two volumes of the
English translation of *Cleveland* to be published before the original French,
so as to bear out the story of a pre-existent English manuscript. See the note
by G. Sherburn in *Modern Philology*, XXV (1927–8), pp. 247–8.

[2] Steele, *The Tatler*, no. 84, 22 Oct. 1709.

a few years later, 'Il est même fort douteux que de Pontis ait existé.'[1]

In the circumstances, one might be tempted to conclude that the whole convention had collapsed. Once the public had realized the deceit involved in 'memoirs', once the novelists themselves began giving away their secrets, then the pretence had surely lost its point. What is more, those critics who charged the novel with being a genre of lies and trickery could now point to such false 'memoirs' as a proof of their rightness. One might therefore expect novelists to abandon the form of the memoir-novel.

But there were a number of reasons to prevent fictional memoirs from dying out quite so quickly. One must remember, first, that many readers, particularly those having no contact with Parisian literary circles, would not be well informed about the truth or falsity of the memoirs they might come across. (Most of the surviving comments on novels are by men of letters; but the fan-mail received by Rousseau after the publication of *La Nouvelle Héloïse* indicates the existence of a reading public which was unsophisticated and, in many cases, gullible to a degree.) Secondly, the loss of faith in the 'memorialist's' claims to authenticity was a gradual process, whose development we have no means of gauging accurately.

Moreover, the myth of 'memoirs', for all its transparency, was useful to novelists and readers alike. More people were reading and enjoying novels, more novels were being published; and yet the socially acceptable attitude towards the genre continued to be one of contempt or condemnation. Disapproval even reached the stage, as Professor May has shown, where Daguesseau, in his function as *Garde des sceaux*, could forbid the publication of new novels in France.[2] Under these conditions, the novelists' claim to be producing something other than novels was a form of face-saving for all concerned. There may be something absurd or irrational about such a situation, but strict logic has never held much sway in the matter of a given society's aesthetic conventions. How many of those who argued that the aim of tragedy was to purge one of evil pas-

---

[1] D'Avrigny, *Mémoires pour servir à l'histoire universelle de l'Europe*, Paris, 1725, *Préface*; and Voltaire, *Œuvres*, ed. Moland, XIV, 446.

[2] Georges May, *Le Dilemme du roman*, Ch. III, pp. 75–105.

sions ever went to the theatre with the intention of being so purged?

There is also a practical, economic reason for the duration of the memoir-form. The novelist who earns a living solely or largely by the sale of his works is a phenomenon scarcely known before the eighteenth century. But once it became possible to make a living by novel-writing, then there was an increase in the number of second-rate authors who, in an earlier age, would hardly have found patrons to support them. Writers of this type tend to follow the current forms which are commercially successful, and throughout the eighteenth century there was a steady flow of undistinguished memoir-novels from such authors.

Finally, there was one purely literary consideration which in all probability helped to confirm and prolong the reign of the memoir-form. This was the fact that autobiographical fiction offered more scope for analysis of thought and feeling than did the third-person narrative of earlier novels, with its quasi-historical limitations on the author's possible knowledge. Admittedly, some seventeenth-century novelists had gone beyond the strict confines of what a third-person narrator might be expected to know, even if we take into account the historian's right to deduce motives, decisions, etc. from observable actions. In *La Princesse de Clèves*, for instance, we are occasionally given some of the protagonists' thoughts, in the form of direct speech, even when these are part of an internal debate which does not lead to action. Such liberties are however comparatively rare; the current standards of *vraisemblance* did not allow for a truly omniscient author who could explain in detail the thoughts and emotions of any or all of his characters. In first-person novels, on the other hand, discussion of the hero's innermost feelings falls naturally within the scope of the narrative. This new method of portrayal was a real advantage to authors like Prévost, Marivaux and Crébillon *fils*. For such writers the memoir-form provided opportunities well suited to their talents. In any case, the fact that all these authors contributed to undermine the authenticity of 'memoirs' shows that this 'truth' was not, for them, the major attraction of the form. Prévost is the most equivocal writer of his generation concerning the 'genuine' sources of his novels. But this tendency to try and sit on both sides of the fence is a characteristic of his thought which we shall meet again in other aspects of his work.

Prévost was not content with the claims to truth which, by convention, provided what one might call an 'external' guarantee for his novels. He pursued the matter further, within his works, by using well-known events and personages. In the *Mémoires d'un Homme de Qualité* this method is at its most obvious in Volume V, which contains the hero's travels through England. Mysie Robertson, in her critical edition of this section of the novel, shows how Prévost drew on his knowledge of English history for background material. The journey takes place in 1716, and after-effects of the 1715 rebellion, in the form of trials and executions, are brought into Prévost's narrative. Similarly, the deportation-episode which is so important in *Manon Lescaut* was based on events which many of Prévost's readers would have heard about or even witnessed.

The plot of *Cleveland* is inseparable from English political events. The hero's mother, who has been Cromwell's mistress, is abandoned by him when she ceases to be politically useful, and the boy later has to be hidden to escape the Protector's plans to get rid of him. (Cromwell is portrayed as a completely unscrupulous, power-seeking hypocrite, a view of his character quite common in French writings of the period.) As a young man, Cleveland goes to France with Lord Axminster, and joins the court of Charles II at Bayonne, where a meeting with Mazarin takes place. Axminster is entrusted with the task of promoting a rising in Charles's favour in the American colonies, and Cleveland follows him there. After further travels and adventures, he settles down in England after the Restoration and is made a Privy Counsellor.

Le Doyen de Killerine has a similar background concerning the efforts of Irish Catholics to help restore James II to the throne.

While Lesage, one feels, manœuvred himself almost inadvertently into a position where he slipped over the brink of fiction into history, Prévost's procedure is clearly part of his general plan. He draws on his wide range of historical knowledge for corroborative details which can contribute to the authentic effect of the whole.

In so far as he is supposedly revealing hitherto unknown 'facts' about well-known events, he is following the practice of some of the *romans héroïques* of the previous century. The difference, of course, is that Prévost utilizes people and incidents of the near-past, a technique which might be thought to produce a more convincing effect. There were precedents even for this approach, in the many *histoires secrètes* and *anecdotes* which appeared from the 1670's onwards. But generally speaking, these took the public figures as their centre of interest. Prévost builds his plot around fictional characters, and makes use of history merely as one method of helping to win the reader's belief.

We may digress here to notice that after claiming reality for imaginary heroes like Cleveland and the Dean of Coleraine, Prévost was hoist with his own petard in the case of his *Histoire d'une Grecque moderne* (1740). This story is narrated in the first person by a Frenchman, never precisely identified, who rescues the Greek girl from a harem in Constantinople, and later falls in love with her and brings her back to France. The first edition of the novel offered no prefatory explanations. In the second edition of 1741, Prévost supplied an *Avertissement* telling his readers that they should not 'confondre l'héroïne avec une aimable Circassienne qui a été connue et respectée d'une infinité d'honnêtes gens'. This comment referred, as the French public would know, to a certain Mlle Aïssé, who had been purchased as a child in Turkey by M. de Ferriol, and sent back to France, where she spent the remainder of her life, dying in 1733. There is every likelihood that it was indeed Mlle Aïssé's story which had inspired the central situation of the *Histoire d'une Grecque moderne*. But when, for once, Prévost had looked to real life for one of his principal characters, he was obliged to deny the process so as to avoid offending those people who had been the protectors and friends of Mlle Aïssé.

In his other prefaces, Prévost regularly defends the truth of his narratives, and thus implies that they are useful contributions to history. In his critical writings, however, he is apt to be more frank about their possible value:

Les Mémoires d'un Homme de Qualité et leur suite, Cleveland, et le Doyen de Killerine, dont je prépare la seconde partie, sont autant de livres inutiles pour l'histoire, et dont tout le mérite est de former une lecture honnête et amusante.[1]

[1] *Le Pour et contre*, 1735, VI, p. 354.

On occasion he even went further, and laid down the principle that history has no place in fiction: 'En général le mélange de l'histoire et de la fiction m'a toujours paru blamable. Tout doit être inventé dans un roman.'[1] Prévost's theory is therefore more strict than his practice. In the novels he not only mixes fact and fiction, but also distorts and alters history in order to suit his plots, and more particularly in order to introduce figures who would lend the narrative an air of 'reality' or 'truth'.

For some of the episodes in his novels Prévost also used a physical setting which many of his French readers would know. This raises the question of his much-discussed 'realism'. Lasserre, for instance, says that one forgets the minor faults of *Manon Lescaut* because, among other reasons, Prévost 'a peint exactement la vie réelle, parfois vulgaire, avec des détails précis et familiers'. This claim, it turns out, is however limited. If Prévost is a 'realist', 'il faut entendre seulement par là que, quand il a l'occasion, au cours de son récit, de donner un détail précis sur les lieux, les mœurs, les personnages, il le donne toujours exact'.[2] Several questions arise from this approach. Are we fully justified in talking about 'realism' when a novelist, mentioning a street-name or a building, chooses to mention one that exists rather than coining a name? How far does such 'realism' matter in its effect on the reader? And what are we to make of supposedly factual details which are inaccurate, that is, false?

Firstly, it seems to me a source of possible confusion to apply the label *réaliste* to Prévost's procedure, and thereby apparently equate it with the methods of some nineteenth-century novelists. Secondly, we must surely distinguish between the effect that his factual details now produce on the reader, and the effect they had on his contemporaries. It seems fair to assume that the mention of such places as 'l'hôtel de Transylvanie' or 'l'Hôpital' had a ring of actuality for Prévost's first readers, and could therefore contribute, in their case, to the illusion of reality. But this effect is a thing of the past. We now have to be told that 'la rue V**' represents 'la rue Vivienne', which was at

---

[1] *Le Pour et contre*, 1739, XVII, p. 75. On the series of *histoires romancées* which Prévost tried—sometimes successfully—to pass off as historical studies, see Georges May, *Le Dilemme du roman*, pp. 156–61.

[2] Eugène Lasserre, *Manon Lescaut de l'Abbé Prévost*, Paris, 1930, pp. 61, 63.

that time 'la rue de la galanterie et de l'agiot'. In the majority of cases, the factual detail which, by its familiarity, might help the eighteenth-century reader to believe in the book has now lost its force and has acquired instead the remoteness of history. (This is a necessary consequence of systematic 'realism' which all too few writers and critics seem to remember.) What is more, a number of the supposed 'facts' which Prévost supplied about New Orleans were inaccurate. But this could be of no particular concern either to his contemporaries or to later generations: in neither case did the average reader possess information to make him doubt Prévost's word.

Instead of discussing Prévost's 'realism' as though it were an element which he could have included or left aside, at his own discretion, one should, I think, remember that much of it arises directly from his initial choice of form and characters and plot. A comparison with *La Princesse de Clèves* may make this point clearer. Here too we have a story turning on an unhappy love, but these characters have no need to worry about money, for instance, or evading the law. To that extent, a certain number of practical preoccupations about daily life have no place in Mme de la Fayette's novel. In *Manon Lescaut*, by contrast, the situation of the lovers, and Des Grieux's continual need of money for Manon, inevitably bring us into the everyday world of practical affairs. That Prévost, in these circumstances, chose to make his milieu a 'real' one, and to call the streets and buildings of Paris by their familiar names, seems to me a part of the memoir-novel convention rather than the literary approach we now call 'realism'.[1]

What is perhaps more interesting is Prévost's concern with another kind of real-life criterion, the question of how the narrator comes by his information and conveys it to the reader. This arises in the case of the long interpolated stories. Prévost tacitly recognizes that a long narrative may suffer in accuracy if it is re-told by a second narrator. On more than one occasion he therefore makes the principal narrator say that the secondary story-teller supplied him with a written text. In *Cleveland*, most of Book III is taken up by the adventures of the hero's half-

[1] Prévost's use of initials for the names of characters is another aspect of the same convention: we are to suppose that real people are involved, whose full names cannot be cited for fear of scandal or unpleasantness.

brother, Bridge, in the secret island-colony near St. Helena. Cleveland closes this episode with the explanation that Bridge had had the kindness to write it out for him, 'et je n'ai fait que l'insérer dans mon histoire'. Similarly, the narrator of *Le Monde moral* (1760), embarking on a long story told to him by his doctor, assures us that the doctor had written down the events in question, which formed 'un petit volume', and that what the public is now being offered is a copy of that manuscript.

Remarks like these show a double preoccupation: the factual accuracy of the stories is guaranteed, since they are in the original story-teller's own words; and the story-telling situation itself is taken seriously, with an attempt at a realistic explanation.

Manon Lescaut resembles *Le Monde moral*, where the doctor's small volume consists of the story which he heard from the Abbé Brenner and immediately wrote down. The Man of Quality likewise insists:

> Je dois avertir ici le lecteur que j'écrivis son histoire presque aussitôt après l'avoir entendue, et qu'on peut s'assurer, par conséquent, que rien n'est plus exact et plus fidèle que cette narration (p. 15).

Such a claim shows a certain desire to create an aura of truth, or at least verisimilitude, about the narrative method itself in interpolated stories of this kind.

The story which is interpolated in a memoir-novel raises a problem of *vraisemblance* by its very presence: is it likely that an autobiographer will go off into long digressions which merely repeat the accounts of other narrators' adventures? Authentic memoirs certainly did not carry the practice so far, and indeed one of the formal elements by which a reader could tell that memoirs were fictional rather than genuine was the intervention of the secondary narrator, so familiar a feature in novels.

The second problem created by interpolated stories is, as we have already observed in *Gil Blas*, that of relevance and structural coherence. That Prévost was at least aware of this problem we can tell from the *Avis* of *Manon Lescaut*, where one of his reasons for giving this story separately is that it has not 'un rapport nécessaire' with the *Mémoires d'un Homme de Qualité*. From this we might be led to conclude that Prévost had moved away from contemporary practice and reached something more like the modern point of view about interpolated stories. Such a conclusion is not however justified. It is at least possible that when Prévost published the volumes of the Mémoires which cover the period to which *Manon Lescaut* belongs by its chronology, he had either not given the final touches to this shorter tale, or else not made up his mind to incorporate it in the larger work.[1] So the ostensibly literary reasons for its separate existence which he offered in the *Avis* may merely cover a belated decision to take advantage of the *Mémoires* as a good opportunity for publishing *Manon Lescaut*.[2] This much is hypothesis. What is demonstrable fact is that within the body of the *Mémoires*, Prévost shows no particular reluctance to interrupt the thread of his story by subsidiary narratives. Several long interpolations, such as the stories of the Marquis de Rosambert and the Baron de Spalding, keep us for considerable stretches at a time from the autobiography of the Man of Quality himself. *Cleveland* has an equal abundance of interpolated stories. The adventures of Bridge have already been mentioned. Admittedly, Bridge's story has some slight connection with the main plot, but much of its detail and minor developments could have been dispensed with if Prévost was really guided by standards of relevance.

A change of method becomes apparent however in *Le Doyen de Killerine*. This novel does still include some passages of narrative by secondary characters, but these are always episodes connected in some way with the main plot, they are kept brief, and generally speaking they are told to the Dean—and by him to the reader—merely because he was not present during the incidents narrated. Such is the account, given by a valet, of the trials experienced in Paris by the Dean's sister, Rose, while the Dean himself was in Ireland. Similarly Milord Linck's

[1] The Marquis's first meeting with Manon and Des Grieux occurs during the period dealt with in the *Avant-propos* of Vol. III. His second encounter with Des Grieux, when the latter tells his story, comes immediately after the stay in England of Vol. V, Book XII. This correlation can be deduced from remarks in *Manon Lescaut*. The *Mémoires* themselves contain no mention of Des Grieux's story.

[2] See *Manon Lescaut*, ed. F. Deloffre and R. Picard, Garnier, 1969, *Introduction*, p. l. All page-references in my discussion refer to this edition.

description of his father's unhappy marriage throws light on Linck's own attitude during his courtship of Rose.

L'Histoire d'une Grecque moderne is also free from irrelevant secondary narratives. One would therefore be tempted to say that Prévost had recognized and learnt to overcome the drawbacks of the interpolated story, were it not that in *Le Monde moral* he produced a work which, like *La Vie de Marianne*, turns aside to allow a second narrator to speak, and leaves both this story and the main plot unfinished.[1]

It seems to me that Prévost's avoidance of secondary narratives in *Le Doyen* and *L'Histoire d'une Grecque moderne* arose not from any desire to achieve structural coherence, but from questions of length and of the scope of the hero's adventures. To see what this statement implies, we shall need to consider the quantity and quality of events in Prévost's plots. The detailed study of a whole novel would take too much space; we may content ourselves with, say, one of the twelve books of *Le Doyen de Killerine*. Book IV may be outlined as follows.

The Dean returns to Paris from Ireland, travelling with Milord Linck, and pausing *en route* to inspect the hiding-place of some church treasure which they intend to convey to France for the benefit of James II and his supporters there.

In Paris, the Dean's first task is to see his sister Rose. After staying for some time in a convent as a *pensionnaire*, she has run short of money and is now earning her living as a seamstress. Linck is in love with Rose, who does not return his love. He has discovered where she is lodging, rented a room in the next house, and arranged for the fabric of the wall between the two rooms to be surreptitiously weakened. His original plan was to abduct Rose, but a scruple of honour made him try to obtain her brothers' consent first. He claims that the elder brother, Georges, has consented to the plan, but the Dean will not agree to Rose's being married against her will. When the Dean visits her, he knocks down the party-wall, and Linck is discovered sitting in the next room. Rose is taken to stay at another convent. Linck then quarrels with, and parts from, the Dean, because he thinks the latter is favouring Des Pesses, Rose's first suitor.

---

[1] *Le Monde moral*, though published in its incomplete form in 1760, had been begun several years earlier.

The Dean goes to see Georges, who is in the Bastille after having fought a duel with Linck; Georges explains why he has been favouring Linck's claim to Rose's hand.

A few days later, while the Dean is visiting Rose, a letter is delivered to her. It is from a nobleman who saw her at a ball and has been writing to her since, but who has not revealed his identity. Rose is in love with him. The Dean arranges to meet her new suitor, who turns out to be the Comte de S . . . He is married, but his wife is much older than himself, and he is prepared to wait for Rose and marry her when his wife dies. This situation presents a moral problem which the Dean tries to solve by consulting various learned clerics. They quarrel and cannot agree on an answer. However, a letter then arrives from the Count saying that his wife is dead, so that he is free to marry Rose.

In the meantime, Linck has challenged another of Rose's admirers, Des Pesses. They fight, Des Pesses is seriously wounded, and on his deathbed he bequeathes all his money to Rose. The Dean has scruples about accepting it, as Des Pesses had been deceived into thinking that Rose favoured him. The Count also disapproves of the legacy, since he wishes Rose's change of fortune to come entirely from him. After consulting Georges on the point of honour involved, the Dean decides to accept the money and hand it to the Count, from whom Rose will receive it.

Linck has been seen in the neighbourhood of the convent where Rose is staying. Fearing for her safety, the Dean agrees that she shall go and stay at the Count's château. But Linck, by bribery, has managed to get himself hidden behind a screen in the *parloir*, and overhears the conversation with Rose about this journey.

Book IV closes here. As might be expected, Book V begins with Linck abducting Rose on the journey, but he is eventually foiled, and Rose marries the Count.

The part of the story outlined above makes up one of the least eventful and complicated sections of the novel. It is easier to follow than much of the remaining plot, as most of the action turns on the fate of Rose, while in the other books there is an interweaving of political intrigues and of the adventures of the Dean's brothers and the four women with whom they are at various times involved.

From the plot of Book IV alone, however, we can draw

certain conclusions. These may seem all too obvious, but call for overt recognition at this stage of our discussion. Firstly, Prévost's narrative is richly charged with incident. The adventures and activities in this one book would have provided Richardson, for instance, with enough basic material for a full-length work. In Prévost the events are close-packed, which also means of course that each separate incident or stage of the story is told with relative brevity.

Secondly, practically all the events are, by real-life standards, striking and unusual. It should be emphasized, for a full appreciation of this point, that the summary given above, while omitting comments and descriptions, left out little that could properly be called 'action'. Prévost's narrative rarely deals with the kind of small incident which is familiar in everyday life. In this respect it is in complete contrast to the novels of, say, Marivaux, where a sprained ankle or the purchase of a new suit of clothes can constitute major 'events' in the plot. Prévost even raises his avoidance of the everyday to the level of a principle. In the *Avis* of the first volume of the *Mémoires d'un Homme de Qualité*, he states:

Si l'on trouve dans cette histoire quelques aventures surprenantes, on doit se souvenir que c'est ce qui les rend dignes d'être communiquées au public. Des événements communs intéressent trop peu pour mériter d'être écrits.

When we speak of the kind of plot used by Prévost, we therefore mean a story in which the events are numerous, relatively fast-moving, and of a striking, not to say sensational character. In this respect Prévost can be said to follow the standards of his predecessors. The quantity and quality of the events in the long seventeenth-century novels were the chief basis for those accusations of exaggeration and *invraisemblance* which critics brought against the genre. Even *Gil Blas*, which by its very approach comes somewhat closer to the norm of everyday life, still relies for much of its effect on a swift sequence of unusual events.

A few words of qualification must be included here. In any given novel, the balance between 'story' on the one hand, and motivation, ethical problems and the like on the other, is obviously only a matter of degree. When we say that Prévost's novels give great weight to action and events, we must add in all fairness that they also offer more in the way of character-drawing and reflective comment than a good many of his fore-runners. *Cleveland*, for instance, provides a study in the gradual acquisition of self-knowledge which makes Gil Blas's development seem superficial. Nor can we suppose that readers like Diderot and Rousseau, both of whom at one time or another commented favourably on Prévost's novels, would have enjoyed these works if they contained nothing but lurid adventures. Nevertheless, the space given up to events, and their multiplicity and unusualness, make the story-line a more important element in Prévost than in many novelists nearer to our own time.

Now any novelist who took the matter of verisimilitude at all seriously could not but realize that if his hero met with too many strange adventures, the reader might find this over-eventful career incredible. One possibility was to keep the novel relatively short, so that even if events moved fast they would not be too improbably numerous. This is the solution adopted for *L'Histoire d'une Grecque moderne*, which is a far briefer work than Prévost's first three novels. It is also the way *Manon Lescaut* is handled, if we consider it for a moment as a separate work.

An alternative, in the long novels, was to reduce the space devoted purely to the hero's own story by admitting interpolations to fill out the work. A still further possibility can be seen in the *Mémoires d'un Homme de Qualité*. By the end of Volume II, the Man of Quality has lived through the major events of his own life and gone into retirement. He leaves this seclusion in order to become the Marquis de Rosemont's tutor, and this step leads to a series of journeys and adventures in which it is often the young Rosemont who plays the leading rôle. There is thus a transfer of interest which enables the novel to continue without loading the Man of Quality with too many more personal sufferings.

The narrative technique of *Le Doyen* is, in essence, an extension of this method, but instead of introducing a second hero to follow the first, Prévost handles his leading characters concurrently and interweaves their stories. The opening sentence of the novel warns us what to expect: 'C'est moins mon histoire que je donne au public, que celles de mes deux frères et de ma sœur.' The Dean's rôle is largely one of comment, advice and supervision. Although he journeys to and fro, and is an active agent in the plot, he is for most of the time acting for other people and trying to forward or frustrate their plans. So while the story is told as a first-person narrative, it is not primarily 'about' the title-character, but follows the adventures of a group of people whose lives intertwine and separate and meet again as the novel progresses. In this way Prévost shares out his generous allowance of incident while making the narrator have an interest in them all. One may notice, *en passant*, that this method is a halfway stage between third-person narrative and the first-person relation of one's own affairs. Prévost has created a compromise between the quasi-historical narrative of the seventeenth century, where the characters' feelings and motives are, as it were, deduced from the outside, and the subsequent memoir-form in which the narrator displays a full knowledge, from within, of one person's ideas and emotions. The Dean can both explain his own sentiments and, through his intimate relationship with the other main characters, account for their behaviour in a way which does not offend against the standards of information possible in real life. (This is, as we shall see, the method used, with some slight extensions, by Bernardin de Saint-Pierre in *Paul et Virginie*.)[1] By sharing out the action in this way, Prévost solved, in part, the problem of the concentration of events in his plot. The modern reader may still find it difficult to accept the sheer amount of complicated adventure which befalls the separate characters, but there is undoubtedly some merit in Prévost's distribution of this quantity of events.

Their striking quality, however, raises problems not merely of credibility, but also of proportion and emphasis—problems, that is, of artistic balance. If everything that happens is exceptional and exciting, how can there be any moments of climax or special significance? This question was not dealt with explicitly in our discussion of *Gil Blas*, but it is easy to see, from our con-

---

[1] It is also the method which Flaubert uses for half a chapter, and then abandons, at the beginning of *Madame Bovary*: 'Nous étions à l'étude . . .' Paradoxically, the last use of this 'nous' occurs in the remark: 'Il serait maintenant impossible à aucun de nous de se rien rappeler de lui.' From this point onwards, the 'companion-narrator' gives way to the omniscient third person.

clusions as to the episodic nature of the plot, that Lesage can create only a minor climax within each episode. He fails to link the separate incidents in any way which might build up to a major climax. In the overall view, therefore, *Gil Blas* suggests a range of hills, none of which rises noticeably above its fellows.

Prévost's plots are more closely knit, and he certainly gives explicit weight to moments of particular stress. But by the nature of these moments—as well as their frequency—he exposes himself to the risk inherent in any 'adventure' story: an unbroken series of striking events tends to become monotonous rather than more striking. We have climbed above Lesage's foothills, only to find ourselves on a featureless plateau. Later novelists, no less fond of vivid and extraordinary action than Prévost, were to utilize the quieter incidents of everyday life as a background which heightened the effect of unusual events and allowed of more contrast. The novels of Balzac and Dickens contain actions which are as rare and strange as much of Prévost, but they also include enough scenes and incidents from the ordinary stuff of life to make their climaxes truly striking.

Prévost's preference for the exceptional in action is linked with the kinds of characters he portrays. They also run to extremes, and tend to be the embodiment of one or two relatively simple traits. In *Le Doyen de Killerine*, for instance, Georges is fiery and ambitious and honourable; Linck is equally fiery but unscrupulous; Patrice and Rose have hearts in which love conquers all; the Dean is all worthy principles and Christian zeal. 'When everybody's somebody, then no one's anybody': the portrayal of so many forceful and extreme characters tends to prevent any of them from emerging as particularly strong or interesting.

Finally, this same fondness for the exceptional comes out, as might be expected, in Prévost's use of language. He has a marked taste for hyperbole and superlatives, and in the long run these again tend to weaken rather than intensify the overall effect. Prévost's characters do not weep, they shed 'des ruisseaux de larmes'; the hero is not merely unfortunate but 'le plus infortuné de tous les hommes'; Cleveland, beginning to describe the obstacles which delayed his marriage, says, 'J'entre dans la mer immense de mes infortunes.' When he is arrested, as a result of his grandfather's well-meaning interference, he cries, 'Je sentis mon cœur se glacer de crainte et frémir de saisissement.' And though he has a moment of joy when he is at last able to set off in pursuit of Fanny, he describes this joy as 'la dernière que j'ai goûtée sans mélange'. The recurrence of such phrases, together with the extremes of feeling they suggest, may lead us to discount their intensity; through familiarity, we cease to respond to them as expressions of deep emotional stress.

Having considered some aspects of Prévost's methods in the three long novels which his contemporaries admired, we can now turn to *Manon Lescaut* to see how these methods were utilized in the one short work which has managed to retain the favour of modern readers.

One conclusion we can draw immediately: there is no great difference, as regards the aspects we have been discussing, between *Manon Lescaut* and the longer novels. The frequent, swift-moving and unusual events are there; the characters are exceptional and not very complex; the emotions described, like the language used to convey them, are consistently intense to the point of exaggeration. How has this novel, or fragment of a novel, come to earn survival?

If we begin by considering the plot in isolation, the problem of *Manon*'s lasting popularity seems to increase rather than diminish, since the action has a repetitive or cyclic quality which might seem guaranteed to produce an effect of monotony, unwelcome to most readers.

Des Grieux meets Manon and falls in love with her. They run away together and settle in Paris. Because their money is running out, Manon becomes M. de B.'s mistress and Des Grieux is forced to return home.

Some eighteen months later, Des Grieux meets Manon again and finds himself in love with her again. They run away together and settle in the village of Chaillot. Because their money is gone, Manon agrees to become M. de G. M.'s mistress. After tricking him, Manon and Des Grieux are arrested and separated by imprisonment.

When Des Grieux has escaped and helped Manon to escape, they settle down again in Chaillot. Ostensibly to obtain revenge on M. de G. M., Manon accepts the advances of his son. After trying to trick this young man, Manon and Des Grieux are again arrested and again separated by prison.

These are three of the book's four main episodes, and they take up just over three-quarters of the Chevalier's narrative. How then does Prévost prevent their basic similarity from becoming tedious?

His chief resource lies in the way he leads up to these apparent repetitions. Thus, the first time Des Grieux meets Manon, he is virtuous with the innocence that depends on ignorance; she has only to awaken in him a capacity for love of which he was unaware. When they meet for the second time, he has gained experience and has, he thinks, conquered his love, so that her fresh immediate conquest of him takes on a different flavour. And by the time Des Grieux sees her in the Hôpital, after their second separation, he has learned to accept both her failings and his own inability to give her up. These differences, which depend on developments in Des Grieux's knowledge of himself and Manon, make the three meetings quite distinct. One may, looking back on the novel, find some difficulty in recalling the order of appearance and the precise rôles of M. de B. and M. de G. M., but the Chevalier seeing Manon for the first time, the seminarist meeting her again in Saint-Sulpice, the young man finding her in a cell of the Hôpital, are clear and memorable stages in the hero's life. What this all boils down to, quite simply, is that the main action springs almost entirely from character; what Des Grieux and Manon do is a consequence of the kind of people they are.

This again would seem so obvious as not to require comment, were it not that Prévost is here carrying out consistently a practice which other novelists of the period—and he himself in other works—observed only sporadically. All too often in seventeenth-century and early eighteenth-century novels, major events in the story are due to coincidence or to outside interventions which are unexplained, so that they appear to be the outcome of chance. And chance was sorely overworked in the early days of the novel. If the hero sets foot on a ship crossing the Mediterranean, the odds are that he will arrive, by capture or shipwreck, in the very town where, unknown to him, his lady-love is languishing (virtuously) in the harem of a local Pasha. Alternatively, if he is heart-whole when he embarks, he will happen to see and fall in love with one of the jealously guarded beauties in the household where he, as a captured Christian, has become a slave. By just such an adventure the Man of Quality meets and marries his Sélima. And years later, when he has lost touch with his wife's family and is travelling from Portugal to Holland by sea, his companions on board happen to be the children of Sélima's brother, that is, his own nephew and niece. Justifiably, Prévost makes the Marquis exclaim, when this relationship is discovered, 'Grand Dieu! me croira-t-on dans cet endroit?' The long heroic novels had abounded in such 'accidents', in fortuitous encounters with momentous results, and the chance re-union of characters long separated by fate. To the modern reader some of these events may seem even more improbable than they did to the contemporary public, who well knew, for instance, the real risk of capture by pirates in the Mediterranean. But even in less sensational incidents the novelist was used to relying heavily on the help of chance for his plot-construction. Book VI of *Gil Blas* can end on a happy note only because Don Alphonse, *en route* for Italy, pauses at the gateway of 'un beau château'. As it turns out, the château not only contains his foster-father, but belongs to his true father (whom he now meets for the first time), and also shelters Séraphine, his bride-to-be. Such a heaping-up of coincidences was soon to pass out of fashion, but Marivaux shows much the same approach when he makes Marianne, with her sprained ankle, be assisted, and later loved, by a young man who turns out to be the nephew of her scheming 'protector', M. de Climal. One of the ways in which the eighteenth-century novel may be thought to have improved is that novelists became less dependent on the overt use of chance as a basis for major events.

'Overt' is the key-word here, since some writers continue to rely on fortuitous events, but have acquired the art of plausible presentation, which distracts the reader's attention from the too palpably convenient workings of chance. The alternative, which is Prévost's way in *Manon Lescaut*, is to reduce the importance of chance and accident by creating a closer causal link between characters and events. Since this trend was to be carried further by several major nineteenth-century novelists, we may term it an advance. More recently, some writers have been challenging what they hold to be an over-simple attitude towards character as a comprehensible 'cause' of actions and events. We shall need to come back to this problem. At this stage it is enough to notice that nowadays a large number of readers have come to expect, and even require, the novelist to provide a pattern of events which is explicable in causal terms. Such readers take an unfavourable view of a novel when they find that its plot depends on a frequent and obtrusive use of chance. Prévost's reduction of the rôle of chance in *Manon* is therefore in accord with modern tastes and expectations.

In his other works, Prévost often resorted to fortuitous events which overtake his heroes and heroines without arising in any way from character. How did he manage to avoid this weakness in *Manon Lescaut?* The answer to this question, and the explanation of various other merits in *Manon*, depend in my view very largely on the shortness of this story. In the three long novels we have discussed, as in the later, lesser-known works, one can see Prévost often utilizing character as a basis for events. It is not too much to say that he tries continually to make the action a consequence of the personalities involved. This is true of *Cleveland,* where the hero frequently points out the causes, in his own temperament, of his behaviour and reactions. Similarly, a number of the events in *Le Doyen de Killerine* are explicitly linked with the way Georges is governed by his sense of honour, with Patrice's inability to resist the passion of love, or with the conflict between the Dean's rectitude and the ways of the world. Nevertheless, it seems that in order to maintain the sheer amount of adventure which Prévost accepted as suitable, he could not, in these works, do without the help of complications introduced by chance. In *Manon Lescaut*, smaller in scope, and containing as its basic plot only three infidelities and a final change of heart, Prévost could, for once, rely much less on such external aids.

The novel's brevity is also a help as regards the space devoted to characterization and discussion of motives. Although, as we have noticed, Prévost allows more room for this element in his long novels than did many of his predecessors, his treatment of such matters may still seem inadequate to modern readers in proportion to the space taken up by events. But *Manon Lescaut* offers comments and analyses which, if not in themselves very lengthy, still make up a significant part of the book and stand in a more satisfactory ratio to the events of the plot. (This fact is of course bound up with the closer link between action and character.)

Finally, the novel's shortness makes both the quantity and the quality of the events become merits rather than potential weaknesses. Here the setting of the narration plays its part: as Des Grieux's adventures are told in the course of an afternoon and an evening, compression and a certain speed of narrative become 'natural'. The concentration of events and their relatively brief treatment, which in the long novels may build up towards monotony, here become acceptable through the circumstances of the telling, and do not in any case go on long enough to become tedious. It is also 'natural'—that is, plausible —that Des Grieux should concentrate on the striking episodes which have led to his present condition; the listener does not feel, in so short a tale, the lack of those calm everyday interludes which may be needed to stabilize longer novels. And since it is the exceptional moments of Des Grieux's life which are described, his intensity of emotion and the corresponding force of his language, can also seem appropriate.

We must not carry the eulogies too far. There may still be moments, even in *Manon Lescaut*, when the reader feels that Prévost's hyperbolic style grows strained and wearisome, or that violent events tread all too swiftly on each other's heels. But considering the work merely as a piece of sustained narrative, one may surely conclude that Prévost has created a small masterpiece; and that its masterly qualities are, judged in the light of his other novels, chiefly due to its smallness.

It has been shown that the setting of the narration contributes to the story's merits by explaining and, in fictional terms, 'causing' its brevity. We may now discuss in more detail how *Manon Lescaut*'s rôle as a tail-piece to the *Mémoires d'un Homme de Qualité* affects the technique of presentation.

The story opens with the incident in which Des Grieux and Manon are first encountered by the Marquis de Renoncour, the 'Man of Quality' of the title.[1] This is an obviously effective plunge *in medias res* which critics have cited with approval. The

[1] In the *Avis* of Vol. I, Prévost says that he obtained the text of the *Mémoires* only on condition that the work would be published without bearing the author's name. The hero is therefore a nameless *Je* during the first volumes, but in Vol. V his name is allowed to emerge.

unusual situation of the couple is calculated to arouse the
reader's interest, and this advantage would have been lost if
we had merely been given Des Grieux's story, in the usual
memoir-fashion, from its chronological beginning. Moreover,
Renoncour's second meeting with Des Grieux, two years later,
then provides an adequate pretext for the narration of the
Chevalier's adventures. (Here Prévost *has* resorted to chance.
It is pure coincidence that Renoncour and Des Grieux, each
bound for a different destination, should 'happen' to be passing
through Calais on one particular day, and should see each other
in the street.) Once they have recognized each other, Des
Grieux can do no less than explain to his benefactor the background and sequel to their first meeting at Passy. In comparison with some of the idiosyncratic and implausible pretexts
supplied by novelists to account for the memoirs they purport
to be 'editing', this situation provides quite a credible reason
for the telling of the tale.

In conformity with the setting he has created, of the long
quiet talk in a private room in the hotel, Prévost makes the
Marquis de Renoncour suggest a break for supper which divides
the story into its two parts (p. 116).[1] Is this an advantage? It
may be argued that Prévost has gained something by making
Part II begin with the fresh start at Chaillot after Manon's
escape. But a good many readers, one can be sure, have in their
time been put off by the sudden reappearance of Renoncour
and his pupil, at a stage when they had been quite forgotten.
By this time most readers have, in a sense, taken the Man of
Quality's place as the listener whom Des Grieux is addressing.
It is no help to be reminded that the Chevalier's story is coming
to us at second-hand, and that the narrator is 'really' Renoncour. Indeed, if we dwell at all closely on the question of how
the story is supposed to be reaching us, the situation may at
times become extraordinarily involved. For instance, when
Manon quotes a remark of the younger M. de G. M., this means
that M. de G. M. said something which Manon repeated to Des
Grieux, which Des Grieux later repeated to Renoncour, and
which Renoncour—with the help of his editor, Prévost—is now

---

[1] This break does in fact contradict the Marquis's undertaking to tell the
story without any further intervention from himself: 'Voici donc son récit,
auquel je ne mêlerai, jusqu'à la fin, rien qui ne soit de lui' (p. 17).

telling us. This difficulty, inherent in the conversation of memoir-novels, is reduced if we forget or ignore the Man of Quality once we are well into Des Grieux's story. The reappearance of Renoncour therefore seems to me more of a hindrance than a help, especially as the novel ends with no further word from him.

Since the question of conversation in memoir-novels has arisen, we may pause here to consider Prévost's technique in this matter. About half of the text of *Manon Lescaut* is taken up by conversation, but the importance of this element may not strike the reader because Prévost generally avoids long passages in direct speech. Instead, his conversations usually consist of an alternation of short passages of direct and indirect speech. In an exceptional case like Des Grieux's long discussion with Tiberge (pp. 90–94), it is worth noticing how the Chevalier's argument is presented in the more lively form of direct speech, while Tiberge's answers, except for two isolated sentences, are left in the indirect form. Prévost's technique with conversations thus has merits which are no less valid for being unobtrusive. Moreover his avoidance of long passages in direct speech is in conformity with real-life standards, since not many people have the ability to repeat, verbatim, conversations which took place months or years previously. We have already observed Prévost's awareness of this aspect of the narrative in Renoncour's claim that he wrote down Des Grieux's story 'presque aussitôt après l'avoir entendue'.

To return to the general question of the presentation of *Manon Lescaut*, one may conclude that the way in which Prévost utilizes the chief narrator and a situation from the *Mémoires d'un Homme de Qualité* is, on the whole, advantageous. Mercifully, he made the link a relatively weak one: it consists of Renoncour's brief allusions to his own affairs, and of the wordless presence of his pupil, the Marquis de Rosemont. Prévost might easily have built up the connection with the *Mémoires* by reminding us, for instance, of those reasons which obliged Renoncour and his pupil to spend a day and a night in Calais; or by showing the effect on Rosemont, himself in love, of Des Grieux's sufferings in the cause of love. Prévost's silence on such points, which would be a fault if we were to consider *Manon* as a part of the *Mémoires*, now make it blessedly self-sufficing.

There is another type of reticence which becomes a merit in *Manon Lescaut*: the paucity of information about Manon herself. This is the moment to recall that in the full title of the work it is the hero who takes pride of place: *Histoire du Chevalier des Grieux et de Manon Lescaut*. And in the *Avis de l'Auteur* there is no specific mention of Manon. The love-affair is discussed entirely in terms of its effects upon Des Grieux. Prévost, it would seem, envisaged Manon merely as the agent of Des Grieux's sufferings. As such, her thoughts and feelings are of secondary importance, and are passed on to us only when they can be seen to affect the Chevalier's behaviour. The result is that she remains, for the most part, an enigmatic and idealized creature whom we see, by the very nature of the story, only through the eyes of Des Grieux.

Generally speaking, Prévost handles his masculine characters with more confidence and skill than he brings to the portrayal of women. His female characters tend to be either insipidly passive or else aggressively passionate. The two most successful feminine creations in his novels are, in my view, the Greek girl Théophé, and Manon herself. In each case the woman is presented through the eyes of a man who is not sure of understanding her completely, and who is always being taken aback by some unforeseen action on her part. This uncertainty stops Prévost from drawing in the character with too categorical a touch, and leaves a measure of vagueness or mystery which enhances the reader's interest.

The narrator of *L'Histoire d'une Grecque moderne* never solves the enigma: is Théophé really modest and pure and virtuous, or is she a coquette who will accept love from others though not from him? In *Manon Lescaut* our doubts are ultimately dispelled; the Chevalier's fidelity is rewarded by the assurance of Manon's complete devotion to him. This new attitude of Manon's is a necessary stage in the plot, and it is here, perhaps, that we do feel the lack of more detailed knowledge about her. From her behaviour up to this point, there is little evidence to support the notion that Manon possesses a capacity for any deep and enduring emotional attachment. Was it, then, to prepare our acceptance of Manon's new, unselfish love that Prévost inserted, in the 1753 edition, the episode of the Italian prince (pp. 118–124)? But her refusal of the Prince's attentions comes at a moment when Des Grieux is not short of money, so that it has little bearing on her changed feelings towards the Chevalier among the hardships of life in America. It seems more likely that Prévost had realized, belatedly, the fascination which Manon exerted over his readers. In his attempt to please the public by giving them more of Manon, he shows that he did not understand the effectiveness of his own reticence in the first version of the story.

Maurice Allem says of this inserted episode, 'Il n'est pas dans le ton du reste de l'ouvrage.' This criticism seems to me not wholly accurate. There is some similarity, surely, between the tone of Manon's gay defiance here, and, for instance, the laughter of the evening when Des Grieux pretends to be her brother so as to dupe M. de G. M. (p. 77). But it is true that by the time the Italian prince makes his appearance, the lovers have undergone separation and imprisonment, and that even worse disasters are impending. The light-hearted addition does therefore seem out of keeping with the moment in the story where Prévost chose to place it.

This is the only major lapse of its kind in *Manon Lescaut*, and it is the result of ill-advised second thoughts on Prévost's part. But his first thoughts, in this matter of tone, are not always above reproach. In the outline of Book IV of *Le Doyen de Killerine*, there was an allusion to the Dean's consultation with a group of theologians concerning the propriety of the Count's offer to marry Rose after the death of his present wife. This episode, which takes up six pages, is a short satirical scene after the manner of Lesage. The oldest of the seven learned doctors takes offence because the Dean does not bow first to him. The remaining six dispute his right to claim precedence. When this quarrel is settled, and the Dean asks for their views on his problem, a fresh argument springs up, with accusations of misinterpreting the Greek and Latin authorities, and counter-accusations of ignorance about the texts in question. Dismayed by this battle, the Dean gives up hope of receiving any advice, and slips away unobserved. The satirical tone of this passage is in complete contrast to the remainder of Book IV, and tends momentarily to make the question of the Count's marriage appear ridiculous. Prévost here displays a lack of sensitivity as to the effect which such a scene produces in relation to its context. There are similar occasions, scattered throughout his novels, which show that his literary taste is not always reliable.

One may have similar doubts about his moral taste. This is not merely a matter of his choosing to describe immoral characters or sinful actions. It is rather that he betrays a penchant for the potentially shocking or equivocal situation for its own sake, as a form of titillation. How else does one explain the hero's near-escape from incest in *Cleveland*, and the same situation in *L'Histoire d'une Grecque moderne*, involving Théophé and a young man who does not know that he is her brother? What else can account for the scene in *Le Doyen* where the Dean visits Mme de S., expecting to discuss religion, while she imagines that he has accepted her invitation as a *rendez-vous galant*?

> Elle passa sur-le-champ à me demander pourquoi, dans les vues qui m'amenaient, j'étais venu avec une robe longue, qui convenait si mal aux circonstances. . . . Nos discours sur cette matière devinrent un tissu d'obscurités.[1]

Prévost does not usually go in for frankly scabrous or pornographic incidents, but skirts round the dangerous subjects, drawing the reader's attention by sidelong glances, and always saving appearances by verbal protestations of innocence.

There is a more fundamental contrast, on the moral plane, between what Prévost's characters do and what they say. We have noticed, in the matter of the 'authenticity' of his novels, that Prévost could apparently maintain opposing views on the same subject. This trait emerges again when we consider the moral code of behaviour in his novels. What happens here is that his characters tend to follow the dictates of 'Nature' and their emotions, while paying lip-service, intermittently, to the conventional standards of society.

Raymond Picard has clarified the ambiguities of this double standard by showing how it depends upon 'la morale de l'intention'.[2] Des Grieux repeatedly insists that his lapses from rectitude, and Manon's, are involuntary, unpremeditated, unavoidable. The young lovers do not deliberately set out to commit crimes or sins; they are forced, or find themselves slipping

---

[1] *Le Doyen de Killerine*, V, 151.

[2] Raymond Picard, 'L'Univers de "Manon Lescaut"', *Mercure de France*, avril 1961, pp. 606–22, and mai 1961, pp. 87–105.

despite themselves, into unvirtuous ways. They therefore remain innocent in intention, and should be judged more on what they are than on what they do. After all he has suffered from Manon's actions, Des Grieux can still say of her: 'Je connaissais les principes de son cœur. Elle était droite et naturelle dans tous ses sentiments, qualité qui dispose toujours à la vertu' (p. 190).

This assumption that what is 'natural' is good and morally defensible recurs constantly in *Manon Lescaut*, and in *Cleveland* the idea was to become an important part of the hero's 'philosophy'. According to this view, our instincts, impulses and desires have nothing inherently sinful in them. In particular, love, as the strongest of our natural feelings, is an innocent passion:

> Il me parut, après un sincère examen, que les droits de la nature étant les premiers de tous les droits, rien n'était assez fort pour prescrire contre eux; que l'amour en était un des plus sacrés, puisqu'il est l'âme de tout ce qui existe; et qu'ainsi tout ce que la raison et l'ordre établi parmi les hommes pouvaient faire contre lui, était d'en interdire certains effets sans pouvoir jamais le condamner dans sa source.[1]

From remarks like these, it is clear that it is 'right' to follow the dictates of love, and that social conventions concerning honour, respect for other people, and so forth should yield to the overriding claims of Nature and love.

As a corollary to this glorification of Nature, Prévost also exalts the capacity for emotion, sensibility. (Like many other disciples of Nature, he does not manage to explain why feelings should be considered more 'natural' than reason in man.) Those who are capable of strong and varied emotions form an élite, superior to their less sensitive brethren:

> Le commun des hommes n'est sensible qu'à cinq ou six passions, dans le cercle desquelles leur vie se passe, et où toutes leurs agitations se réduisent. . . . Mais les personnes d'un caractère plus noble peuvent être remuées de mille façons différentes; il semble qu'elles aient plus de cinq sens et qu'elles puissent recevoir des idées et des sensations qui passent les bornes ordinaires de la nature; et, comme

---

[1] *Cleveland*, I, 197. Prévost's ideas would seem to have changed as he grew older. In *Le Monde moral* the hero discovers that 'tous les goûts naturels, sans en excepter celui de l'honneur, sont moins des vertus que des passions, lorsqu'ils ne sont pas réglés et fortifiés par les grands principes du devoir et de la religion' (*Œuvres choisies*, XXIX, 154).

elles ont un sentiment de cette grandeur qui les élève au-dessus du vulgaire, il n'y a rien dont elles soient plus jalouses (p. 91).

Seen in the light of this system, Des Grieux's anti-social acts need no justification. He is one of the finer souls whose sensibility makes him superior to other men. When love comes to such a person, it 'naturally' dominates his life. In order to fulfil his love, he may commit deeds which society condemns, but since his love is an innocent natural passion, the responsibility for these misdeeds rests not on himself but on those who try to thwart his love.

If this doctrine is shorn of its pseudo-philosophical premises, it amounts to little more than the cry of a spoilt child, for whom the fact of wanting an object implies his right to have it. Like a spoilt child, Prévost's *homme sensible* assumes that his desires should override the desires of others. And Des Grieux's reactions to some of his crimes are indeed childish. After shooting the servant in the course of his escape from Saint-Lazare, he petulantly answers Lescaut's query about hearing a pistol-shot: 'C'est votre faute ; . . . pourquoi me l'apportiez-vous chargé?' (p. 97).

Des Grieux, insisting on the purity of his intentions, continually refuses to accept responsibility for his discreditable actions. If another human being cannot be blamed, then *le destin* is cited as the cause of his undoing. This element of fatalism, or quasi-Jansenist belief in pre-destination has been discussed by several critics, notably Hazard and Roddier.[1] I must confess to a lurking suspicion that in treating this subject as seriously as they do, such critics are accepting an attitude imposed on them by Prévost. In real life, a young man who so consistently blamed everything and everyone else for his faults would probably be considered as immature, self-deceiving, and a source of trouble to others. If one treats Des Grieux's behaviour as a conflict between philosophies and creeds, it is because Prévost has managed to make us forget our habitual standards of judgment. Des Grieux, as Roddier so rightly says, 'nous impose finalement sa vision'.[2]

[1] Paul Hazard, *Etudes critiques sur Manon Lescaut*, Chicago, 1929, pp. 47–69; Henri Roddier, *L'Abbé Prévost, l'homme et l'œuvre*, Paris, 1955, pp. 70–88.
[2] In 'L'Univers de "Manon Lescaut"', Raymond Picard provides an illuminating analysis of the way Prévost wins and maintains the reader's sympathy for the young lovers (pp. 606–12).

With this conclusion we are brought back yet again to the question of 'belief'. In our discussion of Prévost's novels we have seen that several of his methods of procedure are concerned, directly or indirectly, with the creation of an illusion of authenticity. There can be no doubt that he himself took this to be the prime task of the novelist. Writing of a memoir-novel by Mesnier, he said:

L'art suprême dans un livre de cette nature consiste sans doute à se rendre ainsi maître de l'attention et du goût des lecteurs, indépendamment de la vérité des faits qu'on leur raconte.[1]

It is this kind of aim which explains Prévost's use of historical characters and incidents, his vouching for the accuracy of interpolated narratives, his avoidance of long conversations in direct speech, etc. Such factors may well have carried some weight with readers of his own time, but these alone have not sufficed to make his long novels still credible and convincing. If we are to discover why *Manon Lescaut* alone has survived, we must therefore look for qualities which are more important in this short *histoire* than in the full-length novels.

Of such merits the essential ones, in my view, are those concerned with the portrayal of character. In *Manon Lescaut* more attention is given, proportionately, than in the longer works, to three crucial aspects of characterization: the exploration and analysis of lasting traits; the effects of time and circumstance in bringing about changes of feeling and ideas; and the links between personality and action. As a consequence of this treatment, the reader's interest is guided to questions of feeling and motivation as well as to 'what happens next', and Des Grieux and Manon come to life for us as we read. Very few novels written before *Manon Lescaut* possess this power. The one outstanding case is of course *La Princesse de Clèves*, and of this Professor Green has said:

By stressing the importance of psychological analysis as opposed to the mere narrative of physical adventures, Mme de la Fayette plotted the master curve to be followed by later novelists.[2]

[1] *Le Pour et contre*, 1738, XVI, 357. See also the opening pages of *Le Monde moral*.
[2] F. C. Green, *Minuet*, London, 1935, pp. 305-6.

Thus, although Prévost's novels evince a preoccupation with winning the reader's belief by realistic narrative methods, it is in the last resort the 'truth' of character which has kept this one story alive. The modern reader, like those of earlier generations, is caught and held by Des Grieux's revelatory self-portrait, and by his evocation of the eternally fascinating and enigmatic Manon.

VI

Marivaux

CHARACTERS IN DEPTH

IN the opening pages of *La Vie de Marianne*, Marivaux follows the general practice of previous memoir-novelists in presenting their stories. We find an anecdote describing how the manuscript came into the 'editor's' hands. And the reader is assured by the editor and by Marianne herself that this is not a novel but a true story:

> Ce début paraît annoncer un roman: ce n'en est pourtant pas un que je raconte; je dis la vérité comme je l'ai apprise de ceux qui m'ont élevée (p. 10).[1]

Even the explanation that Marianne has undertaken her 'Life' at the request of a friend is not wholly original: Mme de Villedieu's heroine had been made to offer the same pretext in *La Vie de Henriette-Sylvie de Molière*. Nevertheless, Marivaux's book creates an overall impression very different from the memoir-novels of Prévost or Mme de Villedieu. Several elements contribute to this difference. We shall look first at those which arise from Marivaux's style in *La Vie de Marianne*. The most striking characteristics of this style, as compared with earlier memoir-novels, is its wide range of linguistic usage and a certain informality of tone.

The words and sentence-structures used by Prévost, as by Lesage before him, are those of a middle or 'neutral' style. This admits the mention of everyday action and objects, such as taking a cab, and therefore does not aspire to the conscious elevation of *style noble*. At the same time it avoids the solecisms which might be heard from an uneducated person like a cab-driver, so that it does not fall into *style bas*: the *fiacre* with whom Des Grieux has trouble is remarkably temperate in his language

---

[1] Page-numbers for *La Vie de Marianne* and *Le Paysan parvenu* refer to the Garnier edition, edited in both cases by Frédéric Deloffre, and published in 1957 and 1959 respectively.

(pp. 123-4). Marianne's *cocher*, who provides a complete contrast to this restraint, is one of the many characters to whom Marivaux attributes language of a recognizably low or vulgar nature.

The informal tone of *La Vie de Marianne* is not however merely a matter of the novel's containing passages of colloquial and uneducated usage. Throughout the book there is a neglect or a positive flouting of canons of composition, a consistently non-literary approach, an attempt, explicitly avowed, to pursue the level of spoken rather than written French:

Peut-être devrais-je passer tout ce que je vous dis là; mais je vais comme je puis, je n'ai garde de songer que je vous fais un livre, cela me jetterait dans un travail d'esprit dont je ne sortirais pas; je m'imagine que je vous parle, et tout passe dans la conversation (p. 36).

Manon Lescaut also purports to be a word-of-mouth narration, merely reported by the Man of Quality; but there are occasional sentences which have a somewhat rhetorical ring if we keep this situation in mind, and for an extempore narrative the story is admirably composed. *La Vie de Marianne*, by contrast, presents a less coherent sequence of events, and manages more effectively to suggest the tone of the spoken word.

It was something new to find these two elements—the increased linguistic range and the conversational tone—in a romantic novel, though both had appeared, to some extent, in the seventeenth-century *roman réaliste*. What we should notice, however, is that their use in *La Vie de Marianne* is bound up with the initial fiction concerning the creation of the work. Marianne adopts this free and intimate tone because she is writing primarily for a friend, a person whom she addresses and confides in and appeals to throughout the narrative. (In his earlier novels Marivaux had already shown an unusual awareness of the writer-reader relationship.)[1] Secondly, Marianne presents herself as a woman with few fixed ideas about style, with no practice in formal composition, and above all, with no literary pretensions. She therefore opts for the only method

[1] See Wayne C. Booth, 'The self-conscious narrator in comic fiction before *Tristram Shandy*', *Publications of the Modern Language Association*, 67 (1952), pp. 163-85.

of writing she can be expected to command, the quasi-conversational style of letters. And, to complete the circle of the argument, she can limit her aspirations in this way precisely because she is writing for a friend, a reader who will not be over-critical or judge her by professional standards.

We can see now what is different about Marivaux's use of the convention of a real person writing authentic memoirs. Whereas authors like Courtilz de Sandras and Prévost utilized it primarily, it would seem, as a means of winning literal and passive belief, Marivaux makes it account for the stylistic innovations which he introduces by and through the character of Marianne.

Whether or not he was fully aware of the new twist he was giving to this convention, Marivaux certainly knew that *La Vie de Marianne* was in some respects outside the usual run of novels. He even uses the pretext of 'authenticity' to defend himself against criticisms based on the accepted standards of novel-writing, saying in effect: 'Since these are memoirs, you must not judge the book as a novel.'

The particular aspect of the work for which he produces this defence is that of Marianne's reflective digressions. Marivaux discussed these in the *Avertissement* to Part I, obviously fearing that some readers would find them out of place in a novel: 'On ne veut dans des aventures que les aventures mêmes.' (This confirms our observation, à propos of Lesage and earlier writers, that the events of the plot were assumed to be the centre of interest in a novel.) Marivaux's expectations were justified; some critics did object to these asides. Desfontaines is a good example of this attitude, since he attacks Marianne's reflections on every count. Firstly, they are unnecessary and undesirable: Marianne 's'interrompt elle-même fréquemment pour se jeter sans nécessité dans des raisonnements abstraits, dont le lecteur la dispenserait volontiers' (p. lxvi). Then they are sometimes unsound as observations of human nature. Desfontaines cites Marianne's suggestion that if a woman is pretty her conversation is taken to be witty, and rejects it as 'outré et hors de la nature' (ib.). And finally, they are unsatisfactory as to expression: 'Marianne a bien de l'esprit, mais elle a du babil et du jargon'; her reflections 'la font passer quelquefois pour une précieuse'; and she is contrasted with the curé's sister, whose deathbed speech contains 'rien d'affecté, rien de subtil'. The indictment could scarcely be more thorough.

Other critics, including Prévost, were less scathing, and even commended Marianne's asides. This comes closer to the modern point of view. Generally speaking, reflections of this kind are not nowadays condemned as unnecessary or undesirable, provided that they arise from the action and that they are incorporated into the flow of the narrative. Marivaux can scarcely be faulted as to relevance. It is practically always some situation or event in her story which sets Marianne off on her general comments. They do, however, stand out from the surrounding text, and Marivaux makes them even more obvious by the excuses and justifications which Marianne offers. Such apologies are further evidence of Marivaux's awareness that he was diverging from the usual methods of novelists. And they do in fact come under the general fiction that Marianne is writing spontaneously, with no attempt to achieve professional standards of artistic arrangement.

Their matter and manner have, to modern eyes, an incidental merit which contemporary critics seem not to have envisaged. Let us return to the passage which Desfontaines picked out for censure. We may possibly agree with him that Marianne exaggerates the effect of a pretty face, but we can also see that it is a notion which might enter the mind of a woman who had seen her own attractions appreciated. In other words this idea, even if it is unsound or exaggerated, is consistent with the age and situation of the narrator. The same can be said for Marianne's personal manner of expression. It may occasionally seem affected, precious and over-subtle; but is this not in keeping with the character of a woman of fifty, a Countess, who has presumably frequented just those salons and that type of society in which such traits of expression were habitual? Marianne's *babil et jargon* reveal a temper of mind and habits of speech which effectively help to characterize the 'I' of the novel. If the objection should be raised that this is Marivaux's own mode of expression, rather than being distinctively Marianne's, one has only to point to *Le Paysan parvenu*, where Jacob's style is noticeably plainer.

What Marivaux does in the reflective digressions of *La Vie de Marianne* is to exploit the possibilities of exploring and portraying character by oblique methods, in addition to the more obvious use of behaviour and overt self-analysis as sources of information.

Implicit or indirect self-revelation is of course inevitable in any first-person narrative, as it is also in the theatre. The act of speaking gives us information about the speaker. But one scarcely needs to point out that in a work like *Gil Blas* this revelation is minimal. Even in *Manon Lescaut*, whose hero is more reflective, the portrayal of personality depends far more on Des Grieux's actions than on anything he thinks or says about subjects outside the immediate scope of his love for Manon. Marianne carries oblique self-revelation much further. Her comments on *coquetterie*, on the humiliation of receiving charity, or even on the stupid curiosity of a Paris crowd, afford us extra insight on her own approach to life and on her standards of behaviour. As Professor Green has pointed out, Marivaux 'was really the first French novelist to discern the potentialities of *le récit personnel* as an instrument of psychological analysis'.[1] In this domain Marivaux can clearly be seen as a forerunner of Proust.

It seems safe to assume that Marivaux had Marianne's character in mind when he allowed her to make these reflections; the hero of *Le Paysan parvenu* is far less liberal with his comments. But it is also possible that in *La Vie de Marianne* Marivaux was giving way to his own penchant for analysis and generalization, a tendency which is evident in his journals, *Le Spectateur français* and *L'Indigent Philosophe*. Whatever his motives, one effect of Marianne's reflections, and one reason why they may be more acceptable to modern readers, is that they contribute to a more thorough portrayal of her character and give it increased depth and 'reality'.

There was a second point on which Marivaux tried to forestall criticism: his inclusion of 'low' characters, and more particularly the vulgar speech he made them use. In the *Avertissement* to Part II he admits: 'Bien des lecteurs pourront ne pas aimer la querelle du cocher avec madame Dutour.' He tries to justify such scenes not, this time, by stressing the difference

[1] 'Some observations on technique and form in the French seventeenth- and eighteenth-century novel', *Stil- und Formprobleme*, Heidelberg, 1959, p. 210.

between Marianne's memoirs and the usual run of novels, but by indicating the universal human interest of such behaviour. The excuse did not pass muster with all his critics. Desfontaines, again, was the most explicit in his objections:

> La querelle de la lingère avec le cocher de fiacre a paru peu digne d'un esprit aussi élevé et aussi délicat qu'est celui de M. de Marivaux. Son pinceau ne s'est pas exercé ici sur la belle nature: les vils et indignes objets ne se présentent que trop souvent devant nos yeux malgré nous (p. lxviii).

The phrase 'la belle nature', which occurs frequently in discussion of the visual arts at this period, covers a conception of the nature and function of art which has still some partisans: the artist's job is to portray what is noble and beautiful; there are enough ugly, vulgar things in the world without the artist perpetuating them in paint or words.

The basis of Desfontaines' complaint is therefore twofold, that Marivaux made his lower-class characters prominent, instead of keeping them discreetly in the background; and that he did not refine them, when they had to appear, by the use of a correct and educated style. But the reasons for Marivaux offending certain literary standards in this way go deeper than his specific intentions concerning La Vie de Marianne, a fact which may explain why he did not try to bring these practices under the general blanket-excuse of the book's 'authenticity'. They depend on two of Marivaux's abiding interests: firstly in questions of class, and secondly in the workings of language.

Even if we did not know that Marivaux enjoyed walking through the streets of Paris and watching the life around him, we could deduce from his writings that he was fascinated by the differences of thought and behaviour which arise from the structure of society. The privileges of the rich, the servant-master relationship, the struggles of le menu peuple, are recurring themes in his plays and his journalistic writings.

As for language, words were not, for him, mere blank tokens, but instruments deserving attention and respect in their own right. His interest was not chiefly in their sounds and rhythms, as a poet might appreciate them. Nor did he, it seems, feel any temptation to remould and transmogrify them in the manner of Rabelais or James Joyce. Instead, he had a semanticist's interest, especially in the distinctions to be drawn between various expressive effects:

> En voyant cette jeune personne, on eût plutôt dit: Elle ne vit plus, qu'on n'eût dit: Elle est morte. Je ne puis vous représenter l'impression qu'elle faisait, qu'en vous priant de distinguer ces deux façons de parler, qui paraissent signifier la même chose, et qui dans le sentiment pourtant en signifient de différentes (p. 350).

Whenever Marivaux discusses questions of communication and style, he tends to revert to his conviction that an idea is not 'the same idea' if couched in different terms, since any change is bound to affect the emotive reactions it produces in reader or listener.[1] He is, then, continually on the alert for nuances of feeling and for the affective attitudes which a particular choice of words can indicate. And this awareness seems to operate more particularly in situations involving the spoken word, where remarks are uttered to produce an immediate effect, and are a response to the whole complex of circumstances in which the speaker finds himself. For instance, a constant feature of his plays is the sensitivity of many characters not merely to the feelings and ideas of others, but explicitly to the words they use. And the absence of such sensitivity in a character is often a sign that the finer feelings in general are also absent. We can now understand why Marivaux, holding these views about language, was unwilling to forego the use of vulgar speech for his lower-class characters. He would not refine and edulcorate the conversation of Mme Dutour, for instance, as Prévost had done for Manon's uncouth brother and Des Grieux's discontented *fiacre*, because this alteration would falsify a vital element in their portrayal.

He did not go to extremes. An angry coachman would undoubtedly have used even stronger and less grammatical language than that of the *cocher* in Part II of *Marianne*. Marivaux's linguistic 'realism' is therefore only a matter of degree. But he did manage to convey an impression—all too vivid for some of his early readers—of the kind of language liable to be used in such a dispute.

The quarrel of the *cocher* and Mme Dutour is a little scene,

[1] Cf. the passage from *Le Cabinet du Philosophe* quoted in Marcel Arland, *Marivaux*, Paris, 1950, p. 239.

complete in itself. Elsewhere, by incidental exchanges, Marivaux makes the speech of lower-class characters reveal their habitual attitudes and modes of feeling, just as Marianne's reflections throw sidelights on her own personality. Thus Mme Dutour, without active malice or cunning, manages to be offensive to Marianne simply through stupidity and through her inability to imagine what effects her words may have on the listener. Her earlier indiscretions lead up to the crucial moment where she greets Marianne, now a guest of Mme de Fare, with a bubbling stream of reminiscence which effectively destroys Marianne's pretence of being a young lady just up from the provinces (pp. 263–5). Pausing critically over this scene, one might judge that Mme Dutour, a shopkeeper of some experience, could be expected to pay more attention to the remarks of persons of quality like Valville and Mlle de Fare, and that her indiscreetness is here taken to excessive lengths. But Marivaux has previously established this facet of her character so thoroughly that the episode, in its context, carries conviction. And the same type of busy-bodying lack of discretion is shown by the landlady in *Le Paysan parvenu*, again exemplifying an absence of imagination and finer feelings.

The connections between speech-habits and social status are treated in a particularly interesting way in *Le Paysan parvenu* because Jacob, unlike Marianne, is handicapped on arrival in Paris by his uneducated way of talking. However, he is portrayed as being keenly aware of the different effects produced by various kinds of speech, and with his habitual eye to the main chance, he trades upon his ability to use the style that fits the occasion.

Jusqu'ici donc mes discours avaient toujours eu une petite tournure champêtre; mais il y avait plus d'un mois que je m'en corrigeais assez bien, quand je voulais y prendre garde, et je n'avais conservé cette tournure avec Mlle Habert que parce qu'elle me réussissait auprès d'elle, et que je lui avais dit tout ce qui m'avait plu à la faveur de ce langage rustique (p. 85).

This remark skilfully touches in a complex linguistic and psychological situation. Mlle Habert finds Jacob's country speech inferior but engaging, and she—unconsciously?—uses this apparent naïveté of his as a convenient excuse for letting him say things which she wants to hear, but which she would feel obliged to rebuke as forward or impertinent if they were couched in her own everyday language. Jacob has grasped her attitude, and by falling in with the pretence, he exploits it to the full. Thus Marivaux not only illustrates, as might a semanticist, the emotive effects that can be produced by a mode of speech different from one's own, but also makes the case serve the ends of characterization, since Jacob and Mlle Habert behave in ways which extend our knowledge of them as persons.

Both Marianne and Jacob have the task of establishing themselves in the higher reaches of society, starting without the usual guarantees of birth or wealth. For characters like these, the question of forms of address assumes a special importance. Here again, Marivaux makes his personages very sensitive to the terms chosen by others. Some of these distinctions have now lost the connotations which would make them so effective with an eighteenth-century reader, but generally speaking the context reveals the weight attached to such forms of address and helps us to realize, if not fully to feel, their significance. A clear case is provided by the scenes, in both novels, of official opposition to the marriage-plans of the central character. Mme de Miran defends Marianne's right to be addressed as 'Mademoiselle'; Jacobs protests for himself against the humiliating implications of *tutoiement*. In each case it is an attitude which is being attacked, but the debate, instead of becoming generalized and theoretical, continues to centre upon the word itself.

Marivaux is also fond of indicating an alteration of attitude by quoting some word or phrase which sums up the changed point of view. When Marianne is rescued as a baby, the noble ladies of the district all take an interest in her:

Le curé . . . disait souvent depuis que, dans tout ce que ces dames avaient alors fait pour moi, il ne leur avait jamais entendu prononcer le mot de charité; c'est que c'était un mot trop dur, et qui blessait la mignardise des sentiments qu'elles avaient.

Aussi, quand elles parlaient de moi, elles ne disaient point cette petite fille; c'était toujours cette aimable enfant (p. 13).

But fine sentiments wear out with time, and

au bout de six mois, cette aimable enfant ne fut plus qu'une pauvre orpheline, à qui on n'épargna pas alors le mot de charité (p. 14).

The conclusion from all this is that Marivaux was more keenly aware than any previous French novelist of the value of words, both for indicating external distinctions of class and education, and for suggesting permanent traits of personality or changing emotive attitudes. Because he utilizes a wider range of linguistic usage, and because he is skilled in choosing the crucial revelatory phrase, his picture of society has a new depth and precision. It is as though, by his exploration of the resources of speech, he had discovered how to suggest a new dimension in portrayal, never fully mastered by previous novelists.

With this new depth in characterization, and inseparable from it, goes an increase in the credibility of the emotions described. Marivaux achieves this by two complementary methods: he analyses and discusses emotions in detail, and he includes all types and shades of feeling, not merely those which were currently accepted as appropriate in literature.

Examples of his detailed analyses are manifold. Marianne's general reflections often have as their starting-point some observation of her own reactions, which she discusses before and while she is extending her comments to cover the behaviour of others. Once again we can see a contrast between this method and that of Lesage or Prévost. In *Gil Blas* the considerations of motive are summary and often trite. In *Manon Lescaut*, Des Grieux all too often finds that his emotions defy analysis. Marianne's self-communings, as they stand, may not always be the most skilful or artistically satisfying way of presenting such explorations of emotion, but there is little doubt that they make a valuable contribution to the whole picture.

Moreover, by the inclusion of trivial as well as noble feelings, her life acquires an air of completeness which had been lacking in other romantic novels. *Manon Lescaut*, because of its brevity and compactness, can be excused for its constant dwelling on the heights of emotion. But in his long novels, as we have already remarked, Prévost risks monotony and implausibility by concentrating almost entirely on the violent feelings aroused by extraordinary events. Marivaux introduces variety, and highlights the moments of true climax, by mentioning those tamer everyday feelings which are familiar to all readers. And just as, in matters of dialogue, he was not content with the accepted colourless style of 'correct' French, so in the field of emotions, he did not always make his characters conform to the patterns of feeling made familiar by works of literature. In particular, he portrayed those moments of distraction when some flash of emotion, often scarcely creditable by our avowed moral standards, breaks through the stronger and 'higher' feelings which are held to be proper to the occasion. Marianne, shocked and indignant over M. de Climal's propositions, is packing up his presents to send them back:

Cependant le paquet s'avançait; et ce qui va vous réjouir, c'est qu'au milieu de ces idées si hautes et si courageuses, je ne laissais pas, chemin faisant, que de considérer ce linge en le pliant, et de dire en moi-même (mais si bas, qu'à peine m'entendais-je): Il est pourtant bien choisi; ce qui signifiait: c'est dommage de le quitter (p. 131).

This quotation raises a final point concerning the detail and precision of Marivaux's portrait of society: it has, in comparison with the work of many previous novelists, a greater range of visual references, to objects, clothes, movements and gestures. Quite apart from his portraits, which call for separate discussion, Marivaux gives frequent descriptive touches which help to bring the scene before our eyes and to point the significance of some concrete object or physical reaction. The whole business of Marianne's new clothes—their buying, their wearing, and the virtuously indignant sending of them back—makes M. de Climal's attempt on her virtue more concrete and more vivid. And Marivaux has a flair for sketching in a single gesture which is dramatically or ironically effective; as with the Prioress who welcomes Marianne warmly but without undue exertion: 'Eh! ma belle enfant, que vous me touchez! me répondit la prieure en me tendant les bras de l'endroit où elle était' (p. 150).

In speech, in emotions, in its visual aspects, the world of Marivaux's two last novels is altogether more lifelike, more detailed, more 'real', than that of the general run of novels before his time. These are all factors which twentieth-century critics tend to prize, and it is no wonder that Marianne and Jacob have come back into favour after a long period of comparative neglect. But we must not forget the weaker and less original aspects of these two works. Marivaux may well have broken fresh ground in some directions, but there were certain traditional limitations of the novel which he respected all too faithfully.

In plot-construction, particularly as to the use of coincidence and the handling of time, Marivaux was uninventive and often careless. Chance makes Marianne meet Valville, who turns out to be M. de Climal's nephew, and a second chance leads to her meeting Mme de Miran, who is Valville's mother. Similarly, in *Le Paysan parvenu*, when Mlle Habert's new landlady calls in a priest she happens to know, to carry out the wedding-ceremony, he turns out to be the very man who objected to Jacob's presence and sparked off the quarrel between the sisters. One could cite further examples from both novels. It is clear that in working out the events and encounters of his plots, Marivaux neither strained his ingenuity nor took into account the probabilities of everyday life.

As for time, while Marivaux may have achieved a new depth and clarity in character-portrayal, he has little grasp of that further dimension in which the story unfolds. This remark does not apply to the author's or the character's subjective apprehension of time, linked with experience. Marivaux's attitude in this domain has been discussed, from opposing points of view, by Georges Poulet and Leo Spitzer.[1] Our subject here is merely the treatment of measurable time, the chronology of the novel.

Marivaux neglects or ignores the relationship between time, in his story, and the proportions of the novel. The last few pages of Part I, and the whole of Parts II and III, are taken up with the account of a single day in Marianne's life. Granted, this was a momentous day for her, but it is clear that the novel would have stretched out to an inordinate length if Marivaux had been going to finish it on such a scale. The same accusation could be made, for *Le Paysan parvenu*, about Jacob's first day in the Habert household. This failing arises from two points already noticed: the one, usually a merit, Marivaux's penchant for detail; the other, less admirable, his implausible accumulation of chance events.

Secondly, Marivaux does not keep in mind the chronology

[1] Georges Poulet, *Etudes sur le temps humain. II. La distance intérieure*, Paris, 1952; Leo Spitzer, 'A propos de la *Vie de Marianne*', *Romanic Review*, XLIV (1953), pp. 102–26.

he has himself established. Here he is perhaps more excusable, for this was a common fault among eighteenth-century novelists. If one looks closely at the chronology of, for instance, the *Mémoires d'un Homme de Qualité*, one discovers that Prévost at one point allows only a year for travels which, as related in detail, take fourteen months or more; and that the hero's second encounter with Des Grieux is not strictly compatible with the dates and times given for the English journey which it follows. Obviously this matters very little, since scarcely any readers would perceive the discrepancies, but it does show that Prévost's chronology is largely impressionistic, apart from the historical events which are utilized as background. Marivaux too relies on impressions. In Part III, Marianne refers to herself as 'une âme de dix-huit ans' (p. 145), though only a few days earlier in the story, at the time of her first meeting with M. de Climal, she was 'Quinze ans et demi . . . et peut-être plus' (p. 27). Admittedly she has lived through enough excitement in the interval to enrich her experience by several years of 'emotional age'. But could Marivaux not remember, or at least look back to check, the actual age he had given his heroine?

Another of Marivaux's slips concerning time, in *Le Paysan parvenu*, raises larger issues. Towards the end of Part I, Jacob offers us a delightful vignette of the Habert sisters apparently toying listlessly with their food, but really putting it away heartily. The passage begins: 'Jamais elles n'avaient d'appétit . . .' and Jacob, we assume, is describing a scene he frequently witnessed. The sisters complain about the food and their appetites, and Jacob comments:

> Ces discours-là me jetaient la poudre aux yeux de manière que . . . je ne savais les premiers jours comment ajuster tout cela.
> Mais je vis à la fin de quoi j'avais été les premiers jours dupe (p. 52).

What one cannot tell on a first reading, though it emerges when one returns to the book, is that Jacob was in the household only one day, and saw only one meal shared by the sisters.

There are two possibilities here. Marivaux may have been led more or less inadvertently into writing the passage in this frequentative form, with its imperfect tenses, because it follows some sentences describing the habits of the household. This however does not really account for: 'Mais je vis *à la fin*', or the recurring 'les premiers jours'. The second and more likely alternative is that at the time of writing, Marivaux had not worked out in full detail what was to be the next development in Jacob's story.

This in its turn raises two related topics: the amount of care and trouble Marivaux was willing to expend on his novel-writing, and his methods of plot-construction. As to the first, it seems an inescapable conclusion that he felt no particular compulsion either to check whether what he was now writing agreed as to practical detail with what had already appeared; or to see that inconsistencies which had arisen through some new turn in the plot were eradicated in subsequent editions. We may suppose that he could have made such corrections had he wished: Part I of *Le Paysan parvenu*, for instance, which first appeared in 1734, was brought out by the same publisher in a second edition, not a mere reprint, in 1735 (p. li). If Marivaux had wished to amend the passage quoted above in the light of the action in Part II, or had he perceived the slip in *Marianne* concerning a maid who is first called Javotte and a few pages later Toinette, he could presumably have arranged for them to be corrected. That he first made, and then left, these and similar inconsistencies, trifling as they may be, argues a certain insouciance about practical detail in his novels; suggests even that he was prepared to let pass in them the kind of lapse which would never have been tolerated in his plays.

Comparison with his plays is also inevitable when we consider Marivaux's approach to planning the story of his novels. A play such as *Le Jeu de l'amour et du hasard* was clearly thought out as a whole; the end follows logically from the beginning; and the plot is a balanced and carefully contrived structure, 'artificial' in the sense that one can see the skill which has shaped it. Marivaux obviously held that building the plot of a novel is quite a different matter—and so, of course, it may be. Nevertheless, one is left feeling that if only he had been prepared to apply to Marianne and Jacob just a fraction of the art and forethought which went into the planning of his comedies, the result would have produced some improvement in this aspect of his two last novels. Even if he had still not finished them—and I cannot agree with M. Arland's contention that they were bound to remain unfinished—they might yet have acquired, as to plot, those qualities of balance and coherence which are now so conspicuously absent.

In *La Vie de Marianne*, Marivaux succumbs to that familiar feature, the interpolated story. He even warns the reader with repeated promises (which could well have been withdrawn in later editions) that this story is due to appear. In reality, it is not even an interpolation, as he never got back to the main thread of Marianne's life. A similar episode is provided in *Le Paysan parvenu* by the conversation in a coach. This includes the story told by the *plaideur* and some literary criticism directed at Crébillon *fils*, the whole forming an interruption to the main narrative which is reminiscent of Lesage's methods in *Gil Blas*. Moreover the account of Jacob's first job in Paris is almost a separate story from what follows. Admittedly the *cavalier* who breaks in on his tête-à-tête with Mme de Ferval turns out to have seen Jacob during this first period of service, but this, it is all too plain, is merely another instance of Marivaux relying on coincidence, and the encounter does not really manage to link the two parts of the story.

Another element which halts the progress of the plot is the formal portrait. Marivaux does not follow Lesage's habit of offering us the static sketch of a social type, the *caractère*. People who might be considered typical, such as the *cocher*, are shown in action and may in general be said to help the story on its way. But he does give individual portraits, and some of these go on too long, so that they become out of proportion to the narrative proper. From his introductory remarks in several cases, it is clear that Marivaux thought of the *portrait* as an isolated feature which provides a *bonne bouche* for the reader, and which can be brought in or postponed at the writer's pleasure. After the long description of Mme de Miran's character at the beginning of Part IV, he seems to realize that another such account would hold up the action intolerably: 'Il vous revient encore un portrait, celui de la dame avec qui elle était; mais ne craignez rien, je vous en fais grâce pour à présent' (p. 171). But when he does come to portray Mme de Dorsin, he is carried away. The resulting passages which close Part IV and open Part V destroy whatever rhythm of events and comments has so far been established. (The reflections themselves, whose general effectiveness we have discussed, are not always above reproach as to length.)

One final complaint about the portraits, particularly some of those in *Le Paysan parvenu*, is linked with our ignorance of Jacob's subsequent career. On several occasions Marivaux describes and analyses a person in some detail, and then adds an explanatory note such as: 'Ce ne fut pas sur-le-champ que je démêlai tout le caractère que je développe ici' (p. 88); or: 'Je vous la peins d'après ce que j'entendis dire d'elle dans les suites' (p. 143). Marivaux's desire to fill in details of personality and behaviour has swept him on ahead in time, to a point which we poor readers can never know—and which he himself may not have clearly envisaged. On this point of technique Lesage comes off better: he allows Gil Blas, on meeting a new character, to describe his appearance, but discussions of personality are left to people who have known the character in question for some time. Marivaux's relish for creating these set-pieces of character-portrayal leads him outside the limitations of time and plot which he himself has built up.

In fairness, one should balance this by a word of admiration for the subtle and perceptive interplay of the narrator's reactions within the temporal framework of the memoir-situation. Marivaux combines and weaves together all the possible elements: 'How I see things now'; 'How I saw them then'; and 'What I now think about my notions then'. It seems strange that with so sure a touch in this respect, he should have fumbled the time-and-knowledge aspect of his portraits.

As to the provenance of the narrator's knowledge, there is another factor in the plot of *Le Paysan parvenu* which may seem to modern eyes a weakness: the fact that Jacob is more than once reduced to eavesdropping in order to be able to tell us about developments necessary to the plot. The most crucial of these episodes is when the *Directeur* visits the Habert sisters and learns of Jacob's having been taken on as a valet. Whatever may have been the contemporary attitude towards eavesdropping in real life, we should recognize that this was a form of behaviour so thoroughly accepted in literature that most readers would scarcely give it a second thought. Apart from its use and abuse on the stage, it was an easy solution, in novels, to one of the difficulties inherent in first-person narrative: how to let the narrator discover incidents at which he was not present and which no one was likely to report to him. Prévost regularly relies on overheard conversations, though fortunately no occasion for this device arises in *Manon Lescaut*. In the summary of *Le Doyen de Killerine* we saw how Linck obtained vital information by eavesdropping in a convent *parloir*. The Dean himself is wounded in a scuffle when his presence is detected after a similar exploit. Other novelists, then, abused the device even more flagrantly than Marivaux. And Balzac is still using it a century later: the action of *Le Père Goriot* starts with Eugène looking and listening at the keyhole of Goriot's door; Bianchon overhears Poiret and Mlle Michonneau discussing Trompe-la-Mort with Gondureau; and Eugène eavesdrops on the final appeals of Delphine and Anastasie to their father. Eavesdropping, like soliloquizing, is the kind of action which survives in literature even when writers are aiming at a realistic picture of life. The technical usefulness of such devices outweighs the drawback of their often being improbable by real-life standards.

Marivaux's use of eavesdropping, it is worth noticing, is not only relatively restrained, but also selective. While Jacob, a *paysan* not yet aware of social niceties, may resort to listening at cracks and keyholes, Marianne, with her higher standards, finds other ways of discovering and conveying what has gone on in her absence. For instance, Mme de Miran's reactions when Marianne is removed from the convent are passed on at second-hand:

> Mon enlèvement l'avait pénétrée de douleur et d'inquiétude. C'était comme une mère qui aurait perdu sa fille, ni plus, ni moins; c'est ainsi que me le contèrent les religieuses de mon couvent et la tourière . . .
> Je vous avoue que je l'aime, disait-elle en parlant de moi à l'abbesse, qui me le répéta (p. 322).

What the latter repeated was apparently a whole page of conversation, couched in terms which are not particularly plausible if we view them in the light of the supposed situation. One may contrast with this the pages of lively and naturalistic dialogue which Marianne and Jacob report without comment or excuse.

Conversation, possibly more than any other element in novels, would seem to prove that even readers who prefer their stories to be realistic will happily accept much that is frankly improbable by real-life standards, as long as the author does not draw their attention to his infringement of these probabilities. If a novelist does remind us that a character is ostensibly repeating, word for word, conversations which took place years ago or were merely repeated to him, then the reader may be provoked into thinking how unlikely it is that such talk could be faithfully remembered. But if the dialogue is presented without comment, and if—perhaps even more important—it is alive and vivid, the odds are that we shall accept it without query.

In this respect, Marivaux showed rather less literary tact than Prévost. The Man of Quality, it will be remembered, gives an initial brief explanation of how he came to record Des Grieux's story, and he emphasizes that his report, because so promptly written down, is 'fidèle jusque dans la relation des réflexions et des sentiments' (p. 15). Once this point is established, Prévost makes no further comment on the dialogue which occurs in the tale itself. And because our attention is not drawn to the matter, we the readers are not likely to query Des Grieux's accuracy in repeating remarks made to him, or even reported to him at second-hand, by other characters. Prévost's dialogue may be less naturalistic than Marivaux's, but at least he does not offend, as Marivaux does, by occasional maladroit reminders of how a conversation came to be reported.

In a certain sense, the whole of La Vie de Marianne is a kind of conversation with the fictional reader to whom it is addressed. And in discussing Marivaux's work I have chosen to cite examples from La Vie de Marianne more often than from Le Paysan parvenu because the former, in my view, contains more instances of the original and debatable literary traits in Marivaux's practice. But in its general conception and in the personality of its central characters, Marianne itself is more conventional and predictable than the life of Jacob. Marianne admits as much, more than once:

Ce début paraît annoncer un roman . . . (p. 10).
C'est que cet abattement et ces pleurs me donnèrent, aux yeux de ce jeune homme, je ne sais quel air de dignité romanesque qui lui en imposa (p. 80).

The heroine of mysterious origin, the shadowy young man who falls in love with her at first sight, the noble lady who adopts and protects her—these characters had appeared as far back as *La Vie de Henriette-Sylvie de Molière*, and were to go on appearing, in *La Paysanne parvenue* and many another novel, for decades to come. The eighteenth-century reader must have been as familiar with these ingredients of a novel as English theatre-audiences were with the butler who answered the telephone in the first scene of a drawing-room comedy, and with the upper-class family he served. The picture of Marianne's life becomes less conventionally romanesque when Mme Dutour appears, but she and her like remain subsidiary to the heroine and to the group of characters who control her destiny.

Jacob, however, is a new figure in the novel. It is not, I think, either relevant or useful to compare him with Gil Blas or to call *La Paysan parvenu* a 'picaresque' novel. True, he shares with Gil Blas precisely those characteristics which mark him off from the pure picaresque strain: respectable birth and upbringing, the absence of anti-social attitudes, and the like. But what makes Jacob's career diverge from Gil Blas's, as well as from the world of the *picaro*, is that Jacob's fortunes depend largely on his masculine charms. Love is not a dominant theme in the true *picaro*'s life, nor in *Gil Blas*; and *Le Paysan parvenu* is a love-story —of a kind. More accurately, it could be called a study in sex-relations.

Jacob's progress depends on essentially the same factors as that of Marianne: physical attractiveness and personal charm. But it was something new, and not at all romanesque, to admit in a novel that the good looks and taking ways of a young man who was only a servant could win him a place in society. And it was a further step away from literary convention to portray the middle-class spinster Mlle Habert, after her ready yielding to Jacob's charms, as a personage not wholly ridiculous, but understandable and in some ways sympathetic.

Jacob's effect on most women is as immediate as Manon Lescaut's on men. And there can be little doubt that Jacob and the women he attracts are not interested in the sentimental delights of *tendresse* as much as in the physical pleasures of 'the right true end of love'. Those critics who condemn *Le Paysan parvenu* as 'immoral' have therefore some grounds for their

protests, even if Marivaux seems discretion itself when compared with other eighteenth-century authors in the licentious
vein, and mealy-mouthed beside the literary exponents of sex
in our own day.

Marianne, whose rise in society also depends on 'love', has
her virtue to defend and must rely on marriage alone. Jacob
encounters more frequent temptations, and is anyway far
readier to succumb. As it happens he is never physically unfaithful to his wife in the story as far as it goes. But Marivaux
plainly means us to understand that he would have been, if
opportunity had been kinder. In this case the author uses
chance, perhaps with some irony, to protect his hero's 'virtue'.
Jacob's character could indeed be not unfairly summed up in
the phrase 'a sexual opportunist'. This is a far cry from the
fleshless heroes of Gomberville and Mlle de Scudéry, and even
the passionate lovers of Prévost. Marivaux has abandoned the
idealism of earlier romantic novels without descending to the
burlesque or anecdotal level of the satiric type.

However, what can be called his 'realism' or his 'cynicism'
in this domain, depending on the critic's own view of life, is not
confined to Jacob alone. For, like Marianne, Jacob is a person
to whom things happen, towards whom other people take the
initiative. If Jacob trades upon the effect of his physical attractiveness, he can do so only because the women he meets make
the advances. (This again may have been lifelike but was certainly not romanesque.) Jacob's behaviour is further mitigated
by various traits and actions which show him in a favourable
light. He will not accept prosperity through marriage if it means
turning a blind eye to his wife's intrigues; he is kind and con-
siderate to Mlle Habert after marrying her, as well as before; he
is spirited and eloquent in his own defence and hers; and he
shows disinterested generosity in his refusal of a job which another man needs more than he does. He is in fact a quick-
witted, pleasant and engaging creature. Marivaux's originality
lies in recognizing and demonstrating that if a young man of
this type is also endowed with animal charm and a touch of ambition, then his rise in society becomes not merely probable but
assured.

'Society' here means of course a specific kind of society, in
which certain women are influential, relatively independent,

and not overly respectful towards the institution of marriage. There is not much point in asking if this is an entirely faithful portrait of a milieu which Marivaux had observed, but one would be justified in supposing that the world of *Le Paysan parvenu* is *more* like Paris in the early eighteenth century than is the romanesque core of *La Vie de Marianne*. To this extent, Marivaux has revealed possibilities of behaviour about which the novel had hitherto been largely silent, and Jacob's adventures embody his most penetrating and original work as a novelist.

VII

Crébillon

INNOVATIONS IN POINTS OF VIEW

I T was after the memoir-novel had become established as the predominant form of French fiction that a fresh form, the letter-novel, came into vogue in the mid-eighteenth century. Crébillon *fils* is an exception to this general pattern. His first novel was the *Lettres de la Marquise de M*** au Comte de R****, published in 1732, and it was not until 1736 that he began publishing *Les Egarements du cœur et de l'esprit, ou Mémoires de M. de Meilcour*. In this chapter we shall however concentrate largely on the latter work, so as to continue our consideration of the autobiographical novel. In the next chapter we shall deal with the history and theory of the letter-novel, and we can then go on to judge Crébillon's works in letter-form in the light of that discussion.

In his two editions of *Les Egarements*, Etiemble makes high claims for Crébillon, and maintains that he has been treated unfairly by generations of critics and teachers: *L'Ecumoire* and *Le Sopha* have overshadowed the real merits of his other works.[1] There is a good deal of truth in this claim. It is usually these two quasi-Oriental *contes*, with their associations of obscenity, which receive first mention in any criticism of Crébillon, and all too rarely are we reminded that both stories contain an element of political and religious satire, so that obscenity itself was not their only aim. They represent, moreover, only a small part of Crébillon's writings, and it seems unjust that they should play such a disproportionate rôle in the customary verdicts on his work.

On the positive side, and quite apart from the intrinsic qualities of his writings, Crébillon should receive credit for

[1] See the introductions in the editions prepared for the *Club du Livre* (1953) and the *Bibliothèque de Cluny* (1961). For a review of critical opinions of Crébillon, see Clifton Cherpack, *An Essay on Crébillon fils*, Duke Univ. Press, Carolina, 1962, pp. vii–xiv.

originality. He was the first French author to exploit the resources of the letter-novel for portraying character and motives in a full-length work—and well before Richardson in England. *Les Egarements* follows the more familiar memoir-novel tradition, but contains innovations which deserve notice. With *Les Heureux Orphelins* he found an even more unusual method of conveying the interplay of feeling between two characters. And in *La Nuit et le moment* (1755) and *Le Hasard du coin du feu* (1763), he adapted the literary *dialogue* to the ends of fiction. Even if one does not share to the full the admiration expressed by Etiemble, it seems clear that Crébillon deserves serious attention as a literary craftsman.

Already in the preface of *Les Egarements,* where he touches on the matter of 'truth' in the memoir-novel, one can see Crébillon moving away from the standards accepted by an earlier generation. He not only abstains from any claims to authenticity, but goes so far as to admit that these *mémoires* may be invented: 'soit qu'on doive les regarder comme un ouvrage purement d'imagination, ou que les aventures qu'ils contiennent soient réelles' (p. 3).[1] Lesage had denied writing a *roman à clef* but had finished by plunging Gil Blas into history; Prévost and Marivaux, in differing degrees, had both paid lip-service to the notion of authenticity. Crébillon explicitly puts aside truth and/or history as being irrelevant to his ends, and in so doing shows a greater respect for fiction *per se.*

He goes on to defend the novel as a means of instruction, and to describe ways in which it could be improved. This manifesto is worth quoting at some length; its edifying approach may help to counter-balance the cynicism usually attributed to Crébillon, and it cites, with wit and clarity, the kind of undesirable features which had kept the genre in such low repute.

Le Roman, si méprisé des personnes sensées, et souvent avec justice, serait peut-être celui de tous les genres qu'on pourrait rendre le plus utile, s'il était bien manié, si, au lieu de le remplir de situations ténébreuses et forcées, de Héros dont les caractères et les aventures sont toujours hors du vraisemblable, on le rendait, comme la Comédie, le tableau de la vie humaine, et qu'on y censurât les vices et les ridicules.

Le Lecteur n'y trouverait plus à la vérité ces événements extra-

---

[1] The edition cited is Vol. II of the *Œuvres,* ed. Pierre Lièvre, Paris, 1929.

ordinaires et tragiques qui enlèvent l'imagination, et déchirent le cœur; plus de Héros qui ne passât les Mers que pour y être à point nommé pris des Turcs, plus d'aventures dans le Sérail, de Sultane soustraite à la vigilance des Eunuques, par quelque tour d'adresse surprenant; plus de morts imprévues, et infiniment moins de souterrains. Le fait, préparé avec art, serait rendu avec naturel. On ne pécherait plus contre les convenances et la raison. Le sentiment ne serait point outré; l'homme enfin verrait l'homme tel qu'il est; on l'éblouirait moins, mais on l'instruirait davantage.

J'avoue que beaucoup de Lecteurs, qui ne sont point touchés des choses simples, n'approuveraient point qu'on dépouillât le Roman des puérilités fastueuses qui le leur rendent cher; mais ce ne serait point à mon sens une raison de ne le point réformer (pp. 3-4).

In his plea for *vraisemblance* and his attack on exaggerated characters and events, Crébillon might seem to do no more than echo seventeenth-century theorists such as Sorel. There is a difference, however: writers of serious novels in the seventeenth century relied on history as the basis of their *vraisemblance*, that is they dealt, ostensibly, in particular truths, or facts. In this they followed the pattern of contemporary tragedy. But although Crébillon is here referring to the serious novel, as we can see from his examples, he has transferred to it the standards which had hitherto been largely confined to the comic novel and comedy. (His own mention of censuring 'les vices et les ridicules' brings out this parallel.) The serious novelist can still carry out his function of moral improvement, but in Crébillon's view he will win the reader's belief by observing the probabilities of everyday life rather than by depending on specific historical or contemporary events. And the demand for natural portrayal—'Le fait, préparé avec art, sera rendu avec naturel'—would, if satisfied, have done away with the larger-than-life emotions and actions of characters like those of Prévost.

One should not over-estimate Crébillon's originality in drawing this parallel. With the decline of the idealized heroic novel, one or two critics had already perceived the possible similarity of function between realistic fiction and comedy.[1] And among the novelists themselves writers such as Lesage and Marivaux had done much to bridge the gulf between the comic or satiric novel and the more elevated novel of serious feeling.

[1] See May, *Le Dilemme du roman*, pp. 110-16.

In so doing they had also drawn nearer to a naturalistic or realistic portrayal of human behaviour. Nevertheless some credit is surely due to Crébillon for clearly formulating the concept of a serious novel which would not need to rely on the supposed 'truth' of specific events, and whose 'naturalness' would allow sensible people to enjoy and admire the genre.

The preface of *Les Egarements* closes with an outline of the complete story to be unfolded in these memoirs, an outline all the more useful in that Crébillon never got beyond Part III, published in 1738. The general scope of the novel was to be the portrayal of an *éducation sentimentale* in three stages: first the hero's initiation in matters of love, then a period of dissipation and false standards, and finally the discovery of virtue and peace of mind through the good graces of 'une femme estimable'. This programme would presumably have run into a dozen or more parts, as Meilcour is still pretty much of a novice at the end of Part III. As it is, apart from the opening pages which cover a period of several months, these three parts deal with only twelve days of Meilcour's life when he is seventeen. Crébillon's handling of time shows, indeed, a distinct resemblance to Marivaux's: devoted to detail, both authors fall into a pattern of closely succeeding events which fill the hours of each day.

The 'events' of the novel are, in essence, the variations of thought and feeling which Meilcour undergoes in relation to three women. Mme de Lursay, the first of these to appear, dominates the book and also, to a large extent, Meilcour. She is a woman of nearly forty, still attractive, and now respectable and careful of her reputation. Meilcour is attracted to her less from any strong attachment than because there is, to begin with, no woman he likes better. But he is timid and inept, and Mme de Lursay has to lead him on to declare his feelings. Although she is quite ready to yield, she has to proceed cautiously so as not to shatter his illusions about the respect he thinks is due to her.

The affaire is still in its early stages when Versac, a fashionable young roué, gossips maliciously about Mme de Lursay in front of Meilcour, who thus discovers that his idol is by no means as pure as he had believed:

et je courus chez Mme de Lursay, dans l'intention de me venger, par ce que le mépris a de plus outrageant, du ridicule respect qu'elle m'avait forcé d'avoir pour elle (p. 126).

This ends Part I.

Meilcour's vengeance is to take the form of winning Mme de Lursay and then throwing her over. But she is more skilled in manœuvres of this kind than he. His first attempt to put his new boldness into practice is rebuffed, but after regaining her ascendency over him, she relents and begins to initiate him into 'l'étude des gradations', a study which is however interrupted by the arrival of callers.

Under the pressure of fresh interests Meilcour's renewed affection for Mme de Lursay begins to decline. At first she reacts with pain and anger. After a few days, however, she appears no longer to care, and one evening she seems to be on the verge of starting an affaire with another young man. Meilcour's wounded vanity prompts him to return after the other guests have left, and demand an explanation. Mme de Lursay again wins him over, and this time he is granted complete satisfaction:

Grâces aux bienséances que Madame de Lursay observait sévèrement, elle me renvoya enfin, et je la quittai en lui promettant, malgré mes remords, de la voir le lendemain de bonne heure, très déterminé, de plus, à lui tenir parole (p. 331).

On this note the book ends.

Woven into the main plot, and affecting its progress at various points, are Meilcour's reactions to Hortense de Théville, a beautiful young girl whom he first sees in the box next to his own at the Opera. Her effect on him is immediate:

Je ne sais quel mouvement singulier et subit m'agita à cette vue: frappé de tant de beautés, je demeurai comme anéanti. Ma surprise allait jusqu'au transport. Je sentis dans mon cœur un désordre qui se répandit sur tous mes sens (p. 48).

When Meilcour at length discovers the identity of this girl he learns, too, that she is on terms of such friendly familiarity with the Marquis de Germeuil that he, Meilcour, would seem to have no hope. It is in moments of despair over this situation that he returns to Mme de Lursay, and it is because of Hortense that he feels remorse even while enjoying Mme de Lursay's favours.

The older woman knows nothing of Meilcour's feelings for Hortense, but becomes jealous of Mme de Senanges, an ageing coquette who openly sets her cap at Meilcour. He speaks of her, when she first enters the story, as the person 'à qui . . . j'ai eu le malheur de devoir mon éducation', but their association has scarcely begun in the novel as it stands. However, it is strongly favoured by Versac, who, towards the end of Part III, has become Meilcour's mentor and model.

From this description it can be seen that the action of the novel consists almost entirely of changes and developments in personal relationships. There are certainly no 'événements extraordinaires et tragiques' of the kind Crébillon deprecated. What we have here is a novel of purely psychological interest, a *roman d'analyse*. Nor was it Crébillon's first effort in this type of work; as we shall see, his letter-novel of 1732 can be described in the same terms.

The characters in *Les Egarements*, then, are observed not under the stress of exceptional and fantastic events, but in the course of their everyday activities: paying social calls, holding dinner-parties, going to the opera, walking in the Tuileries. Yet in the midst of these ordinary pursuits they are still at the mercy of chance. However *vraisemblable* Crébillon has made his characters and the scenes they enact, he has still relied heavily on coincidence for the operation of his plot. Before Meilcour has learnt the identity of his fair Unknown, he happens to hear her talking to a companion in a secluded path in the Tuileries. The conversation on which he then eavesdrops happens to concern a young man, never named, who seems to have aroused Hortense's interest and who might, from the way she refers to him, even be himself. Later it turns out that Hortense's mother happens to be not only a friend of Mme de Lursay, but also a distant cousin of Meilcour's mother. Add to all this the pat arrival of a new character each time there is some need to give the story a fresh impetus—Versac, Mme de Senanges, etc.—and it becomes clear that in matters of plot-construction Crébillon is still far from respecting everyday standards of probability.

The same accusation could be made, if we think of the book as memoirs, concerning the way the plot unfolds, day by detailed day, and even, on occasion, with supplementary accounts of

Meilcour's night thoughts. It is simply not to be believed that an elderly man, looking back on himself when young, could recall with such precision the events of one fortnight when he was seventeen. The convention of the autobiographer's powers of recall is here strained beyond its limits.

Crébillon oversteps the convention in another and possibly a more interesting way. Instead of keeping strictly to the narrator's point of view, describing his own thoughts and feelings but confining himself to an external view of others, he frequently enters the mind of these other characters. It is permissible, of course, for the first-person narrator to infer intentions and reactions from the behaviour that he observes, but Crébillon goes beyond this. During the whole course of the novel, Meilcour is in the position of a naïve youth who does not understand the desires and machinations of Mme de Lursay. He does not say, nor can we reasonably suppose, that at some later stage of his life she explained to him exactly how she decided to lead him on, or to out-manœuvre him in the conduct of their affaire. Yet Crébillon repeatedly makes Meilcour speak in definite and precise terms about Mme de Lursay's thoughts and intentions. A passage like the following shows the procedure clearly:

Elle avait toujours espéré qu'elle me reverrait, mais sûre enfin que je l'évitais, elle commença à craindre de me perdre, et se détermina à me faire essuyer moins de rigueurs. Sur le peu que je lui avais dit, elle avait cru ma passion décidée: cependant je n'en parlais plus. Quel parti prendre? Le plus décent était d'attendre que l'amour, qui ne peut longtemps se contraindre, surtout dans un cœur aussi neuf que l'était le mien, me forçât encore à rompre le silence; mais ce n'était pas le plus sûr. Il ne lui vint pas dans l'esprit que j'eusse renoncé à elle: elle pensa seulement que, certain de n'être jamais aimé, je combattais un amour qui me rendait malheureux. . . . Mais comment me faire comprendre son amour, sans blesser cette décence à laquelle elle était si scrupuleusement attachée? (pp. 58–9).

The presentation of feelings is complete, and is made even more vivid by the use of *style indirect libre* for the questions she put to herself: 'Quel parti prendre?' etc.

This insight into other people's minds is not confined to Mme de Lursay. In spite of his naïveté at the time of the events, Meilcour now shows an omniscient penetration into the thoughts of those he met, and only occasionally does Crébillon remember the conventional limits of his hero's knowledge, in a phrase such as, 'Ces réflexions, *que vraisemblablement il fit*, le calmèrent.' At such moments the artifice is all too obvious. But for most of the time Crébillon is moving away from the point of view of the first-person narrator to that of the omniscient third person.

The rise of the memoir-form meant that the *roman* came to be associated with first-person narrative, while third-person narrative was viewed as a characteristic of the *conte* and the independent *nouvelle*. By the second half of the century this association was so firmly established that we can find a writer explaining, in the preface of her novel, why she has written in 'le style du conte', that is, in third-person narrative.[1] Generally speaking, such narrative was offered in a quasi-historical manner. The writer could describe actions, but only infer thoughts and feelings. Crébillon himself outlines the historical method accurately, if sarcastically:

> Vous ne me montrez que l'extérieur de l'homme, ou ne m'offrez, pour percer plus loin, que des conjectures que je puis, si je veux, ne pas adopter, et qui, quelques fines qu'elles puissent être, n'en sont peut-être pas mieux fondées.[2]

However, neither the historians nor the writers of third-person fiction had ever clung slavishly to this convention. As well as deducing the emotions and mental processes which 'must have' led to certain decisions and actions, they also, occasionally, presented inner debates which did *not* lead to action, and which were therefore not strictly within the scope of historical narrative, even allowing for inference. Such 'illegitimate' discussions of a character's inner life occur not only in *La Princesse de Clèves*, which we have already mentioned, but in the heroic novels of, for instance, Mlle de Scudéry. What is noticeable in such cases, however, is that the usage is limited in extent and, as it were, surreptitious. In the serious novel, at least, writers generally attempted to preserve the appearance of an historical approach.

The authors of comic or burlesque novels enjoyed greater

[1] Mme Benoist, *Agathe et Isidore*, Paris, 1768, *Préface*.
[2] *Œuvres complètes*, London, 1772, 7 vols., V, 293.

freedom. Their stories did not as a rule lay claim to historicity, and when such claims were made, they were obviously face- tious. So there were no barriers of *vérité* to stop these writers moving into the minds of their characters and describing ideas or emotions as they saw fit. Cervantes, for instance, displays such omniscience in *Don Quixote*, and Sorel took advantage of it in *Francion*. By the eighteenth century, therefore, the omniscient narrator was nothing new in the novel as a genre. The fresh development came when this approach was exploited fully and unashamedly by writers of serious novels, a stage which was not reached until the early nineteenth century.

Crébillon's procedure in *Les Egarements* does however present a variant which had not, to my knowledge, occurred before. When first-person narrative began to be utilized for fiction, the novelists who adopted this method obeyed its conventions strictly. They did not enter the minds of any character except their narrator, or describe any incidents at which he was not present. (This, as we have seen, sometimes entailed excessive reliance on devices such as eavesdropping.) We can therefore view Crébillon's contraventions of the 'rules' of first-person narrative either as a reversion to the freedom enjoyed by seventeenth-century comic novelists—and *Les Egarements* does, after all, contain elements of satire—or else as a foreshadowing of the nineteenth-century omniscient narrator.

He was, one might judge, forced into such omniscience by his preoccupation with the analysis of feelings, and by the very nature of his story. After the ironical remarks cited above, on the 'external' historical method, he goes on to say:

Moi, c'est le cœur que je développe, son délire particulier, le manège de la vanité, de la fausseté dans la plus intéressante des passions que j'expose à vos yeux.

This aim is attributed to one of his characters, but could very well be taken as Crébillon's own. And one can see its consequences in the case of *Les Egarements*. The duplicity, scheming and secret intentions of the characters surrounding Meilcour are vital to the plot and, in Crébillon's eyes, interesting in themselves. They must therefore be conveyed to the reader. Meilcour is the only mouthpiece of the novel, so that even if he is supposedly too young and simple to know what his associates are thinking, it is still through him that this information must reach us. In the circumstances, it is hardly surprising that Crébillon has slipped over the brink into omniscience.

The author's occasional attempts to revert to the rules of memoir-writing, in phrases such as 'que vraisemblablement il fit', only remind us of a situation we could otherwise happily ignore. He is wiser in the matter of conversations, where he makes no attempt to explain how or why he can recall every word. Dialogue does play an extremely important part in the work, occupying about half the text. In most cases it is decisive in producing some new development of feeling, and is therefore intrinsic to the plot; the conversations count as events in themselves. In *Le Sopha* which, according to Crébillon's own account, was written at the same period as *Les Egarements*, he discusses and defends conversations both as being a kind of event and as providing a method of characterization:

— Vous avez tort de vous plaindre, lui dit la Sultane; cette conversation qui vous ennuie est pour ainsi dire un fait par elle-même. Ce n'est point une dissertation inutile et qui ne porte sur rien, c'est un fait . . . n'est-ce pas 'dialogué' qu'on dit? demanda-t-elle à Amanzéi en souriant.

— Oui, Madame, répondit-il.

— Cette façon de traiter les choses, reprit-elle, est agréable; elle peint mieux et plus universellement les caractéres que l'on met sur la scène.[1]

These are the kinds of arguments which Marivaux too uses to defend both a conversational style and conversations as such, though in the latter case his main interest was to justify the use of lower-class speech. Crébillon, by contrast, keeps firmly to the upper levels of society. Within this more limited range he produces varied and individual styles of talk which are usually quite convincing. Mme de Lursay's veiled encouragement to Meilcour is in well-bred contrast to the vapid provocations of Mme de Senanges. The insolence and malice of Versac's remarks make it clear why he is both feared and admired. Most of these conversations are vivid and keep the story moving, though occasionally they do fall into the minutiae which Crébillon himself saw as one of their possible drawbacks. They

[1] *Œuvres*, ed. Pierre Lièvre, Paris, 1930, III, 234.

are usually clearer and more interesting than the passages where Meilcour simply describes his feelings.

One conversation in particular calls for special comment, the long passage towards the end of the book in which Versac outlines his philosophy of action to Meilcour. The tone, of advice and persuasion, is that of Vautrin to Eugène de Rastignac in *Le Père Goriot*, but Versac is not an outlaw from society. Having come to understand the factors which make for success in *la bonne compagnie*, he has not rejected the vice and hypocrisy they involve, but has learnt to handle them as a master.

> Entré de bonne heure dans le monde, j'en saisis aisément le faux. J'y vis les qualités solides proscrites, ou du moins ridiculisées, et les femmes, seuls juges de notre mérite, ne nous en trouver qu'autant que nous nous formions sur leurs idées. Sûr que je ne pourrais, sans me perdre, vouloir résister au torrent, je le suivis. Je sacrifiai tout au frivole; je devins étourdi pour paraître plus brillant; enfin, je me créai les vices dont j'avais besoin pour plaire: une conduite si ménagée me réussit.
>
> Je suis né si différent de ce que je parais, que ce ne fut pas sans une peine extrême que je parvins à me gâter l'esprit (p. 271).

This account of a conscious change of character in order to fall in with the requirements of society suggests not Vautrin but Mme de Merteuil of *Les Liaisons dangereuses*, and she can indeed be seen as a feminine counterpart of Versac. Thinking of men as instruments for her power and of her pleasure, she obviously aspires to the same kind of ends as Versac. He states his aims to Meilcour:

> Je suppose d'abord, et avec assez de raison, ce me semble, qu'un homme de notre rang, et de votre âge, ne doit avoir pour objet que de rendre son nom célèbre. Le moyen le plus simple et en même temps le plus agréable pour y parvenir, est de paraître n'avoir dans tout ce qu'on fait que les femmes en vue, de croire qu'il n'y a d'agrément que ce qui les séduit et que le genre d'esprit qui leur plaît, quel qu'il soit, est en effet le seul qui doive plaire (p. 265).

We are dealing here with the type of person for whom sexual relationships are the chief, perhaps the only, interest in life. And this kind of sex-warfare—for it is success, not happiness, which is at stake—necessarily involves secret negotiations, bluff and hypocrisy. Marivaux's Jacob, using his physical attractions for social advancement, seems honest and practical in comparison with these creatures for whom a 'conquest' is an end in itself. According to the standards of most modern readers, the life led by Meilcour and Versac seems strangely empty. Meilcour himself, at the beginning of his story, sums up the various reasons—economic, social and political—which are partly responsible for such behaviour:

L'idée du plaisir fut, à mon entrée dans le monde, la seule qui m'occupa. La paix qui régnait alors me laissait dans un loisir dangereux. Le peu d'occupation que se font communément les gens de mon rang et de mon âge, le faux air, la liberté, l'exemple, tout m'entraînait vers les plaisirs (p. 12).

Apart from the two mothers, Mme de Meilcour and Mme de Théville, all the characters in the book appear to spend most of their time thinking about love and love-making. Versac brings out into the open, and analyses, the assumptions and motives which govern their behaviour. His treatment of the subject, which Crébillon obviously found an absorbing one, takes on almost the proportions of a lecture—or a tutorial.

Crébillon's view of sexual relations in the upper reaches of French society is very similar to that of Laclos. But while *Les Liaisons dangereuses* provides an effective treatment of this subject, *Les Egarements* is, for various reasons, a less satisfactory novel. The plot, first of all, has a see-saw regularity: Mme de Lursay wins Meilcour's attention, he breaks free; she wins him back, he breaks free again—and so on. And while Prévost managed to vary the equally repetitive pattern of *Manon Lescaut* by the development of the Chevalier's character, Meilcour scarcely grows up at all, and could hardly be expected to in the time covered by the novel. If Crébillon had fulfilled his plan for the whole work, a different impression might have emerged, but the three parts we have are weak in this respect.

Secondly, Crébillon has a tendency to envisage his theme in an abstract and theoretical fashion. There is a particular danger here, that of coming to consider the human race merely as two opposing masses, Men and Women.[1] Writers who fall into this trap tend to generalize widely and even wildly, and Crébillon is no exception. 'Une femme, quand elle est jeune,'

[1] See the chapter of this title in Cherpack, *An Essay on Crébillon fils*, pp. 34–47.

he begins, 'est plus sensible au plaisir d'inspirer des passions, qu'à celui d'en prendre.' The idea is developed, and followed by a further paragraph on the woman who has reached 'cet âge où ses charmes commencent à décroître'. This kind of generalization has several drawbacks. It is difficult, for instance, to produce observations of any complexity which really apply to the behaviour of every man, or every woman, in love. While reading, we may therefore be brought up short by the patent falsity of some of Crébillon's comments, judged in the light of our own experience. The trouble here is that instead of merely describing how certain kinds of people may act in certain situations, Crébillon has been tempted, by his fondness for theorizing, into writing of them as though they were typical of all mankind.

The habit of generalizing about the two halves of humanity even leads him into seeing some actions as typically masculine or feminine when they could as well be considered as typically human: 'Les femmes adorent souvent en nous nos plus grands ridicules, quand elles peuvent se flatter que c'est notre amour pour elles qui nous les donne' (p. 98). Surely this comment would be equally true if it ran, *mutatis mutandis*, 'Les hommes adorent souvent . . .'? Feminine readers may have special cause to notice, and be annoyed by, this tendency, since it would seem to be *la Femme* who is the more frequent subject of such generalizations-by-sex. However, it is not merely the quality of such remarks which can be criticized in Crébillon— many a novelist gets away with generalizations which do not bear close consideration—it is their sheer quantity, and the space they occupy, which may become wearisome. *Les Egarements* might have been a better novel had we been shown more of the interplay between characters, and heard less of the narrator's abstract theorizing.

Crébillon's tendency to abstraction goes even deeper, and is inherent in his very vocabulary. It seems to be his natural mode of expression to deal in abstract nouns and general terms rather than in the concrete and specific. A passage like the following is typical of his discursive manner:

Cependant il restait encore à Madame de Lursay bien des ressources contre moi, si elle eût voulu s'en servir. Ce caractère de sévérité qu'elle s'était donné, et qui, tout faux qu'il était en lui-même, l'arrêtait sur ses propres désirs, la honte de céder trop promptement, surtout avec quelqu'un qui, ne devinant jamais rien, lui laisserait tout le désagrément des démarches; la crainte que je ne fusse indiscret, et que mon amour découvert ne la chargeât d'un ridicule d'autant plus grand qu'elle avait affiché plus d'éloignement pour ces sortes de faiblesses; sa coquetterie même, qui lui faisait trouver plus de plaisir à s'amuser de mon ardeur qu'à la satisfaire, et qui avait vraisemblablement causé ses inégalités, plus encore que tout le reste (pp. 95-6).

(Crébillon's skill in using language is a subject to be pursued later; readers may already have noticed, however, from this and earlier quotations, certain weaknesses as to rhythm and even as to clarity of sense.)

In description he follows the same pattern of abstractions. Here is how Hortense de Théville appeared to Meilcour on their first meeting:

Qu'on se figure tout ce que la beauté la plus régulière a de plus noble, tout ce que les grâces ont de plus séduisant, en un mot, tout ce que la jeunesse peut répandre de fraîcheur et d'éclat; à peine pourra-t-on se faire une idée de la personne que je voudrais dépeindre. . . . Elle était mise simplement mais avec noblesse. Elle n'avait pas en effet besoin de parure: en était-il de si brillante qu'elle ne l'eût effacée; était-il d'ornement si modeste qu'elle ne l'eût embelli? Sa physionomie était douce et réservée. Le sentiment et l'esprit me paraissaient briller dans ses yeux (pp. 47-8).

Now it would be foolish to suggest that abstraction and lack of visual detail are, in themselves, major faults in a novelist; Prévost shares these characteristics with Crébillon, and we find Manon no less fascinating because her character is discussed with abstract nouns and we do not know the shape of her nose. The fondness for the general and the abstract goes back, of course, to the seventeenth century. *La Princesse de Clèves*, for instance, in its descriptions and discussions, has much in common with this aspect of Crébillon's style. But when such a style is combined with the theoretical, generalizing tendencies we have already observed, the overall effect may well be excessively remote and intellectual.

With his abstract approach Crébillon combines a liking for analysis. Nuances of feeling are distinguished and classified, motives are brought out into the light and carefully examined.

Mme de Lursay denies that she is afraid of Meilcour falling in love with her:

> Non, reprit-elle, ce n'est pas que j'en aie peur; craindre de vous voir amoureux serait avouer à demi que vous pourriez me rendre sensible: l'Amant que l'on redoute le plus est toujours celui que l'on est le plus près d'aimer; et je serais bien fâchée que vous me crussiez aussi craintive avec vous (pp. 32–3).

She is of course playing a part, so that the passage has overtones of dramatic irony. Even without this, the notion is complex enough, and Crébillon, one feels, is sometimes too subtle by half.

Finally, despite all this reflection and analysis, the moral and emotional values of the book remain curiously equivocal. From the preface and his general comments on characters like Versac and Mme de Senanges, Crébillon seems to condemn the futility of devoting all one's time to the pursuit of love. Yet he describes Meilcour's struggles with patient detail, thereby implying that they are worthy of interest and attention. A character like Mme de Meilcour, who receives explicit praise for her virtue and for devoting herself to bringing up her son, not only plays a minimal rôle in the action, but would seem to have left Meilcour ignorant both of the conventional moral principles and of the hazards of society life.

On the emotional side, we are first led to believe that Mme de Lursay's affection for Meilcour may be sincere; it is she who gives rise to the remark: 'Ce qu'on croit la dernière fantaisie d'une femme est bien souvent sa première passion' (p. 41). Yet she is later portrayed as no more than a schemer, motivated by pride and physical desire rather than by *tendresse*. As for the one supposedly profound emotional situation of the novel, Meilcour's love for Hortense, this is likewise attenuated and ridiculed, by ironical references to love-affairs in novels. The hero speaks of himself as 'd'autant plus persuadé que j'étais vivement amoureux que cette passion naissait dans mon cœur par un de ces coups de surprise qui caractérisent dans les Romans les grandes aventures' (p. 52). And when she is leaving the Tuileries he observes—with a passing thrust for Marivaux:

> Je me rappelai alors toutes les occasions que j'avais lues dans les Romans de parler à sa Maîtresse, et je fus surpris qu'il n'y en eût

pas une dont je pusse faire usage. Je souhaitai mille fois qu'elle fît un faux pas, qu'elle se donnât même une entorse . . . (p. 86).

The general effect of the traits we have noticed is to give an abstract and artificial air to Crébillon's world. His characters react, like puppets, to each fresh move of their manipulator, and their feelings are fully explained to us. But conceived and presented as they are in general analytical terms, they tend to remain mere creatures of the intellect, without emotional consistency. Crébillon does not even succeed in making them appear to care whole-heartedly about the loves and intrigues which are ostensibly the main interest of their existence. It is scarcely surprising, then, if the reader, however willing he may be to co-operate, finds it difficult to accord to such tenuous beings a continuous measure of imaginative belief. In spite of Crébillon's enlightened literary theories, in spite of his technical innovations, this memoir-novel does not wholly fulfil its promise.

It is even more unlikely that a modern reader will enjoy the curious hotch-potch of *Les Heureux Orphelins* (1754), though here again Crébillon's handling of the story is of considerable interest from a technical point of view. Part I of the novel is translated from Mrs Eliza Haywood's *The Fortunate Foundlings* (1744). The heroine, Lucy, runs away from home because of the attentions of her adoptive father. She is seen, in London, by a rich nobleman who plans to seduce her, but she manages to escape, and ends up in Bristol under the protection of the Duchess of Suffolk. Part I ends with Lady Suffolk declaring to Lucy:

Je me sens un besoin extrême de parler, et de mon amour et de mes malheurs; et je crois ne pouvoir pas entretenir quelqu'un qui veuille bien s'y intéresser autant que vous (V, 119).[1]

Part II, where Crébillon begins to invent for himself, turns out to be Lady Suffolk's account of how she fell a victim to the wiles of Lord Durham, an unprincipled young rake brought up in France. Since the Duchess is virtuous and deeply in love with Durham, the effect is rather as though we were to hear about

[1] *Les Heureux Orphelins* does not appear in any modern edition of Crébillon's works. I therefore quote from the *Œuvres complètes*, London, 1772, 7 vols.

Valmont's seduction of Mme de Tourvel from the latter's point of view. When Durham has abandoned her, Lady Suffolk still feels some affection for him. In order to disabuse her completely, the Queen sends her a packet of Durham's letters, intercepted in the post to France. These letters take up the remaining two Parts of the novel.

The work thus consists, ostensibly, of a third-person narrative, a story in memoir-form, and a sequence of letters. In reality, these letters are merely another first-person account of past events, since they retail, firstly, Durham's plan to win the favours of three court ladies, and then his progress in these intrigues. Lady Suffolk is one of the three, and her sincerity and virtue are contrasted with the other two victims, an experienced coquette and a *fausse prude*. Durham's manœuvres show him to be as lucid and pitiless as Laclos's Valmont, and rather more successful, since he remains unpunished.

From a technical point of view, the interest of these letters lies in the way that Durham presents us with his version of events which we have already seen through the eyes of the Duchess.[1] Crébillon seems to have worked over the two accounts with some care. The details are accurately correlated, and we repeatedly find that one narrative provides elements not available in the other, so that the two versions are truly complementary. Lady Suffolk, for instance, repeats verbatim her first conversation with Durham. He in his turn reports:

Quoiqu'elle parût se prêter peu à la conversation, et qu'elle ne me laissât ni lui dire tout ce que j'aurais voulu, ni lui parler aussi longtemps que j'aurais désiré, il ne me fut pas difficile de juger, moins encore à son embarras, qui fut extrême, qu'à la promptitude avec laquelle elle termina notre entretien, de l'impression qu'il faisait sur elle (V, 258).

On other occasions it is Durham who fills in the details of a scene to which the Duchess has merely alluded. Similarly, she tells how he looked and behaved, and how this affected her, while he reveals the motives for his conduct and his diagnosis of her reactions.

A further parallel between the accounts is that in each case there is a sympathetic 'listener', and this fictional audience

[1] Cf. Cherpack, *An Essay on Crébillon fils*, pp. 104–7.

affects the way the story is presented. Lucy does not yet know what it is like to be in love, and Lady Suffolk therefore comments on her own feelings and behaviour in remarks intended to warn the girl about the pitfalls of passion. Durham, on the other hand, is writing to a French nobleman who has been his tutor and guide in sexual intrigue. His 'progress reports' refer to the theories on which he acts, describe in detail the practical outcome of his manœuvres, and include passing reflections on subjects such as the differences between society women in France and in England. Like Marivaux, Crébillon makes his narrator's tone depend on the fictional listener or reader, so that we are offered the story in two versions which are differentiated not only by the point of view but by overall distinctions of tone and attitude.

As in *Les Egarements*, Crébillon apparently wishes us to penetrate fully into the thoughts and feelings of both participants in the love-affair. In *Les Heureux Orphelins* he manages to do this without infringing the conventions of his chosen form of narrative; neither the Duchess nor Durham exceeds the limits of what each could be expected to know. (In this context I am accepting, as conventionally possible knowledge, the narrator's memories of long conversations, letters, etc.) But the two narratives together provide us with a double version of events, from the point of view of the deceived and the deceiver. This method is unusual, and shows Crébillon's desire to extend the author's resources in describing both the 'truth' of a given set of events, and also his characters' inner life.[1]

The main plot of *Les Heureux Orphelins* reaches no conclusion, though it turns out that the nobleman who pursued Lucy in London was Durham himself, under his new title of Count of Chester. Crébillon's weakness in plot-construction has already been noticed. Clearly the linking together of events to form a complete and coherent structure was an aspect of his craft which he found unimportant. The chief interest of his memoir-novels lies not in the story as such, but in his efforts to

---

[1] A very early example of this technique comes in Hélisenne de Crenne's *Les Angoysses douloureuses* (1538), where the hero relates in Part III his side of the love-affair which Hélisenne has told more fully in Part I. In our own time, Lawrence Durrell's *Alexandria Quartet* utilizes the device on a larger scale.

grasp nuances of thought and feeling, and to find adequate and if necessary new methods of conveying them to his readers. For these aims, if not always for their execution, Crébillon still merits serious consideration.

VIII

Letter-Novels

HISTORY AND TECHNIQUE

L ETTERS, in verse and prose, had long been used in fiction before a novelist finally wrote a full-length story consisting of nothing but letters.[1] The earliest known prose novel of this kind is Juan de Segura's *Precesso de Cartas*, which appeared in 1548. Spain can therefore claim primacy in the epistolary genre as well as in the picaresque novel. A few years later, in 1563, Italy produced another novel in letters, *Lettera amorosa* by Pasqualigo. Kany says of this work (p. 74): 'It is thought that these were real letters, written, copied and preserved with the intention of being published, "quasi a modello di epistolario amoroso".' Should we then not consider this work as fiction? A similar problem arises for a far earlier work, Jean Froissart's *La Prison amoureuse* (1372–3). This consists of twelve prose letters set in a verse narrative, and according to Kany it is possible that some of these were real letters exchanged between Froissart and his patron Wenceslas.

All this should strike a familiar note. In the early stages of the memoir-novel too, we have seen a real-life form which was imitated in fiction, producing some works which were partly fictional and partly true, as well as others which were wholly invented but might deceive some readers as to their origin. The late seventeenth century saw the publication of several sets of letters whose authenticity has been a matter of debate. There were, for instance, the *Lettres de Babet* (1669), attributed to Edmé Boursault. (This collection also contains answers addressed *to* the lady in question, and Colombey's edition of

---

[1] Most of the information in this section comes from Charles E. Kany, *The Beginnings of the Epistolary Novel in France, Italy and Spain*, Berkeley, California, 1937. Also useful, though less reliable, is G. F. Singer, *The Epistolary Novel*, Philadelphia, 1933. On the English novel in particular, see Frank G. Black, *The Epistolary Novel in the late Eighteenth Century*, Univ. of Oregon, 1940.

1886 appeared under the title *Lettres à Babet*.) The original preface of this work maintains that Babet was a real person and that her letters were authentic. Hoffman, in his biography of Boursault, comes to the conclusion that they were genuine private letters. Other critics persist in thinking them to be completely fictitious.

The classic case in this kind of debate is that of the *Lettres d'une religieuse portugaise* (1669). There have always been some sceptical readers to dispute the authenticity of these five long love-letters, supposedly written by the nun to a French officer who had been her lover and who had now left her to return to France. By the majority of readers, however, these had been accepted as genuine letters, the impassioned outpourings of the nun herself. This case was apparently strengthened by researches which identified the heroine as Mariana Alcoforado, a nun of the Convent of the Conception at Béja, and her lover as the Comte de Chamilly, who had taken part in the Portuguese campaigns. In his edition of the *Lettres portugaises* Deloffre outlines this long controversy and cites the arguments used on both sides.[1] He concludes that the letters were written by Guilleragues, ostensibly the translator, and points out the common-sense view, generally ignored by the partisans of authenticity, that Guilleague's being the author of the letters does not conflict with the facts of Mariana's existence or of her love-affair with Chamilly. Guilleragues had only to hear about the incident, through gossip, and then use it as the basis for his own imaginative rendering of Mariana's feelings.

Deloffre also links the publisher's claims of authenticity with the contemporary distaste for, or distrust of, fiction: 'Ainsi le public exige qu'on le trompe, en faisant passer pour vraies les œuvres de fiction.' This attitude we have already noticed as a contributory factor in the development of the memoir-novel.

The *Lettres portugaises* were extremely popular. Translations, sequels and imitations of the work began appearing soon after its publication, and it was the immediate cause of a vogue, in both France and England, for using letters as a form for narrative fiction. But there were other causes, such as the long-established tradition of using the letter-form for any and

[1] Guilleragues, *Lettres portugaises, Valentins et autres œuvres*, Paris (Garnier), 1962, Introduction, pp. v–xxiii.

every kind of subject. An Italian author of the sixteenth century, Luigi da Porto, had chosen to write works on history in this way. Pascal wrote letters on religion, Valincour and Bellegarde on literary criticism, Montesquieu on French society, Muralt and Voltaire on the English. One could extend *ad nauseam* the list of authors, famous or obscure, who utilized the letter-form for various themes and purposes.

Apart from these literary precedents, there was also the influence of social usage, about which modern readers may need to be reminded. It was common practice to preserve all letters, sometimes including copies of those one had sent, and to pass on to one's friends copies of any missives of general interest which one might have received. The letter was both a more durable document and more of a social institution than it is nowadays. To the eighteenth-century reader there was nothing inherently improbable in someone's having kept a whole series of letters which might later be found and published. It was this fact which enabled fictional letters, like memoir-novels, to masquerade as real-life products.

As we might therefore expect, letter-novels share with memoir-novels the habit of claiming, usually in a preface, that they are printed from authentic documents, discovered through some happy chance, and published for the (moral) benefit of the public. We can also surmise, judging from developments in the public's attitude towards memoir-novels, that as time went on and the bookshops were flooded with letters from this Marquise and that Peruvian Princess, this Milord and that peasant, a general scepticism about the pretence would become manifest among writers and readers alike. Indeed, evidence of such scepticism is not lacking. When the *Lettres de Ninon de Lenclos* came out in 1750 there were some readers who, in spite of the *Envoi* implying that the letters were genuine, recognized the work as fiction. (The author was most probably a lawyer named Damours.) The Abbé de la Porte, for instance, spoke of the

prétendues Lettres de notre moderne Laïs. Celui qui les compose est, à ce qu'on dit, un avocat, qui m'a paru entendre à merveille le Code de Cythère. Il parle de l'amour aussi bien qu'aurait pu faire Ninon elle-même; et s'il avait eu la précaution ou l'adresse de ne pas employer certaines expressions de nouvelle fabrique, on aurait pu croire que ses lettres étaient réellement de la personne à qui il les attribue.[1]

But such insight was not universal. Elizabeth Griffiths translated these *Lettres de Ninon de Lenclos* into English, and published them in 1761 with notes and comments which make it clear that she thought she was dealing with a genuine text.[2] It might be said in her defence that she presumably missed the significance of the neologisms and other linguistic traits which helped La Porte to diagnose the work as a recent fabrication; but one could also argue that the mere fact of the letters constituting a story should, at that time, have aroused her suspicions. However, a later Frenchman—or later Frenchmen—also failed to observe these signs: as late as the 1880's, the *Librairie Garnier* was issuing the work as part of its *Collection des Classiques*, with 'Ninon de Lenclos' listed as its author, and no indication that the letters might be by another hand.

In a few cases, therefore, letter-novels have proved as successful in deception as pseudo-memoirs. Generally speaking, however, this became less and less likely as successive novelists introduced new complications in the form. The primacy of the story, and the devices involved in its presentation through letters, made these novels plainly unlike the general run of Collected Correspondence.

We shall now go on to consider some of the techniques employed in narration by letters.[3] This discussion will also be utilized as an opportunity for looking at some of the minor novels of the mid-century.

Marivaux's last contribution to *La Vie de Marianne* is dated 1741, and *La Nouvelle Héloïse* appeared in 1761. Between these two dates there is an apparent hiatus in the history of the French novel. (Voltaire's fictional works, as previously explained, come more properly under the heading of *contes*.) It was not that novelists ceased to produce new works. From 1741 to 1750, for instance, there were 318 fresh publications

[1] La Porte, *Observations sur la littérature moderne*, V, 1751, p. 118.

[2] See A. O. Aldridge, *Essai sur les personnages des Liaisons Dangereuses en tant que types littéraires*, Paris, 1960, pp. 7–8 (Archives des lettres modernes, no. 31).

[3] For a discussion of epistolary technique, see Jean Rousset, *Forme et Signification*, Paris, 1964, IV, 'Une forme littéraire: le roman par lettres', pp. 65–103. See also below, p. 277n.4.

in the field of prose fiction. But even the brightest lights among novelists in these twenty years before *La Nouvelle Héloïse* were minor authors who now achieve only the barest of mentions in histories of literature, and with good reason. They include Mme de Grafigny, whose *Lettres d'une Péruvienne* (1746) is sometimes cited as a 'philosophical' novel in the tradition of Montesquieu's *Lettres persanes*; Mme Riccoboni, who produced a sequel to *La Vie de Marianne* and wrote several letter-novels; and still lesser names like the Chevalier de Mouhy and Jean François de Bastide.[1] From the point of view of literary merit, the novels which appeared in this period are not worth detailed consideration. We shall therefore be utilizing them as sources of illustrations for specific points, rather than analysing and discussing them for their own sake.

During these twenty years French readers were also being offered an increasing number of translations of English novels, and in particular of the works of Richardson. *Pamela* was first published in a French version in 1742, and *Clarissa Harlowe* in 1751, and both inspired a good deal of interest among French readers. The question of Richardson's possible influence on specific authors like Rousseau and Laclos has been studied by Professor Green, who concludes that this influence has been generally overrated.[2] Nevertheless it is safe to say that in one respect Richardson's success influenced the whole genre, in France as well as in England. It is in the 1740's that the number of new letter-novels in France begins noticeably to increase, and by the 1760's the vogue of the form is firmly established.[3]

Such a development can have strange consequences. It may mean, for instance, that a novelist adopts the form of the letter-novel without seriously considering whether the story he wants to tell is particularly suited to this method of narration. He may even persist in forcing into this mould a plot which

---

[1] For further information about novels published between 1750 and 1760, see S. Etienne, *Le Genre romanesque en France depuis l'apparition de la 'Nouvelle Héloïse' jusqu'aux approches de la Révolution*, Brussels, 1922, pp. 59–135; and A. Martin, V. Mylne and R. Frautschi, *Bibliographie du genre romanesque français, 1751–1800*, London, 1977.

[2] F. C. Green, *Minuet*, pp. 365–430.

[3] See Martin, Mylne and Frautschi, *Bibliographie du genre romanesque français*; and Y. Giraud, *Bibliographie du roman épistolaire en France des origines à 1842*, Fribourg, 1977. Both bibliographies include translations into French.

would clearly be better handled in memoir-form or in third-person narrative. The epistolary convention presents certain difficulties and problems of execution which make it something of a challenge to the novelist interested in the technical aspects of his craft. But such an interest was rare among French novelists of the eighteenth century; works which were written as letter-collections, presumably in the cause of naturalness and verisimilitude, often contain a host of implausible details arising from the letter-form itself.

Before discussing specific problems of technique, we must establish, and distinguish between, the two main ways of using letters as a method of narration.

One kind of letter-novel has a good deal in common with memoirs. In this type of story the central character writes to a friend or relation and tells this confidant, day by day or stage by stage, about the events which are going on. Richardson's *Pamela* is for the most part narrated in this way. Pamela does not often correspond with the wicked Mr B. herself; they are usually living under the same roof with all too many opportunities for private conversation. Her letters to her parents merely provide a running commentary on her relations with Mr B., and his various attempts on her virtue.

Fundamentally there is only one difference between this type of narrative and that of the memoir-form: the perspective of time. The memorialist knows, at the moment of writing, how all his adventures turned out. Seeing them from a distance, he can now distinguish the incidents and actions which mattered. He can explain things which puzzled him at the time, and can judge how far his own hopes and fears were justified or mistaken. The character in a letter-novel, on the other hand, usually writes under the pressure of immediate events, and cannot see their outcome. His or her letters often come very close to being a kind of diary. Indeed, when Pamela cannot send off her letters she takes to keeping a journal instead, and the change is not particularly noticeable. So letters of this kind are a first-person descriptive account of events and reactions, and the addressee may be a relatively passive confidant, contributing little or nothing to the main action.

A novel composed chiefly of this kind of letter does not exploit all the possibilities of the genre, though it may on that account be easier to plan and work out. A large number of works were constructed on these lines. The bulk of the *Lettres d'une Péruvienne* consists simply of a first-person account by Zilia of her experiences when she was captured and taken to France. In her *Lettres de Myladi Juliette Catesby à Lady Henriette Campley, son amie* (1759), Mme Riccoboni makes her heroine relate how, after a long period of separation and estrangement from Lord Ossery, she is reconciled with him and marries him. In 1764, De Rozoi published the *Lettres de Cécile à Julie, ou Les combats de la nature*. Here Cécile pours out to Julie the long tale of her sufferings, which finally lead her to conclude that most of the conventions of civilized society, including marriage, are unnatural and indefensible. This type of letter-novel continued to appear occasionally, even when the vogue of the whole form had declined. In America Jean Webster's *Daddy-long-legs* (later filmed as *Love from Judy*) and its sequel *Dear Enemy* achieved considerable popular success in the early years of this century. More recently, in 1957, Paul-André Lesort published *Le Fer rouge*, a series of nine letters in which a woman recalls and analyses her relations with her husband and finally decides to leave him.

Novels like these are, in essence, monologues. The form is extended and enriched when the letters are addressed not to an observer who is outside the plot, but to another protagonist. Montesquieu said that one could find in *Les Lettres persanes* 'une espèce de roman', and the parts of the book which seem to merit this description are Usbek's letters to the harem and the answers he receives from his wives and their guardians. The important thing about novels using this kind of letter is that the missives become not merely an arbitrary method of narration, but 'events' themselves, a necessary and integral part of the plot. Pamela's adventures would have been no different if she had not told her parents what was going on. But in *La Nouvelle Héloïse* the fact that Julie did write a letter in answer to Saint-Preux's opening appeals, as well as what she said in this and subsequent letters, can be seen as a direct cause of fresh developments in the story.

It must be emphasized that it is the nature of the letters, and of the person to whom they are addressed, which makes this difference, not merely a multiplicity of correspondents. Crébillon's *Lettres de la Marquise de M**** can show how the letters of a single character become events in a story, not mere *reportage*. However, the letter-novel does tend to be more complex and interesting if it includes contributions from two or more of the characters involved. It then turns into a true dialogue or a series of exchanges, having a good deal in common with plays and often deserving to be called 'dramatic' in construction if not in content.

The most highly-developed form of the letter-novel contains both 'event-letters' and 'memoir-letters', and these have a direct parallel in two types of scenes in plays: the ones where the verbal exchanges on-stage are crucial happenings, like a quarrel or a declaration of love; and the others which are merely confidences or messenger-speeches concerning past events. Letter-novels also share with plays certain technical problems concerning the presentation of the material. We shall now go on to consider how these were handled by various French novelists. (The examples will in the main be cases of failure and lack of technical skill, partly because these were so common, and partly because they highlight the difficulties in question.)

Letter-novels and plays have much the same problems to solve in the matter of their beginnings. In the absence of a narrator, how is the public to be informed who is who, and what has happened so far? The unskilled playwright may fall into the trap of making characters tell each other, for the benefit of the audience, things they already know and have no reason to repeat. (Sheridan neatly hit off this 'You know that—' device in *The Critic*.) Letter-novelists not infrequently commit the same offence. Mme de Grafigny makes her Peruvian Princess remind Aza that the day the Spaniards arrived was the date fixed for their wedding: 'Tu le sais, ô délices de mon cœur! ce jour horrible, ce jour à jamais épouvantable, devait éclairer le triomphe de notre union' (*Lettre* I). And Saint-Preux writes, in his first letter to Julie, 'Vous savez que je ne suis entré dans votre maison que sur l'invitation de votre mère.'

One may contrast with this the effective exposition of *Les Liaisons dangereuses*. In the first two letters, from Cécile and Mme de Merteuil respectively, we are provided with all the essential information about Cécile herself, her forthcoming marriage, Mme de Merteuil's plans to wreck it, and Valmont's rôle as seducer. All this is conveyed with apparent naturalness in the course of the letters, though Laclos does help himself out by footnotes, notably to explain the Marquise's animosity towards Gercourt.

The use of footnotes is not exceptional. Mme de Grafigny frequently inserts them to elucidate some Peruvian term in the text. Rousseau too takes advantage of his 'editorial' status to explain local Swiss terms, translate quotations from Italian poetry, or even to apostrophize his characters and comment on their remarks. If some of this apparatus seems tedious and out of place to the modern reader, we should recall that it is part and parcel of the whole pretence that these letters were not originally intended for the general reader, and that the editor must help out the public when necessary.

Another problem which faces both playwright and novelist is that of getting the characters into the appropriate place to make their exchanges. The dramatist needs to bring them together, and has to arrange their entrances and exits in a plausible fashion. The novelist using letters has usually to separate his characters. This is so obvious a condition that it would not be worth mentioning except that many novelists broke even this rule. Once the love-affair of Crébillon's Marquise is in full progress, it is difficult to see why some of her letters are written at all, since the lovers are both in Paris and in constant touch with each other. Even more flagrantly against common-sense are letters exchanged when both characters are living in the same house, as happens at the beginning of *La Nouvelle Héloïse*. Saint-Preux is made to offer some kind of explanation: Julie's reserve and coldness during their occasional moments alone together reduce him to stuttering incoherence. But the excuse is pretty weak, and it would not cover, for instance, the subsequent letters about Julie's programme of studies, since this subject could have been discussed openly before Julie's mother or Claire. Laclos, on the other hand, makes Valmont write to Mme de Tourvel, staying under the same roof, only when she has refused him any chance of a tête-à-tête. The delivery of these letters later becomes a minor intrigue in itself, and the first time she answers one of them we realize that she has signed her own capitulation. Laclos thus manages to turn his infringement of the separation-convention to good account.

The dramatist and the letter-novelist have also to try to

maintain some standards of probability about the circumstances in which their characters address each other. Among the kinds of lapse with which we are all familiar in plays, and even more in operas, are the interminable dying speech, the long aside, and the revelation made precisely when someone concerned is eavesdropping. All these have their parallels in letter-novels. Characters often write exhaustingly long letters when they are on the point of death; Crébillon's Marquise, and Julie, are obvious examples. Or they write when feverish and ill: Julie breaks off a letter to succumb to smallpox; Mme Riccoboni makes Mistress Fanni Butlerd head one of her letters, with more force than elegance: 'Lundi, dans mon lit, malade comme un chien.' But there are even graver faults in the choice of an occasion, moments when we cannot imagine a person writing a letter at all. Here is De Rozoi's Cécile, apparently opening a long-awaited letter from her lover with one hand, and writing a running commentary on it with the other (the *points de suspension* are the author's):

> Ouvrons enfin celle-ci . . . Mérité-je bien de la lire? ah! je le mériterai mieux. Je ne sais pourquoi je tremble en l'ouvrant: qu'ai-je à craindre? Lisons: *Mademoiselle* . . . ah! Julie, quelle expression! n'ai-je plus que ce nom-là pour lui? Je n'en lirai pas davantage. Barbare, aie moins d'urbanité et plus de tendresse! Non, je n'achèverai point; je veux déchirer sa lettre (*Lettre* V).

She ends not by tearing it up, but by transcribing it for Julie's benefit, interspersed with her own comments on the text. Scarcely less ridiculous than this is the letter written by Saint-Preux when he is in Julie's dressing-room waiting to spend the night with her (*Lettre* LIV). In both these examples, it may be noticed, we have something closely approaching the modern device of *monologue intérieur*; it is only their being cast into letter-form which makes them seem ridiculous. The trouble here is a clash between the author's desire to let us know about a character's reactions at some crucial moment, and the conditions under which people can be expected to sit down and write letters. Laclos is not easily faulted in this respect. While the writing of a letter in Emilie's bed may be improbable (*Lettre* 48), it is well within the scope of Valmont's perverse imagination as we have so far come to know him. As for Mme de Tourvel's dying letter to him (*Lettre* 161), it is carefully superscribed, 'Dictée par elle et écrite par sa Femme-de-chambre', and turns into a flow of delirious appeals and reproaches which could well be compared with Goriot's death-bed scene.

One practical aspect of the letter-writer's situation which does not, of course, affect the playwright is the simple need for writing materials to be accessible. A fine example of misplaced ingenuity on this subject comes from De Rozoi. Cécile, in disgrace after her attempted elopement, is shut up for three days in a darkened room. At last the servants bring a light. Almost immediately she finds 'une écritoire échappée à tous les regards', which enables her to resume her letters. However, Mme de Grafigny might be thought to surpass even this: Zilia's first seventeen letters are recorded by means of *quipos*, or knotted cords of different colours which the Peruvians used for keeping accounts, sending messages, etc. Fortunately, by the time she came to the end of her *quipos* she was learning to read and write in French, so that she could then 'translate' the earlier letters and pursue her correspondence in a normal European fashion. (There is the added inconsistency that her first 'letter' was delivered to Aza, who unknotted and re-tied the cords to convey his answer; properly speaking, therefore, she had no copy of her first letter to translate.)

There are other invitations to implausibility inherent in the letter-form. It is surely unusual, for instance, for a person writing a letter to report a long conversation verbatim. Yet if the novelist is not to forgo the vividness of dialogue he must occasionally quote conversations. As already indicated for memoir-novels, such quoting is usually inoffensive as long as we are not reminded of all that is involved in its recording. Here it is the writer too obviously trying to obey the conventions who upsets the delicate balance of the illusion. In Restif de la Bretonne's *Le Paysan perverti*, Edmond gives three pages of dialogue, and then goes on: 'Ici notre conversation a été interrompue par l'arrivée de M. Parangon; et je suis venu sur-le-champ te l'écrire, de crainte d'en oublier quelque chose. J'achèverai tantôt' (*Lettre* XIV).

Stylistically too, some of the attempts to achieve verisimilitude were misplaced and excessive. This is most noticeable when the novelist tries to convey strong emotion by making his character fall into an exclamatory and disjointed style. This might, conceivably, seem natural in speech, but is less credible in writing. Zilia, in *Les Lettres d'une Péruvienne*, already shows a tendency in this direction. As the century progressed the trend became more marked. One feels that the recipient of a *Billet* like the following could hardly have gained much comfort or assurance from it:

On entraîne votre amante . . . où? dans quel lieu? . . . je ne sais; —on me laisse à peine le temps de vous écrire . . . mon désordre, mes larmes . . . quand vous recevrez mes lettres, quand vous apprendrez . . . Sort barbare, je te pardonne tout si tu épargnes ce que j'aime . . .[1]

The kinds of problems and devices we have been discussing all arise from the special conventions of the form itself. To suppose that a story was fortuitously built up by the writing of a series of letters, is to impose certain peculiar restrictions on the manner of its presentation. Yet we should notice that most of these problems are minor ones, mere matters of ingenuity and contrivance, not involving literary talent in the widest sense. We have not, for instance, needed to touch on the novelist's major tasks: effective characterization, the linking of events, coherent organization, etc. In fact details such as where or when or with what the characters wrote their letters are, to the modern reader, questions of common-sense and craft rather than art. The observance of a chosen convention and all the practical details this involves depends on the kinds of technique which are now taught by schools of journalism or by courses in 'creative writing'. If such courses now exist, it is because of current attitudes and requirements: the reader of today expects the rules to be kept. If we remember that both the *Lettres d'une Péruvienne* and *La Nouvelle Héloïse* were highly popular works, it becomes evident that eighteenth-century readers were far less exigent in this respect. However vigorously novelists of the period might proclaim that their works were true, or true-to-life, it was to be some time before common-sense, attention to detail, consistency and obedience to the conventions of the chosen form were accepted as part of the basic equipment of any competent novelist.

[1] Dorat, *Les Sacrifices de l'amour*, in *Œuvres*, Amsterdam, 1772, XIII, p. 82.

IX

Crébillon's Letter-Novels

TRUE to type, Crébillon's first letter-novel, the *Lettres de la Marquise de M****, starts with an editorial explanation:

> Je viens de faire une découverte, qui me donne une joie sensible: j'ai trouvé dans les papiers du Comte de R*** les Lettres de la Marquise de M***, et j'ai été charmée de voir la seule chose qui reste d'une personne illustre par sa naissance, et célèbre par son esprit et par sa beauté. Je les ai lues avec plaisir, et peut-être vous en feront-elles autant qu'à moi. Je ne serais pas même fâchée qu'elles vissent le jour (p. 3).[1]

The letters, we are to believe, were authentic. Whereas Crébillon departed from the current fashion by admitting that *Les Egarements* might be fiction, this earlier work puts forward the usual claims to 'truth'. As we shall see, Crébillon's use of the convention of authenticity varied with the nature of the novel he was presenting.

This work consists of seventy letters and a score or so of *billets*, all written by the Marquise. We have here, then, the simplest form of the letter-novel, and the most 'probable' by real-life standards. Although he had relatively few precedents from which to judge, Crébillon had realized that one of the risks inherent in this method of writing was monotony, especially as his plot in this case was limited to the events in the Marquise's love-affair:

> Quelque bien que les Lettres amoureuses soient écrites, les mêmes termes y sont souvent employés, les mêmes situations reviennent; c'est toujours le même objet présent aux yeux du lecteur: . . . C'est toujours l'amour que l'on voit sous des formes différentes, et il ne serait pas possible que l'uniformité du fond ne dégoûtât, malgré la variété des sentiments (p. 5).

His fears were not entirely groundless, and one may well sigh

---

[1] The edition cited is Vol. IV of the *Œuvres*, ed. Pierre Lièvre, Paris, 1930.

occasionally as one reads, and wish for a change of subject-matter.

But he has done a good deal to allay tedium. Sometimes the variety is in the nature of ornament applied to the main structure, and comes from devices with which we are by now familiar. Letter LV, like one or two others, is really an interpolated story. Mme de la G***, faithful to her lover for four years and seemingly inconsolable when he ends the affair, finds swift comfort in the arms of a young duke instead of dying of a broken heart. She has nothing to do with the Marquise. The only personal note in this letter is the last sentence: 'Adieu, Comte, avant de me faire une infidélité, souvenez-vous de l'aventure de notre ami et de la façon de se consoler de Madame de la G***' (pp. 210–11).

Apart from this type of diversion, there are also one or two letters devoted to Paris gossip, largely about people who are never mentioned elsewhere.

Depuis que vous êtes à la campagne, il s'est passé à la ville des choses fort extraordinaires. Madame de *** est devenue dévote, T*** est devenu libertin. L'une a quitté son amant, l'autre son bénéfice: on croit qu'ils se repentiront tous deux. Le Comte de ***, aussi désagréable que jamais, est accablé de bonnes fortunes, et la prude Madame de *** se divertit à être amoureuse. La sèche Marquise médit toujours, met toujours du blanc, joue sans cesse, a conservé son goût pour le vin de Champagne, son teint couperosé, sa taille ridicule, son babil importun, sa vanité, ses vapeurs, son page et ses vieux amants. C'est une femme immuable, celle-là! (pp. 241–2).

This touching-in of town-talk, followed by general reflections on contemporary manners, is Crébillon's way of bringing into his personal narrative some satirical sketches, which are comparable to the *caractères* in *Gil Blas*. There is even, on occasion, something verging on the formal individual portrait, as in the case of the *petit magistrat* of Letter XLVIII, or the Marquise's philosophy teacher, 'le plus joli pédant du monde, frisé, poudré, et qui, à ce qu'on m'a dit, a le bonheur de parler l'hébreu avec toute la politesse possible' (p. 144).

These elements, which in other novels have so often seemed irrelevant or not sufficiently blended into the narrative, take on a rather different air in Crébillon's story. Firstly, they are rarely long, and never long enough to disturb the main flow. Secondly, these light-hearted and entertaining diversions are introduced at moments when all is going well between the Marquise and the Comte, when she is neither disquieted by his fickleness nor worried by any other crisis in their love. One should notice that the stories, gossip and portraits practically all occur after the protagonists have become lovers, not during the shifting uncertainties of the early letters. In the opening stages, plausibly enough, the Marquise's whole concern is devoted to their personal relations, first of all in her unwillingness to fall in love with him, and then in her reluctance to grant him the final favours.

Apart from any other justifications for these digressive elements, the letter-novelist has a theoretical excuse denied to the memoir-writer; that it is true-to-life for people writing letters to discuss whatever is of immediate interest to them at a given moment. This, it can be argued, is the 'natural' and even the probable thing for the letter-writer to do, since it is a basic supposition of the form that he does not know, while writing, that he is creating a complete story; considerations of relevance or structural coherence are therefore precluded. However, the natural thing may bear little relation to what is artistically effective, and disquisitions like those of Saint-Preux on Italian music or domestic economy show clearly enough what abuses this theoretical approach may lead to. Crébillon's digressions seem models of literary tact in comparison, and do have the desirable effect of varying the tone and content of the letters.

In any case, these traditional devices are of subsidiary importance only. Crébillon's chief resource for avoiding monotony lies in the change of mood and tone from letter to letter, and of course in the events which the letters relate. In this he is, it seems to me, extremely skilful. The first twelve letters, for instance, show the Marquise refusing to yield to her suitor's pleas, and denying that she will ever fall in love with him. Within the limits of this situation, her tone varies from the serious to the frivolous, from annoyance to teasing, from the unequivocal to a hint of uncertainty.

After two letters which begin to admit that her feelings for him have gone beyond mere friendship, she brings herself, in

Letter XV, to the point of writing, 'Je vous aime'. The argument now shifts. Unlike the majority of Crébillon's characters, the Marquise cannot see any need to proceed to physical love-making.

Je ne doute pas que cela ne vous paraisse extraordinaire, mais soit que les romans m'aient gâté l'esprit sur cet article, soit que j'aie reçu en naissant cette façon de penser, je ne vois point que ce que vous avez la bonté de me proposer soit une chose si essentielle à mon bonheur (p. 54).

For a further dozen letters she maintains this attitude, again with lively shifts of tone and mood. A letter may begin imperiously: 'En un mot, Monsieur, vous le prendrez comme il vous plaira, mais il n'en sera que ce que je voudrai' (p. 57). And it then moves on to a plea for virtue which would not be amiss in the mouth of Rousseau's Julie:

Je vous aime, n'ajoutons pas à cette faute des fautes plus odieuses. Il n'a point dépendu de moi de ne vous pas aimer: les mouvements du cœur ne sont pas soumis à la réflexion, mais il dépend de moi d'être vertueuse, et l'on ne cesse pas de l'être malgré soi (p. 59).

By Letter XXIX she has however yielded. The remainder of the book is then taken up by the progress of the love-affair in all its moments of ecstasy, doubt, jealousy, caution, etc.

The last five letters tell how her husband has obtained an official post far away from Paris and is taking her away with him. She finds separation from the Comte unbearable, and we finally see her ill and on the point of death.

There are, one must admit, certain tedious patches in the second half of the novel, however conscientiously Crébillon has tried to vary its tone. And the heroine's death is perhaps more satisfactory for the way it rounds off the story than for its inherent pathos. Crébillon has made her thoroughly credible in her persiflage and even in moments of serious argument, but the pages of passionate despair over separation do not carry the same conviction. However, it is only the truly great author who has an equal command over the whole scale of sentiment, and we must not ask too much of Crébillon.

What should be pointed out to his credit is that the novel does go beyond the range of feelings and attitudes usually associated with his name. As Pierre Lièvre has indicated in his preface, the Marquise stands out among Crébillon's characters as a woman who, without being unduly prudish, recognizes and respects the idea of duty and fidelity in marriage. She is not the only one: Meilcour's mother, even when widowed, does not comply with the standards of a society based on *galanterie*; and there is a virtuous wife even in *Le Sopha*. But such people are usually only minor figures in Crébillon's writings, isolated and insignificant defenders of the moral standards which everyone else, secretly or overtly, flouts. The Marquise of the *Lettres* occupies the centre of the stage, and it is her point of view which pervades the book. When she is unfaithful to her husband—who has often been unfaithful to her—she feels guilty. The remorse which assails her from time to time as the book proceeds gives a depth to her character which is lacking in most of Crébillon's coquettes and their partners.

This element is all the more important since, like *Les Egarements*, this novel deals almost entirely with the play of thought and feeling, and tends towards abstraction. Crébillon, as we have already observed, does little to make the world of his novels a visual one. In *Les Egarements* we are usually told where the characters are: in a corner of the *salon*, walking in the Tuileries, or the like. But we rarely see a gesture, a turn of the head, a facial expression; all this is left to our imagination. The setting of the *Lettres de la Marquise* is even vaguer. There is no hint, for instance, of the surroundings in which the lady writes her letters. One may however question Lièvre's verdict that there is scarcely more than one sentence 'où il use de mots qui fassent voir des choses et des gens' (p. xvi). On the contrary, there are perhaps more references to the concrete visible world in this novel than in *Les Egarements*, and a vignette like the following shows Crébillon's capacity for making a scene visual when he thinks fit:

Mon mari, comme vous savez, se croyait malade hier, et le soin de sa santé étant le premier de ses plaisirs, je pensais avec raison qu'il ne sortirait point de toute la semaine. Cela nous aurait contraints: il a changé d'avis. Il s'est éveillé ce matin le teint frais, et les yeux vifs, il est venu dans mon appartement avec un air nonchalant et douloureux, pour voir ce que je lui dirais de son visage. Je l'ai trouvé tel qu'il était, c'est-à-dire un peu meilleur que le mien, je

l'en ai félicité, et l'ai assuré que ce qu'il prenait pour une indis-
position n'était qu'un ennui qui, répandu sur ses charmes, en
obscurcissait une partie. Il a insisté, je l'ai conduit à mon miroir, il
a ri en se regardant, et tout d'un coup il m'a dit qu'il était mieux
(p. 100).

Such small scenes provide a positive, if infrequent, contribution to the real-life effect of the story. A negative factor of no
less importance is the absence of strange and singular events in
the plot. Although Crébillon had not yet published his criticism
of the 'situations ténébreuses et forcées' of most novels, he was
already demonstrating, in these *Lettres*, his gift for building
a story without having recourse to extraordinary actions or
crucial coincidences. In this respect the work is clearly superior
to *Les Egarements*, where the manipulations of chance so clearly
shape the plot. In the Marquise's story the rôle of chance is
slight. Her husband may happen to arrive when she is just
about to yield to the Comte's entreaties: 'Oui, je l'avoue, si mon
mari arriva hier à propos pour lui, il vint fort mal à propos pour
vous. Ma vertu chancelante ne se défendait plus que faible-
ment' (p. 91). But this chance arrival merely postpones the
Comte's satisfaction for a few pages. Such external events as do
affect the plot, including even the Marquis's appointment
abroad, are well within the bounds of *vraisemblance* as established
in this small world.

However, we are still left ignorant on one vital matter, the
question of time. Instead of the over-precise account of successive days which he was to give in *Les Egarements*, Crébillon here
provides scarcely any indications of the passing of time. This
means that we have no idea how long the various stages of the
affaire took to happen. Did the lady take weeks or months to
admit that she loved him, and then only a few days to become
his mistress, or *vice versa*? The speed, or delays, of the crucial
events in this story should be one of the factors on which we
base our view of the Marquise's character, but Crébillon has
offered us no dates. The possible bearing of this element had
already been realized by some writers of fictional letters: Montesquieu had made his Persians date their missives, though admittedly foxing French readers by using the Persian calendar.
But even with this complication, the attentive reader can see
that the last fifteen letters, giving the dénouement of the harem

story, spread back over a period which has already been covered by previous letters on general subjects. The notion of dating the letters in a novel was therefore not unheard of, and Crébillon's *Lettres de la Marquise* would, I think, have gained considerably if this small touch of precision had been added.

Apart from the minor failings we have noted, it is a novel of some merit. Paradoxically, considering Crébillon's reputation for the superficial and the salacious, it is a work which needs to be read slowly and with full attention. Only in this way does one come to appreciate its real qualities of insight and feeling.

To conclude our review of Crébillon's letter-novels we must now move on nearly forty years, to a period after the publication of best-sellers in the form by Richardson and Rousseau.

In 1768 Crébillon brought out his *Lettres de la Duchesse de *** au Duc de ****, and three years later came the *Lettres athéniennes*.[1] The latter is a thoroughly boring collection of amorous intrigues, episodic in structure, and held together only by the character of Alcibiades. The love-affairs involve Aspasia, Pericles, and various other notable Greeks. (Alcibiades, as might be expected, at one point consults Socrates, who sends him a firm rebuke for unmannerly behaviour.)

Presumably because of the inherent implausibility of the stories in this collection, Crébillon has not attempted a guaranteeing preface. He merely added an explanatory phrase to the title so that it reads, with some insouciance, *Lettres athéniennes, extraites de la portefeuille d'Alcibiade*.

In the *Lettres de la Duchesse de **** we have a more realistic story, set in the France of 1728–30, and bearing some resemblance to the early *Lettres de la Marquise*. The Duke of the title is not married to the Duchess, but she is his friend and adviser. He eventually declares his love for her, which takes her by surprise. Her husband is unfaithful to her, but she does not see this as a reason for starting a love-affair of her own. She does come gradually to love the man who is wooing her but when, after her husband's death, he makes a proposal of marriage, she refuses him. Because of the numerous infidelities in his past, she feels that she could never trust him.

[1] For a more detailed discussion of these two works, see Cherpack, *An Essay on Crébillon fils*, pp. 122–48.

This simple plot is complicated by sub-plots concerning other characters, and by more action and intrigue than we find in the *Lettres de la Marquise*. And although the Duchess is another virtuous heroine, her letters lack the intensity of feeling which is one of the merits of the earlier novel. Crébillon seems to be re-working his first theme, but in a rather jaded fashion.

In the decades since the *Lettres de la Marquise*, the letter-novel had developed in scope and complexity. In the 1768 novel, Crébillon fell in with fashion to the extent of including letters from more than one correspondent. But even at this relatively late date he still maintains firmly in his preface that this is not a novel, and sets truth above mere verisimilitude:

> Ces lettres sont-elles factices, ne le sont-elles pas? . . . Il ne saurait être au lecteur de la même indifférence qu'elles soient véritablement d'une femme, ou qu'elles n'en soient pas.
>
> La raison en est, à ce qu'il nous semble, que le vrai a toujours sur nous plus de droits que ce que nous savons n'en être que l'imitation; et que rien n'est plus fondé en raison que cette façon de voir et de sentir.
>
> Jamais, dans les livres du genre de celui-ci, l'auteur ne se décèle, que l'intérêt n'y perde considérablement.[1]

Later in the preface, the 'editor' points out that no professional novelist would have let his story end in so unsatisfactory a way as this one does. He admits that readers who are used to the works of Richardson and his imitators may find these letters cold and unfeeling, but adds: 'Il est sûr que dans leur système [ils] auront raison, mais encore une fois, ce livre-ci n'est pas un roman' (p. ix).

One can therefore perceive a direct relation between the plausibility of form of Crébillon's novels, and his claims concerning their authenticity. With the *Lettres athéniennes*, obviously only a fantasy laced with historic names, he makes no more than the barest ironic gesture towards complying with the convention. In *Les Egarements*, which does not strictly fulfil the qualifications for genuine memoirs, he lets the reader choose between fact and fiction. But with the two letter-novels which do obey all the rules of the form and could conceivably be genuine, he makes the claim to authenticity in explicit and unequivocal

[1] *Œuvres*, 1772, VII, iv–v.

terms. He justifies the claim on theoretical grounds, and points to the internal evidence of the books themselves as proof of his good faith in advancing the claim.

One of the types of internal evidence which Crébillon cites for both the letter-novels in question is the stylistic weakness which reveals that the letter-writer is not a professional author. In the *Lettres de la Marquise*, the reader is warned: 'Vous n'y trouverez pas cette correction de style dont se parent nos écrivains.' The 'editor' of the *Lettres de la Duchesse* gives an even more detailed account of the stylistic faults—over-long letters, poor sentence-construction, too-frequent parentheses, etc.— which lead him to conclude: 'Il n'est pas raisonnable de penser que si un auteur de profession les eût écrites, il ne se fût point aperçu de tous les défauts que nous-mêmes y avons remarqués, et qu'il eût voulu les y laisser subsister' (p. v). This is ingenious but misguided. To make a character write bad prose so as to prove his non-professional status is scarcely good policy; it is somewhat like portraying a bore in such a way that he bores the reader. Crébillon is here on the verge of a much larger problem, that of using style as a means of characterization in first-person narrative, but his preoccupation with 'authenticity' limits him to this negative approach.

He has however given us the right to look closely at his own style. Do his women letter-writers betray 'les négligences d'une femme spirituelle', and if so, should we admire them? Does Crébillon, when writing as himself or Meilcour, avoid such carelessness and produce a style which is noticeably better?

One of the Marquise's most striking stylistic traits is her frequent use of a *que* clause or phrase at the close of a sentence. In the following passage, for instance, only one sentence—the shortest—avoids this construction:

Mais, sans aller chercher dans le passé, tâchez de me persuader que cette joie qui vous animait, quand vous jouiez hier, n'était que pour moi. Rappelez-vous cette froideur avec laquelle vous me parlâtes, ces regards inanimés et contraints, ces soupirs que vous donniez plus au chagrin d'être loin d'elle, qu'au plaisir d'être auprès de moi. Ne me dites pas que c'était pour cacher aux yeux des autres votre véritable passion, que vous en feigniez pour elle. Quand on aime, l'amour perce au travers de la contrainte; un regard, un geste, prouve plus, en certaines occasions, que les discours les plus étudiés. D'ailleurs ce serait pour vous une excuse frivole. Quand vous m'aimiez, vous étiez moins circonspect, et quelque peine que j'eusse à contraindre vos empressements, je vous aurais plutôt pardonné mille imprudences, que tant de froideur (pp. 81-2).

Admittedly these *que*'s are not all fulfilling the same grammatical function, but once one has noticed the repetitive fall of the successive sentences, the effect may become obsessive and somewhat distracting. One is justified therefore in concluding that Crébillon does display a certain insensitivity to the rhythm and ring of words in his writing. Even when the imperfect subjunctive was still in current use, surely there was an unwelcome echo in a sentence such as this, from the Duchess: 'Si ce malheur arrivait, il serait tant dans mon caractère, que mon ami et moi fussions les seuls qui le sussions' (p. 36)?

If we concentrate however on sense rather than sound, we find that these complex clausal structures are highly effective in conveying subtle nuances of thought and emotion. Bernadette Fort has shown, in her careful analysis of Crébillon's syntax, how by embedding qualifications and doubts and restrictions within each other and within the main framework of the sentence, he creates effects of ambiguity and shifting perspectives of feeling.[1] It follows that one needs to read such passages patiently and attentively in order to appreciate their merits to the full. Such an approach can compensate for the surface 'faults' of apparently unwieldy sentences.

We have discussed three of Crébillon's novels in some detail, and given passing consideration to two others. His work also includes three Oriental tales, and the *contes dialogués*, *La Nuit et le moment* and *Le Hasard du coin du feu*. These two quasi-dramatic pieces do not come within the province of this study, but they are undoubtedly Crébillon's best and liveliest work in his vein of *galanterie*, showing great skill in their conversational manœuvres and nuances.

As for the novels proper, we may conclude that it is the two early works—*Les Lettres de la Marquise de M**** and *Les Egarements*—which have the most to offer to a modern reader. They have the merit of providing a vivid picture of certain aspects

---

[1] Bernadette Fort, *Le Langage de l'ambiguïté dans l'œuvre de Crébillon fils*, Paris, 1978, pp. 45-89.

of Parisian society at a given period, and possess marked qualities of insight and penetration. They also contain technical developments which make them worthy of a place in the history of literary forms.

X

Rousseau

A NEW SERIOUSNESS

THE so-called 'second preface' of *La Nouvelle Héloïse*, which was published separately in 1761, is sub-titled: *Entretien sur les romans entre l'éditeur et un homme de lettres*.[1] Although it purports to be a general discussion of novels, this preface is more in the nature of an apologia for Rousseau's own novel. The *éditeur* of the sub-title is of course Jean-Jacques himself, and his choice of the word implies that the letters of which the work consists are authentic. The question of authenticity is raised several times during the discussion. Indeed the interlocutor, N., makes his final verdict on the book depend on this factor:

> Certainement, si tout cela n'est qu'une fiction, vous avez fait un mauvais livre; mais dites que ces deux femmes ont existé, et je relis ce recueil tous les ans jusqu'à la fin de ma vie (p. 756).

Rousseau refuses to resolve this uncertainty by a categorical answer, but he does repeatedly imply that the people and the letters were 'real'.[2] He admits that he has worked on the book, but urges that it should not be judged by the standards usually applied to fiction:

[1] This is given as an *Appendice* (pp. 737–57) in the 1960 Garnier edition, edited by René Pomeau, from which I quote. For further discussion of the *Entretien* see the comments by Bernard Guyon in Rousseau, *Œuvres complètes*, Bibliothèque de la Pléiade, Paris, 1961, II, *Introduction*, pp. LXII–LXIV, and *Notes*, pp. 1345–55.

[2] Rousseau's attitude closely resembles that of Richardson. Bishop Warburton, in his preface for *Clarissa Harlowe*, discussed the work openly as fiction, and Richardson wrote to him: 'Will you, good Sìr, allow me to mention, that I could wish that the *Air* of Genuiness [*sic*] had been kept up, tho' I want not the Letters to be *thought* genuine; only so far kept up, I mean, as that they should not prefatically be owned *not* to be genuine: and this for fear of weakening their Influence where any of them are aimed to be exemplary; as well as to avoid hurting that kind of Historical Faith which Fiction itself is generally read with, tho' we know it to be fiction.' (19 April 1748; quoted in: McKillop, *The Early Masters of English Fiction*, p. 42.)

Je reviens à nos lettres. Si vous les lisez comme l'ouvrage d'un auteur qui veut plaire ou qui se pique d'écrire, elles sont détestables. Mais prenez-les pour ce qu'elles sont, et jugez-les dans leur espèce. Deux ou trois jeunes gens simples, mais sensibles, s'entretiennent entre eux des intérêts de leurs cœurs . . . (p. 742).

This method of attempting to disarm criticism is nothing new; we have met it in the writings of Marivaux and Crébillon. Both these authors used the plea of authenticity to explain and excuse certain aspects of their work which critics might be expected to view unfavourably: a careless or conversational style, reflective digressions, an unexpected dénouement. Rousseau's tactics are the same, but he extends and amplifies the argument by linking it with his ideas on the corrupting influence of urban life. What he says, in effect, is that this book shows how people do feel, behave and express themselves when they have led a simple, quiet existence away from the turmoil and hypocrisy of the towns. If sophisticated critics cannot recognize and appreciate the truth of the picture, it is because their standards of morality are vitiated by 'civilization', and their taste has likewise been contaminated by the false and showy literature which is produced by such a society. Rousseau's argument is therefore not merely defensive. It suggests that readers who do not believe in and enjoy his story are themselves at fault.

His refusal to give a clear Yes or No to the question concerning the literal truth of the story meant that some readers could accept it as authentic. For the less gullible section of his public, Rousseau's argument could have an alternative interpretation: if the reader does not believe that Julie and Saint-Preux were real people, then he should at least be prepared to accept that the book offers a faithful picture of a certain kind of person following a specific way of life.

Rousseau thus claims that if his story is not true, it is realistic. In the *Entretien* the characters, the events and the style of the novel are considered, in turn, as Rousseau pursues his contention that the book is true-to-life.

N. argues that if characters are to seem 'real', they must display the universal traits of mankind: 'Dans les tableaux de l'humanité, chacun doit reconnaître l'homme' (p. 738). Rousseau's answer is shrewd enough: 'J'en conviens, pourvu qu'on sache aussi discerner ce qui fait les variétés de ce qui est essentiel à l'espèce.' His point is that these essential or universal qualities may be found, and portrayed, in people who are in other respects exceptional. One can scarcely disagree with this theoretical formulation. We shall however need to ask, later on, whether the leading characters of La Nouvelle Héloïse do in practice fulfil their author's own requirements.

When the discussion turns to the events of the plot, N. complains that they are too ordinary: 'des événements si naturels, si simples, qu'ils le sont trop' (p. 379). Rousseau retorts by exposing the apparent paradox in current ideas about the novel: 'C'est à dire qu'il vous faut des hommes communs et des aventures rares. Je crois que j'aimerais mieux le contraire.' His point of view is thus in direct contrast to Prévost's justification of the unusual incidents in his plots.[1] In so far as the modern serious novelist no longer relies on sensational events to provide the main interest of his work, one may say that posterity has agreed with Rousseau. However, it is not only 'des hommes rares', but the unexpected actions and reactions of more ordinary people which are nowadays seen as an appropriate source of interest.

Rousseau's discussion of character and plot is brief compared with his defence of the style of the letters. He admits that they do not conform to the accepted canons of literary elegance, but argues that, by the very nature of things, a genuine love-letter cannot be expected to do this: 'Une lettre que l'amour a réellement dictée, une lettre d'un amant vraiment passionné, sera lâche, diffuse, toute en longeurs, en désordre, en répétitions' (p. 741). Such a description clearly assumes that all people in love develop the same kind of literary style, an assumption we may find too sweeping. But here, as elsewhere, it is real life which Rousseau cites as the criterion for judging the letters.

Now Rousseau is not usually put forward as a practitioner of 'realism' in the novel. His style and approach are more often

[1] In the unfinished story Emile et Sophie, Rousseau's plot is however more eventful and closer to the practice of Prévost. After learning that Sophie has been unfaithful to him, Emile takes up a wandering life, is captured by pirates in the Mediterranean and made a slave, leads a revolt of his fellow-slaves against a cruel overseer, and ends up in the service of the Dey of Algiers.

For a general account of similarities between the novels of Prévost and Rousseau, see Claire-Eliane Engel, 'L'Abbé Prévost et Jean-Jacques Rousseau', Annales Jean-Jacques Rousseau, XXVIII (1939–40), pp. 19–39.

qualified as 'poetic', an attribute sometimes taken to be in contrast, or even in opposition, to literary realism. 'L'éloquence est
une sorte de mensonge', says Diderot, 'et rien de plus contraire
à l'illusion que la poésie.'[1] It may be as well, therefore, to attempt some clarification of the poetic elements in La Nouvelle
Héloïse before we decide how far Rousseau's claims to realism
are justified.

We may begin with those effects of sound and rhythm which
in the finest poetry both appeal to the ear and enrich the sense.
Rhyme, of course, is not involved. But a number of critics have
analysed and praised the 'lyrical' quality of Rousseau's prose.[2]
Now it seems to me quite evident that Rousseau did possess a
sensitive ear for the flow of his sentences, for their rhythms and
cadences. His talent for achieving balance without monotony,
and a subtly-patterned texture, can be seen at its best in his
descriptions of natural scenery and in the letters where the
lovers express strong emotional reactions. For this reason a passage such as Saint-Preux's first letter from Meillerie (Part I, 26)
may be more effective when read aloud, with its full appeal to
the ear, than when it is taken in by the usually faster method of
visual reading.

There may, however, be some risk in using this kind of critical
assessment as the basis for the further conclusion that Rousseau's
style is 'poetic'. If one judges merely by effects of rhythm, ca-
dence, syllabic grouping and the like, then it would not be
difficult to find passages in the prose of, say, Montesquieu or
Voltaire, let alone Diderot, which would qualify for the same
epithet. Indeed, Voltaire occasionally displays an aptitude for
alliterative or echoic effects which suggests a livelier awareness
of words as sounds than anything one can infer from Rousseau's
prose. If we do not usually think of analysing the 'poetic' elements in Montesquieu and Voltaire, it is because they lack
certain other qualities which Rousseau possessed and which, in
conjunction with his 'lyrical' style, evoke the notion of poetry.
The most striking of these qualities is what may be called his

---

[1] Œuvres romanesques, p. 791.

[2] See Pierre-Maurice Masson, 'Contribution à l'étude de la prose métrique dans la Nouvelle Héloïse', Annales Jean-Jacques Rousseau, V (1909),
pp. 259–71; and Bernard Guyon, 'Un Chef-d'œuvre méconnu: "Julie" ',
Cahiers du Sud, 49 (1962), pp. 336–8.

'non-literal' approach. I use this possibly cumbersome term to cover the fact that at the level of linguistic expression, Rousseau frequently prefers metaphor and other figures of speech to literal terms; and on the plane of character and situation, he is apt to stress symbolic or idealized aspects of the subject-matter.

This second type of non-literal approach can perhaps best be illustrated by an instance where it is taken to excess. In the famous letter at the end of Part IV, about the lake trip to Meillerie, there comes a point where the men in the boat are struggling for their lives against the danger of being swept on the rocks. Rousseau makes Saint-Preux describe how Julie behaved in this crisis:

> C'est alors que, retrouvant tout son courage, Julie animait le nôtre par ses caresses compatissantes; elle nous essuyait indistinctement à tous le visage, et mêlant dans un vase du vin avec de l'eau de peur d'ivresse, elle en offrait alternativement aux plus épuisés (p. 499).

Now if one takes this quite literally, and visualizes Julie indiscriminately wiping the faces of the oarsmen in a small boat threatened with disaster, the effect is ludicrous. Rousseau has failed to perceive the bathos because his interest is concentrated on the notion of Julie as a ministering angel, or as fulfilling the universal rôle of Woman when her menfolk are in danger. His attention is focused so exclusively on this idealized or symbolic aspect of the situation that the literal viewpoint is forgotten.

As a more successful example of the same approach, one may cite the passage, a few pages later, where Saint-Preux takes Julie to see the spot among the rocks of Meillerie where he spent some days while they were still avowedly in love with each other. For him the place is rich in memories and associations. But its fresh summery appearance is different from the ice-bound rocks he knew, and symbolizes, in a paradoxical fashion, the change which has taken place in his relations with Julie. For the reader, as for Saint-Preux, the two aspects of Meillerie acquire a significance far beyond the literal importance of the place in the events of the plot.[1]

---

[1] Rousseau also uses symbolism of a more overt kind, such as the *voile* in Part VI. And modern critics tend to interpret the whole story on a symbolic level, an approach which will be discussed later.

Rousseau himself explains how this subjective, idealizing view arises: 'L'amour n'est qu'illusion; il se fait, pour ainsi dire, un autre univers; il s'entoure d'objets qui ne sont point, ou auxquels lui seul a donné l'être' (pp. 741–2). He continues: 'et comme il rend tous ses sentiments en images, son langage est toujours figuré'.[1] Again one may baulk at the generalization that all love-letters are rich in images and figures of speech, but there is no doubt that the love-letters of *La Nouvelle Héloïse* do conform to this description. When dealing with his characters' emotions, Rousseau is more generous with metaphor and simile than any of the eighteenth-century novelists we have so far considered.

Literary imagery plays no significant part in Lesage's style, being largely confined to a few well-worn metaphors which occur in the high-flown language of his *nouvelles*. Crébillon, as we have seen, tends to express himself by abstractions rather than in a figurative way. Marivaux is somewhat more interesting in his figures of speech. In particular, he provides extended passages in which an emotion is personified and shown in action. A propos of Mme Dutour's quarrel with the cab-driver, Marianne says:

> Quand l'amour-propre . . . n'est qu'à demi fâché, il peut encore avoir soin de sa gloire, se posséder, ne faire que l'important, et garder quelque décence; mais dès qu'il est poussé à bout, il ne s'amuse plus à ces fadeurs-là, il n'est plus que le plaisir d'être bien grossier et de se déshonorer tout à son aise qui le satisfasse (p. 94).

Apart from this usage, however, *Marianne* and *Le Paysan parvenu* contain relatively few images and comparisons.

Among the novelists who preceded Rousseau, it is Prévost who most nearly resembles him in tone and feeling, and this resemblance extends to their use of imagery too. Prévost is more liberal with figurative devices than his contemporaries. Nearly all his metaphors would have been familiar to his readers, since they are generally drawn from the stock of images established in the *style noble* of seventeenth-century tragedy. We find the 'chains' and 'fires' of love, the 'glaive suspendu'

[1] In the *Essai sur l'origine des langues* Rousseau had argued that emotive language is inevitably figurative: 'Comme les premiers motifs qui firent parler l'homme furent des passions, ses premières expressions furent des tropes' (Chap. III).

and—the most frequently occurring metaphor in *Manon Lescaut*—the image of a 'fall' from virtue:

Cependant, un instant malheureux me fit retomber dans le précipice, et ma chute fut d'autant plus irréparable que, me trouvant tout d'un coup au même degré de profondeur d'où j'étais sorti, les nouveaux désordres où je tombai me portèrent bien plus loin vers le fond de l'abîme (p. 46).

Prévost makes only slight use of overt similes with *comme*, and in most cases these comparisons are commonplace: 'Elle tremblait comme une feuille.' Very occasionally he develops a simile more fully. Talking of persons who are completely trustworthy, Des Grieux says:

Le cœur, qui se ferme avec tant de soin au reste des hommes, s'ouvre naturellement en leur présence, comme une fleur s'épanouit à la lumière du soleil dont elle n'attend qu'une douce influence (pp. 63–4).

Even allowing for the rare touch of vividness imparted by similes of this kind, one must conclude that Prévost's use of imagery is relatively restrained and cautious.[1]

Rousseau is not always liberal with images; when he discusses ethical problems such as duelling or suicide, for instance, his vocabulary tends to be literal and abstract rather than figurative. In other parts of the work, however, and noticeably in the love-letters of Julie and Saint-Preux, his use of imagery is both more ample and more varied than that of Prévost.

To understand the effect of this element in Rousseau's style, we must take a closer look at the quality of the metaphors. For although the love-letters are studded with phrases such as 'le feu qui me consume', 'un torrent de délices', 'un voile de tristesse', etc., not all of these can properly be called figurative. In some cases the metaphor has become so familiar, through

---

[1] When he does attempt a more complex simile, the result is not always felicitous. The much-imitated Virgilian image of the wounded stag becomes: 'Jamais la comparaison du cerf blessé, qui porte, en courant, le trait dont il veut se délivrer par sa fuite, ne convint mieux qu'aux tristes efforts de ma raison, pour secouer le joug de mes sens' (*Le Monde moral*, p. 619). Rousseau was also to utilize this image, but rather more tactfully: 'Je sors, je marche à grands pas, je m'éloigne avec la rapidité d'un cerf qui croit fuir par sa vitesse le trait qu'il porte enfoncé dans son flanc.' (*Emile et Sophie*, in *Œuvres*, Paris, Hachette, 1873, III, 8.)

frequent use, that it no longer operates as an image. The most obvious example of this is *feux*: the comparison of love to a 'burning' in the heart had become so commonplace that the term *feux* would be liable to express and evoke the concept of 'love' rather than the mental image of 'fire'. That Rousseau himself used the word in this conceptual sense can be seen on the occasions where he combines *feux* with other images. When, for instance, Julie says: 'Tout trahit des feux que le ciel eût dû couronner' (p. 119), it is clear that not 'fires' but love itself has been betrayed and should have been crowned. The same comment would apply to many of Prévost's well-worn metaphors such as *lumières* and *fruits*, and, like Prévost, Rousseau sometimes revives the full metaphorical sense of such terms by extending the image with the help of other nouns and verbs. Thus Saint-Preux tells Julie: 'Les feux dont j'ai brûlé m'ont purifié' (p. 666).

(The fire/flame metaphor is frequently linked, by Rousseau, to the notion of purity: the fire is pure itself, or is a means of purifying. This recurrent combination of two images therefore serves to emphasize the innocent aspect of the love-affair. But Rousseau generally uses the singular *feu* for such extended figures, keeping *feux* for the more limited conceptual usage.)

For his metaphors Rousseau relies on expressions which were already familiar or even hackneyed. In his similes, however, he is more original. It is as though the accepted images can be used without drawing attention to them, but his freshly invented comparisons call for the overt recognition of a *comme*. Julie, claiming the right to advise Saint-Preux on his actions, says:

N'avez-vous jamais remarqué que si la raison d'ordinaire est plus faible et s'éteint plus tôt chez les femmes, elle est aussi plus tôt formée, comme un frêle tournesol croît et meurt avant un chêne? (p. 29).

Earlier in the same letter we have a passage on the 'magnetism' of love, in which not only *comme*, but also *pour ainsi dire* may be seen as excusing the unfamiliar image:[1]

[1] Cf. the comments by Boileau and La Motte on the use of phrases like *pour ainsi dire* to excuse 'daring' metaphors: Boileau, *Réflexions critiques sur . . . Longin*, XI; La Motte, *Réponse à la onzième réflexion de M. Despréaux sur Longin*.

Nos âmes se sont pour ainsi dire touchées par tous les points, et nous avons partout senti la même cohérence. . . . Nous n'aurons plus que les mêmes plaisirs et les mêmes peines; et comme ces aimants dont vous me parliez, qui ont, dit-on, les mêmes mouvements en différents lieux, nous sentirions les mêmes choses aux deux extrémités du monde.

Some of these similes contain the kind of images from nature which are conventionally associated with poetry:

Dieux! quel ravissant spectacle . . . de voir deux beautés si touchantes s'embrasser tendrement, . . . leurs douces larmes se confondre, et baigner ce sein charmant comme la rosée du ciel humecte un lis fraîchement éclos! (p. 90).

Others are more striking because less conventional:

L'amour s'est insinué trop avant dans la substance de votre âme pour que vous puissiez jamais l'en chasser; il en renforce et pénètre tous les traits comme une eau forte et corrosive, vous n'en effacerez jamais la profonde impression sans effacer à la fois tous les sentiments exquis que vous reçutes de la nature (p. 174).

The modern reader may occasionally find such comparisons strained or incongruous; he is scarcely likely to complain that they are difficult to understand. We have grown accustomed to far more complex and ambiguous images than these. Some eighteenth-century critics, however, maintained that Rousseau's figures of speech were obscure or even incomprehensible.[1] It is from comments of this kind that we can appreciate how daring and original Rousseau's figurative language must have appeared to his contemporaries. Even today it is this aspect of his style, together with his idealized or symbolic treatment of character and incident, which provides the chief justification for saying that his prose is sometimes 'poetic'.

The novel contains some further elements which have come, largely through the influence of the Romantic movement, to be associated with poetry. One of these is the uninhibited revelation of reactions and feelings, a trait which can be linked with the now popular concept of poetry as a form of self-expression.

---

[1] Cf. 'Voltaire . . . se déclare incapable de comprendre ce que signifie cette phrase: "nos âmes coulent et fondent comme de l'eau".' (Ch. Bruneaux, 'L'image dans notre langue littéraire', *Mélanges de linguistique offerts à Albert Dauzat*, Paris, 1951, p. 57).

Another is Rousseau's manner of appreciating and exalting the beauties of the outdoor world of Nature, as poets like Wordsworth taught us to see it in English. The presence of these factors in *La Nouvelle Héloïse* contributes to a general impression that Rousseau's novel is more 'poetic' than other fictional works of his time.

If we now ask whether such an approach is bound to be in conflict with 'realism', we come upon one of the paradoxes inherent in the accepted usage of the term. A poet is no less 'real' than non-poets, his feelings need be no less a part of everyday life; nor need an observation elaborated by a simile be any less true than an unadorned statement. Indeed, if the 'realistic' novelist is aiming at a balanced portrait of his own society, he should in all fairness include the poet's point of view, as a relevant aspect of current ideas and feelings. Such a notion does not however come within the generally accepted sense of 'realism', which for most people entails a literal, prosaic approach to life. The mere fact that Rousseau's handling of his love-story can be described as 'poetic' would therefore disqualify him, for many readers, from being a *romancier réaliste*.

We can nevertheless disregard this label, and ask the more general question, whether Rousseau's novel does possess the qualities of a faithful portrayal of real life, whether it creates the effect of 'truth' he claimed for it.

In the major events of the plot there is relatively little that one can object to as being 'not like life'. The love-affair and the obstacles to the lovers marrying are lifelike enough, by the standards of the time. Saint-Preux's adventures in Paris and on his journey round the world do not approach the strange and violent episodes which other writers of the period habitually related in such cases. And after his return, one might be justified in saying that scarcely anything happens until the death of Julie. There are possibilities and plans and projects, such as Julie's notion of Claire and Saint-Preux marrying, or Wolmar's invitation to Saint-Preux to live at Clarens as tutor. But these plans come to nothing. (The critics who are scornful or ironic about the proposed *ménage à trois* sometimes seem to have forgotten that Rousseau did not allow the project to be fulfilled in the novel; when Saint-Preux returns to Clarens in Part IV, he comes only as a visitor.)

The two crucial events which might arouse query by real-life standards are Julie's quasi-mystical experience on her wedding-day, and her death. The latter in particular may seem insufficiently explained: with the increase of medical knowledge, we now expect more precise and convincing causes of death than the immersion and shock which lead to Julie's unspecified 'fever'. Her death, however, like the moral crisis of her wedding-day, is presented by Rousseau as an instance of divine intervention. One may object to this method of shaping the plot as a kind of cheating by the novelist, but from Rousseau's point of view the reader's verdict should presumably depend not on literary criteria of this kind, but on one's acceptance or rejection of the religious concepts involved. And even if one does not, in real life, believe in a personal God who acts in ways like these, there is still a case for imaginative belief. If we can accept the divinely motivated incidents of Greek plays such as *Oedipus* and *Hippolytus*, whose gods are foreign to our everyday beliefs, why should we refuse to make the same kind of effort for a more modern work?

It is therefore arguable that the plot of the novel is credible, by everyday standards, so long as the reader is prepared to accept Rousseau's religious standpoint. But to consider the events of the story *in vacuo* is to neglect the effect of the novelist's presentation of these events. Everyday incidents can become bizarre or fascinating or merely dull, depending on their treatment. What Rousseau does with the events and actions of *La Nouvelle Héloïse* is to endow them with a hectic sensibility which is their chief drawback for the modern reader.

By 'sensibility', I mean here that the characters' emotional reactions are both swift and intense; and that Rousseau shows a preference for what one may call the 'softer' emotions—love, pity, sympathy, distress—which are readily displayed and expressed, often with the accompaniment of tears.

Now Rousseau's argument, it will be recalled, is that even exceptional characters can be lifelike and credible so long as the author has discerned and portrayed the universal aspects of their personality. But the sugar-coating of sensibility which covers so much of his characters' behaviour is not a universal or timeless element in human conduct. It was a trait peculiar to Rousseau's epoch: the reaction to, or the complement of, the eighteenth century's expansive faith in Reason. This particular vogue for the display of the softer feelings has now lost ground, and the symptoms of sensibility are liable, nowadays, to seem not merely dated but weak or quaint or even ridiculous.

Our modern attitude is a matter of habit rather than reasoning, and one can scarcely hope to affect it by logical comparisons. Yet it can be argued that the sentimental eighteenth-century authors are not so much blameworthy as simply unlucky in relation to twentieth-century feelings and ideas. Critics of our time *can* praise attitudes which fall outside the scope of their everyday reactions. In particular, the last half-century has witnessed a growing appreciation of artistic naïveté, a quality foreign to the thoughts and feelings of most of the critics who commend it. But we laugh at the sentimentality, *sensiblerie* and easy tears of the eighteenth century, even though most of us know and recognize this appeal of the emotions. There is a suggestion here of the 'odd perverse antipathies' felt by Butler's bigots, who

> Compound for sins they are inclined to,
> By damning those they have no mind to.

However this may be, as things now stand, Rousseau is condemned out of his own mouth. Julie and Saint-Preux may experience the basic emotions of love which are common to all mankind, but their ways of showing this love, in words and behaviour, are not 'universal' and do not fulfil Rousseau's claims for them. From the modern point of view, Rousseau is at his weakest when he is dealing with the emotional relationships of his characters. We are tempted, time after time, to complain that his people are whipping up their own feelings, or making more show of emotion than the situation warrants. A scene like Claire's arrival, when she is coming to live at Clarens, is a case in point. After the exclamations, tears, faintings and joyful confusion of the first few moments, Saint-Preux adds:

> Il fut impossible de songer à rien de toute la journée qu'à se voir et s'embrasser sans cesse avec de nouveaux transports (p. 586).

One cannot help but feel that this is magnifying a happy occasion beyond the appropriate limits.

As well as being exaggerated in tone, the letters concerning

the characters' emotions are often long-winded. This again
Rousseau tried to excuse by real-life standards: lovers, we have
seen him saying, *are* prolix and repetitive. One can only retort
that this is a case where literature must rise above real life.
The artless outpourings of a pair of lovers may be of absorbing
interest to themselves. But the novelist must think of keeping
the reader interested too, and this involves, among other things,
avoiding *longueurs*.

Our attention has so far been concentrated on the passages
concerned with the characters' feelings. To judge the work
fairly, we must also look at Rousseau's handling of straightforward narrative, of description, and of the sections which
deal discursively with religious, moral and social problems.

Sustained narrative of events does not occupy much of the
text, since the developments of the plot depend more on ideas
and feelings than on physical action. When the need arises,
however, Rousseau can relate a scene vividly and effectively.
The passage in which Claire describes Saint-Preux's quarrel
with Bomston is a lively, succinct piece of reporting, even if it
does depend on the hackneyed device of eavesdropping (pp.
125–6). Julie's account of her father's anger over the notion of
Saint-Preux aspiring to marry her is also well executed (pp.
147–51). These are 'memoir-letters', where the narrators are
keeping each other informed of the latest developments. They
are more practical than the love-letters, and their mundane
details are for the most part presented without metaphor or
high-flown language. Indeed the description of Julie's fall, her
nose-bleeding, and the subsequent meal, is both clearly visual
and, in its small way, dramatic. In this sober style even the
emotional reactions seem less exaggerated, and the general
effect is quite realistic.

It is however in his descriptions of outdoor scenes and scenery
that Rousseau comes closest to modern expectations in the matter of realism. He scarcely ever supplies us with information
about the indoor settings of the action: even in the case of the
salon d'Apollon it is the view from the two windows which is
described; as for the room itself, we are merely told that it is
'ornée de tout ce qui peut la rendre agréable et riante' (p. 528).
By contrast with this assumption that rooms and furnishings do
not call for any detailed description, Rousseau takes pains to

portray a mountain landscape, a lake, or a garden with sufficient care for us to be able to visualize them. Julie's *Elysée* is of course the most outstanding example (Part IV, 11). An additional merit of such descriptions is that they present places which have some significance in the plot, places where decisions are taken or events occur. Several of the main stages in the story are thus linked with these natural settings, which Rousseau's descriptions enhance and make more memorable.

The question of relevance to the plot comes to the forefront again when we turn to the overtly instructive letters. These long discussions and debates are not, strictly speaking, digressions or interpolations like the subsidiary stories of Lesage, since they are bound up with situations involving the main characters. On the other hand, it is sometimes only too clear that these situations have been arranged as pretexts for the discussions. The pretexts vary in their bearing on the main plot: the subject of Italian music, for instance, is clearly gratuitous, while the debates on duelling and suicide do at least appear to have some relevance to the course of events. As for Saint-Preux's account of life in Paris, this is a necessary part of Rousseau's town-versus-country argument, but there is nothing in the plot which makes it necessary for Saint-Preux, when he leaves Julie, to go to Paris rather than elsewhere. The author's didactic preoccupations become even more evident in the second half of the book, with the essays on domestic economy, education and religion. Again they rise from the situation of the characters: Julie and Wolmar lead a full and satisfying life, and we must be shown, in detail, how it differs from and rises above the wastefulness and hypocrisy of Parisian society. In real life, a reflective person like Saint-Preux might well devote some space in his letters to comments on such topics. But although these descriptions are ostensibly seen through the eyes of Saint-Preux, the way of life he explains and eulogizes is not one of his own devising, but one that has been prescribed by Julie. Saint-Preux, at best never a strong or decisive personality, here becomes merely an instrument for relaying Julie's theories and their outcome. And most readers will of course be aware that Julie, in this case, is only a mouthpiece for Rousseau himself.

Apart from the manner of their introduction, these discussions now tend to appear either commonplace or else unacceptable in their content of ideas. Rousseau puts forward the notion that childhood should be, as far as we can make it so, a period of happiness, security and relative liberty. This attitude is now so widespread in modern society that Julie's preaching on the subject sounds trite to a degree. On the other hand, his plans for the running of a self-sufficing country estate, under the benevolent autocracy of the landowner, are largely irrelevant to twentieth-century social and economic conditions.

Yet a novel does not necessarily lose its appeal if it handles problems that no longer concern the modern reader: *La Religieuse* can still hold our interest. Diderot has chosen, however, to present his criticism in action, through the events of the plot. It is Rousseau's weakness, as a novelist, that so much of the theme of corrupt urban life and virtuous 'natural' country life is not worked out in events but presented, at best, as animated tableaux. There are minor exceptions; Saint-Preux's seduction in Paris might be cited. But considering the schema of the whole work, one can say that the first half, where the love-interest predominates, has an adequate allowance of incident to keep the story moving along. The second half lapses into little more than the portrayal of a state of affairs. There are repeated suggestions that something may happen, but all the plans and emotional crises fail to produce any new development. The love-story yields pride of place to the idyllic conditions of every-day life at Clarens. And scenes such as the *vendanges* are merely a description of typical events which, from a structural point of view, are comparable to Lesage's *caractères*. They fill in the background of the fictional world, but do not help the novel to progress.

Having concluded that these didactic passages are unrealistic in their presentation and delay the plot, we may pause, before considering Rousseau's defence of them, to recognize their merits as a part of the structure of the novel. Rousseau is exceptional among eighteenth-century novelists in his ability to organize a long work as a coherent whole, and in his evident sense of the inter-relationships of the various parts. It may be argued that Laclos's technical mastery in this respect was even greater, but Rousseau is clearly superior to his predecessors. The structural deficiencies of *Gil Blas* have already been assessed. Marivaux and Crébillon left their memoir-novels unfinished. *Manon Lescaut* is effectively put together but retains traces, however slight, of its dependence on the *Mémoires d'un Homme de Qualité*; and in his long novels Prévost shows little talent for organizing a plot so that one can see it as an ordered whole. We are left with Crébillon's *Lettres de la Marquise* as the sole example, among the works we have discussed, of a complete, independent and well-ordered story. By pure coincidence, it shares a basic similarity of plot with *La Nouvelle Héloïse*. In each case the heroine, after admitting her love, is at first unwilling to yield to the lover's desires; when she does yield, they have a brief, unquiet love-affair; and she dies, at the end of the novel, still loving him. This superficial resemblance of key-events is a proof, if any were needed, that the 'same' story can make two very different novels. With all its merits, Crébillon's work is slight. Rousseau has attempted far more; both the range of the subject-matter and the sheer length of *La Nouvelle Héloïse* are indications of his ambition.

Concerning the way his plot is shaped and articulated, we have explicit proof that he distinguished and appreciated the significance of the various stages of the novel within the pattern of the whole. A remark in his own hand, on a copy of the work, reads:

N.B. Il importe que ce roman, quoique ne formant qu'un seul volume, y soit divisé en six parties ou livres comme dans la première édition. Cette coupure est nécessaire et sert au meilleur effet de l'ouvrage (p. 775).

If we look at the divisions which Rousseau requires, we find that each of the six parts closes with an incident or scene which decisively rounds off that particular 'movement'. At the end of Part I, Saint-Preux leaves for Paris; although he does not know it, he is never again to meet Julie as her lover. Part II finishes with the discovery of Julie's letters by her mother, an event which contributes to her renunciation of Saint-Preux. Julie's marriage, the centre and pivot of the whole work, comes in Part III; it inspires thoughts of suicide in Saint-Preux, but when Bomston has cured him of these, he announces to Claire, at the end of this Part, that he is setting off on his voyage around the world. Between Parts III and IV comes an interval of several years. When Saint-Preux finally returns and visits Clarens, the conflict between Julie's former love and her present duties is revealed and resolved in the course of the lake-trip, and this episode closes Part IV. After the details of life at Clarens which take up most of Part V, we come to Julie's suggestion that Claire should marry Saint-Preux. But this solution is rejected in Part VI, which culminates in the death of Julie.

This kind of awareness of the crucial stages of a long story, and of the effectiveness of divisions and fresh beginnings, is something one does not find again in the novel until the nineteenth-century novelists, with their third-person narrative, re-establish the use of chapters. Flaubert, in particular, has a flair for the kind of comment or narrative detail which both crowns one chapter and leads the reader on to the next. Rousseau's skill in this field is comparatively rudimentary, but it is still unique among his contemporaries.

As well as shaping his story so that the divisions between the Parts emphasize crucial points in the plot, he has also managed to balance the various parts in terms of length. If the first Part is the longest, this is because it must contain the whole of the love-affair until Saint-Preux is forced to leave Julie. The remaining parts are more or less equal in length, except for Part III; this, being a little shorter, redresses the balance for Part I, and means that the novel does fall into two approximately equal sections, before and after the gap in time of Saint-Preux's voyage. The static and discursive passages of the second half therefore have a part to play in holding the quantitative balance between these two sections of the whole work.

Rousseau must surely have been aware of their usefulness in this respect; so symmetrical a structure can scarcely have been accidental. But he doubtless valued these passages primarily for their moral and didactic function. The first half of the novel, up to the wedding, portrays a situation which is impermanent and unsatisfactory. It is emphasized that the lovers are acting through weakness and error rather than wilful sin, but the fact remains that their behaviour can be blamed. The sequel reverses these conditions, shows Julie regenerated and fully virtuous, and describes the kind of life in which a couple can best fulfil their duties towards each other and society. To drive home the positive merits of life at Clarens, Rousseau devotes as much space and detail to this section of the work as he had allowed for the earlier and less virtuous episodes.

He himself defends the plan of the book in the section of the *Entretien* which deals with the novelist's task of moral instruction. But N. is made to accept without query the teachings of the second half, which are most likely to evoke the criticism of the modern reader, and blame instead the allegedly reprehensible events of the early love-affair. Rousseau's answer may seem a rather forced justification, particularly if we know something about how the novel came to be written. However, it does show that he had thought out for himself some of the problems involved in the whole concept of literature as a means of edification.

Rousseau takes into account the ideas and circumstances of his potential readers, and seriously considers the process by which a book is likely to affect people's moral standards and behaviour. As a first consequence of these reflections, he eliminates several categories of readers as being unable to benefit from his book. The novel is not for virtuous *jeunes filles*, since 'Une honnête fille ne lit point de livres d'amour' (p. 750). Innocent girls have not had their ideas tainted by the reading of other novels, and therefore do not need the kind of lesson offered by *La Nouvelle Héloïse*. At the other end of the scale, sophisticated town-dwellers are likely to be so fixed in their prejudices that they are beyond being helped by a single work of this kind. Rousseau therefore expects that his moral teaching will be effective with mature readers who are also provincials and country-dwellers. People of this kind must be encouraged to appreciate and enjoy their way of life, and to grasp the opportunities of doing good which arise from it. This aim, of course, justifies the long descriptions of how the Clarens estate is organized and managed, and of the satisfaction it offers to all those concerned in its running.

As for the love-affair, Rousseau again relates its effectiveness to the readers' own standards. People who are so virtuous that they find the opening episodes repugnant do not stand in any need of improvement in their ideas about love and marriage. Readers who do find Julie and Saint-Preux's behaviour interesting or attractive will be led on to the more edifying events of the end of the novel, and may thus be brought to change their ideas. This argument absolves Rousseau from the charge of portraying sensual love for its own sake, and also justifies the length of the second half, as a necessary element in the final effect of instruction and improvement.

In this section of the *Entretien*, discussing the moral usefulness of the novel, Rousseau has carried over to prose fiction some of the ideas on the possible moral effects of plays which he had expounded in the *Lettre à d'Alembert*. By querying several of the accepted notions on which the Improvement-theory of literature was based, he brought common-sense modifications into this hitherto over-simple theory.

But the *Entretien*, although ostensibly about 'les romans', is a piece of special pleading for *La Nouvelle Héloïse*, and Rousseau evades the issue on two points which seriously weaken his case. There is first the fact that people do not go to works of art *for* instruction and edification. Rousseau says of his ideal public of simple country-dwellers: 'Ils lisent pour se désennuyer et non pour s'instruire' (p. 749). Obviously then, the novelist must disguise his teaching so that it does not stand out as the prime reason for the book's existence; and he must at all costs avoid boring the reader. Rousseau occasionally sins against one or the other, or both, of these precepts.

Secondly, he recognizes, in the *Lettre à d'Alembert*, that the noble and virtuous feelings aroused by a play may have no after-effects in the spectator's own life:

> En donnant des pleurs à ces fictions, nous avons satisfait à tous les droits de l'humanité, sans avoir plus rien à mettre du nôtre. . . .
> Au fond, quand un homme est allé admirer de belles actions dans des fables et pleurer des malheurs imaginaires, qu'a-t-on encore à exiger de lui? N'est-il pas content de lui-même? . . . Ne s'est-il pas acquitté de tout ce qu'il doit à la vertu par l'hommage qu'il vient de lui rendre?[1]

This argument can obviously be transferred to novels: one may admire Julie's perfection without feeling moved to imitate it; or escape imaginatively into the idyllic calm and order of Clarens without deciding to re-organize one's own way of life. In attacking the moral usefulness of the theatre Rousseau had distinguished between our reactions to a work of art and to a

[1] *Œuvres complètes*, I, 193-4.

real-life situation, in a way which undermines the whole theory that art improves people directly by its 'lessons'. In defending *La Nouvelle Héloïse* as a morally useful novel he forgot or suppressed this facet of his aesthetic theory.

Nevertheless, even if one can find weaknesses in Rousseau's argument about moral usefulness, one must still acknowledge that *La Nouvelle Héloïse* does treat major moral and religious problems with a new seriousness. Rousseau, more than any previous French novelist of his century, has subordinated his story to the moral lessons it proclaims.[1] One must limit the comment to *French* novelists, for the same approach—with similar weaknesses—had already appeared in the English novel, notably in works such as Richardson's *Clarissa Harlowe*. And it is worth remarking that while Richardson's French translators, including Prévost, tended to prune their text of many practical and concrete details in order to suit French taste, they retained for the most part the reflections which carry Richardson's moral argument. The similarity of the effects produced on readers by Richardson's and Rousseau's works can be seen in favourable comments on the respective authors. Diderot's opening of the *Eloge de Richardson* is well known:

> Par un roman, on a entendu jusqu'à ce jour un tissu d'événements chimériques et frivoles, dont la lecture était dangereuse pour le goût et pour les mœurs. Je voudrais bien qu'on trouvât un autre nom pour les ouvrages de Richardson, qui élèvent l'esprit, qui touchent l'âme, qui respirent partout l'amour du bien, et qu'on appelle aussi des romans.[2]

This was published in 1762. In the previous year, the critic of the *Journal encyclopédique* had already written, à propos of *La Nouvelle Héloïse*:

> Du jargon, des portraits, une intrigue et quelques situations touchantes, voilà, à peu de choses près, ce qui fait le fonds des romans ordinaires; ... Les cœurs corrompus qui ne veulent que des romans, les âmes communes pour lesquelles l'amour n'est qu'une faiblesse, tous ceux qui ne croient enfin ni au sentiment ni à la vertu ne s'amuseront point à la lecture de ces *Lettres*.
> ... Celui qui après avoir lu ces lettres, ne se sentirait pas porté à

[1] Some seventeenth-century novelists such as Camus had sought to edify.
[2] *Œuvres esthétiques*, p. 29.

devenir meilleur, donnerait bien mauvaise opinion de son cœur. Honneur! Vertu! Bonheur! voilà sur quoi roule toutes ces lettres. Gens du monde, ne les lisez pas; elles ne seront qu'un roman pour vous.

Comments of this kind express a realization that the genre has taken a new turn. Plot is no longer the prime source of interest, nor even adventures larded with moralizing. It is the fusion of events and reflections which matters, so that ideological implications emerge as the burden of the work.

However, there had long been another type of fiction whose chief purpose was the presentation of ideas and theories on subjects such as religion, morals and philosophy. A line of writers stretching back to Rabelais and beyond had used fictional narrative as a vehicle for ideas of this kind. In the seventeenth century this practice had led to the development of a minor genre, the *voyage imaginaire*, and in Rousseau's time the same function was being fulfilled by the *conte philosophique*. But these works which dealt with serious topics generally did so in a tone of humour and fantasy; their characters, and more particularly their settings and events, were conspicuously unrealistic. One can see this as a precaution—conscious or conventional— taken to disguise the dangerous nature of the ideas being expressed, since these were often, by the standards of the time, unorthodox or subversive or immoral. Serious subjects were thus handled in an un-serious way, avoiding realism, and utilizing fantasy, farce or satire.

The seventeenth-century *anti-roman* and *roman satirique* had some affinity with this type of literature, since they sometimes offered serious criticism of society and of moral standards in a humorous manner.

In contrast to this, the serious novel, although ostensibly providing moral lessons, generally steered clear of the major human problems. It was the eighteenth century which was to see the non-satirical *roman* gradually taking over religious, ethical and social problems as subject-matter. And such topics were then treated seriously, and presented with the help of the techniques of realistic portrayal which were evolving throughout this period. Similarly, the writers of *contes philosophiques* sometimes abandoned fantasy—if not satire—and adopted a realistic manner. These twin tendencies produced a small group of works which seem to lie halfway between the conventional *roman* and the *conte philosophique*. Montesquieu's *Lettres persanes* can be cited as an early example; the *Lettres péruviennes* of Mme de Grafigny follow the same trend, with rather more stress on the *romanesque* element; and Voltaire's *L'Ingénu* shows the process continuing. The contrast between *L'Ingénu* and Voltaire's other *contes* is pointed out in a recent edition of the work:

> As a result of its dramatic structure, its realism of characterization and its rich variety of emotional tone, *L'Ingénu* is, then, very different from *Candide* and the earlier *contes*, and of all Voltaire's experiments in the *genre* it comes closest to having the characteristics of a novel.[1]

In the end, however, it was the *roman* which triumphed and took over the functions of the *conte philosophique*. During the nineteenth century one no longer finds French writers utilizing a satiric approach and a deliberately unrealistic fictional world as a means of expressing their views on serious topics. (England provided at least one honourable example in the tradition of the *conte philosophique*, Butler's *Erewhon*.) And while twentieth-century writers of fiction have invented or rediscovered various forms of fantasy or anti-realism for the handling of serious themes, one no longer thinks of classifying these works in a separate category, since the *roman* is now accepted as a suitable genre for discussing any of the major issues in human life and thought.

Consequently it is now justifiable and pertinent to consider the ideas of a serious modern novelist in terms of religious beliefs, philosophic systems or moral codes. Such an approach would be pointless in the case of the *roman héroïque*. It is with Prévost that we come to the first novelist who attempts to treat, as a major element in the plot of an otherwise conventional *roman*, a subject such as religion. But his handling of this theme, in *Cleveland*, is overshadowed by the hero's multifarious adventures and absorbing love-life. Not until Rousseau do we find a novel whose plot develops in such a way that it expresses and illustrates the full range of the author's ideas on human nature, society, religion and ethics.

In the light of our previous discussion, one reservation should

---

[1] Voltaire, *L'Ingénu* and *Histoire de Jenni*, ed. J. H. Brumfitt and M. I. Gerard Davis, Oxford, Blackwell, 1960, pp. liv–lv.

perhaps be made: while the interwoven themes of *amour-passion*, marriage and religion are worked out in the action of the book, the other major problem—town-life versus country-life—is, as we have seen, presented in a more static and descriptive way. Apart from this, one can say that the events of the story illustrate Rousseau's beliefs just as, for instance, the plot of *Candide* illustrates Voltaire's reactions to *Optimisme*. In a very general sense, the actions of the characters in *La Nouvelle Héloïse* symbolize the argument which Rousseau is unfolding.

Modern critics tend to stress this type of symbolism in the novel, and this approach has, in my view, certain dangers. One may be too ready to find a symbolic significance in every incident, and strain the interpretation of the story accordingly. Robert Osmont, for instance, attaches great importance to the theme of *l'absence* (which would seem to cover 'separation' of any kind), and interprets various incidents somewhat freely, to say the least, in pursuance of his thesis:

> La perspective de l'œuvre réclamait de Rousseau qu'il découvrît cette forme subtile de l'absence, que seul le mariage avec M. de Wolmar rendait possible. . . . Déjà, dans la IIIe partie, avant même le mariage, Rousseau a voulu symboliser cette présence effacée de l'être aimé, lorsque après sa maladie, revenue de son délire, Julie croit avoir rêvé au plus secret de son âme l'image que ses yeux ont bien vue, l'image de Saint-Preux.[1]

This is, to my mind, a clear case of taking the search for symbolism too far.

Osmont also assumes, rather rashly I feel, that Rousseau consciously aimed at certain symbolic effects. The whole question of Rousseau's motives and intentions in shaping his story is fraught with problems. But discussion of this subject can be unduly limited or distorted if the critic assumes that Rousseau was influenced only by the desire to symbolize his ideas and theories. The element in the plot which most clearly illustrates the

---

[1] R. Osmont, 'Remarques sur la genèse et la composition de la *Nouvelle Héloïse*', *Annales Jean-Jacques Rousseau*, XXXIII (1953–5), p. 115. The same issue of the *Annales* contains an article by Jean-Louis Bellenot, 'Les formes de l'amour dans la *Nouvelle Héloïse* et la signification symbolique des personnages de Julie et de Saint-Preux' (pp. 149–208), which is more restrained in its handling of 'symbolism' and provides a perceptive account of the different aspects of love to be found in the novel.

drawbacks of this approach is Julie's admission, in her last letter to Saint-Preux, that she is still in love with him. This avowal may strike the reader as inconsistent with her behaviour in the second half of the book, and with the aura of saintliness with which Rousseau has surrounded her. Various critics have attached different meanings to this confession, in the light of Rousseau's views on love and religion.[1] The fact that they do not all agree is an initial indication that the symbolic significance of this situation is no simple matter.

An alternative method of explanation is to look for Rousseau's motives in the events of his own life while he was writing the novel. Professor Green, for instance, sees Julie's admission that she still loves Saint-Preux as a literary specific for Rousseau's wounded pride over Mme d'Houdetot's rejection of his love.[2] Suggestions of this kind at least remind us that Rousseau could have been influenced by considerations other than the desire simply to express his theories through the medium of fiction. But need we suppose that an element such as Julie's admission of love was dependent on only a single motive? And if we allow a multiplicity or a mixture of motives for an ambiguous situation like this, may we not reasonably include not merely ideological or personal motives, but aesthetic ones too?

Let us for a moment consider the dénouement of the novel merely as a matter of effective story-telling. If Saint-Preux had settled down at Clarens as tutor, and the chief characters had all lived happily ever after, this would have been something of an anti-climax, in view of the previous sufferings of Julie and her lover, as well as implying that true love can be tamed or even disappear. It is a more satisfactory and conclusive ending that Julie should die, and die realizing that she still passionately loves Saint-Preux. This brings the wheel of the story full circle, back to his first trembling avowal of love for her. Rousseau was

---

[1] See A. Schinz, *La Pensée de Jean-Jacques Rousseau*, Paris, 1929, pp. 309–15; M. B. Ellis, *Julie or La Nouvelle Héloïse*, Toronto, 1949, pp. 77–8; R. Grimsley, *Jean-Jacques Rousseau*, Cardiff, 1961, pp. 146–51.

[2] F. C. Green, *Jean-Jacques Rousseau*, Cambridge, 1955, pp. 189–93. Professor Green provides several corrections of detail to the earlier important account of the genesis of the novel by Daniel Mornet; this appears in Mornet's critical edition of the work (Paris, 1925), I, pp. 77–90. See also Bernard Guyon's Introduction to *La Nouvelle Héloïse*, and in particular his discussion of the dénouement, pp. XLIII–XLV.

not, we may agree, first and foremost a story-teller, but both
the ending he finally gave us, and his earlier plan of making
Julie and Saint-Preux drown in each other's arms, show him
trying to find a strong finish rather than a mere tailing-away.

Julie's continuing love of Saint-Preux, and her death, therefore answer an artistic requirement. This does not preclude the
episode from also being a kind of wish-fulfilment on Rousseau's
part; nor from illustrating his notion that God may allow or
even direct some minor misfortune in order to prevent a greater
evil. Julie voices this thought:

> Nous songions à nous réunir: cette réunion n'était pas bonne.
> C'est un bienfait du ciel de l'avoir prévenue; sans doute il prévient
> des malheurs (p. 728).

When there is any doubt about the meaning or symbolism of an
incident, we should therefore do well to seek for an explanation
not only in ideological or personal terms, but also, possibly,
in terms of effective story-telling.

Yet when one has argued as best one may for the recognition
of those literary values which make *La Nouvelle Héloïse* a novel
rather than just a collection of theories, one is forced in the last
resort to admit that practically everyone who nowadays reads
the book does so because of these theories. It is utilized, moreover, largely as a source of illustrations for ideas which Rousseau
expounded in other, non-fictional works, and one is justified in
suspecting that if Rousseau had written nothing else, then *La
Nouvelle Héloïse* might well have sunk without trace, as did
scores of its contemporaries. A modern reader may realize and
admit, intellectually, the merits of Rousseau's novel as a construct, as an ordered story, as the vehicle for intelligent and
sometimes original social criticism, as the demonstration of a
deeply-felt religious creed. But the overt teaching on so many
subjects turns it gradually, as one reads, from a novel into a
document in the history of ideas. And when Rousseau does
allow his characters to speak for themselves, they are so masked
by sensibility that their voices come through to us with strange,
distorted and sometimes comic overtones. The illusion has not
lasted.

XI

Diderot

THEORY AND PRACTICE

ROUSSEAU'S chief contribution to the theory of the novel
lies in his fresh thinking about the moral effects of literature; on the question of realistic presentation of the story
he did little except try to justify his own practice. By contrast,
Diderot accepted all too easily the current assumptions about
literature as a means of moral improvement, but cast new light
on possible methods of winning the reader's belief.

The problem of illusion, in the different arts and in the different genres of those arts, was one which occupied Diderot
during the whole of his career as a writer. A full-scale review of
his evolving opinions on the subject would take us beyond the
scope of this study. However, some of his scattered remarks
have a particular bearing on the novel, and may help us to see
how far *La Religieuse* carries out his own aims and requirements
in the genre.

Diderot has not provided us with any detailed theoretical
analysis of what 'illusion' means in terms of an experience
undergone by the reader, but the *Eloge de Richardson* contains
numerous suggestions of how he saw it at work in himself and
others. At times the deception would seem to be complete, and
the reader is apparently convinced that he is involved in a real-
life situation:

> O Richardson! on prend, malgré qu'on en ait, un rôle dans tes
> ouvrages, on se mêle à la conversation, on approuve, on blâme, on
> admire, on s'irrite, on s'indigne. Combien de fois ne me suis-je pas
> surpris, comme il est arrivé à des enfants qu'on avait menés au
> spectacle pour la première fois, criant: Ne le croyez pas, il vous
> trompe. . . . Si vous allez là, vous êtes perdu.[1]

But we must allow for a certain degree of lyrical exaggeration.
When he has fallen into a calmer vein of reminiscence, Diderot

[1] *Œuvres esthétiques,* p. 30.

shows that he was fully aware that he was not living through the adventures but reading a book: 'Combien cette lecture m'affecta délicieusement! A chaque instant je voyais mon bonheur s'abréger d'une page' (p. 31). And later, even though he is discussing the apparent impossibility of reading Richardson with critical detachment, he reveals, by the use of the word *imaginé*, that he is conscious of the book's fictional nature:

L'intérêt et le charme de l'ouvrage dérobent l'art de Richardson à ceux qui sont le plus faits pour l'apercevoir. Plusieurs fois j'ai commencé la lecture de *Clarisse* pour me former; autant de fois j'ai oublié mon projet à la vingtième page; j'ai seulement été frappé, comme tous les lecteurs ordinaires, du génie qu'il y a à avoir imaginé une jeune fille remplie de sagesse et de prudence, qui ne fait pas une seule démarche qui ne soit fausse (p. 40).

Without perhaps having thoroughly clarified his ideas on the nature of illusion as an experience, Diderot shows—if only inadvertently—that he does not equate it with literal belief.[1]

Moreover, with an insight quite exceptional at the time, he realized that susceptibility to illusion varies from individual to individual. Each play-goer or reader has his own standards:

Quand je dis que l'illusion est une quantité constante, c'est dans un homme qui juge de différentes productions, et non dans des hommes différents. Il n'y a peut-être pas, sur toute la surface de la terre, deux individus qui aient la même mesure de la certitude, et cependant le poète est condamné à faire illusion également à tous.[2]

Diderot is prepared to admit, however, that certain types of fiction do not need to create an illusion of reality. In an important passage at the end of *Les Deux Amis de Bourbonne*, where he discusses the art of the story-teller, fiction is classified under

---

[1] In *Les Bijoux indiscrets*, the remark that a spectator should be 'trompé sans interruption' by the stage illusion is later qualified; Sélim suggests that the audience are aware they havè come to see 'l'imitation d'un événement et non l'événement même' (*Œuvres romanesques*, pp. 142, 145). Later, in *Le Paradoxe sur le comédien*, Diderot maintained that the spectator does not forget himself so completely as to think that the play is real life (*Œuvres esthétiques*, pp. 369–70). Even in the first of the passages from the *Eloge* cited above, the phrase 'pour la première fois' implies that experienced spectators will not be deceived in this way.

[2] *Œuvres esthétiques*, p. 215.

three headings. The second of these includes fantasies, fairy-tales, all kinds of stories which are not tied down to the conditions of real life:

> Il y a le conte plaisant à la façon de La Fontaine, de Vergier, de l'Arioste, d'Hamilton, où le conteur ne se propose ni l'imitation de la nature, ni la vérité, ni l'illusion; il s'élance dans les espaces imaginaires. Dites à celui-ci: Soyez gai, ingénieux, varié, original, même extravagant, j'y consens; mais séduisez-moi par les détails; que le charme de la forme me dérobe toujours l'invraisemblance du fond: et si le conteur fait ce que vous exigez ici, il a tout fait.[1]

(This definition is obviously the one we shall need to recall when we come to discuss *Jacques le Fataliste*.) Although it is far more usual to find Diderot praising the kind of fiction which does create an illusion for the reader by 'imitating nature', this explicit recognition of the rights of fantasy should not be forgotten.

The two remaining types of fiction could be designated as 'lifelike', and 'larger-than-life'. Of these, the latter makes its effects by imposing on the reader a new scale of actuality, so that he accepts an 'unreal', heroic world because everything in it conforms to its inherent established pattern of grandeur:

> Je distingue le conte à la manière d'Homère, de Virgile, du Tasse, et je l'appelle le conte merveilleux. La nature y est exagérée; la vérité y est hypothétique: et si le conteur a bien gardé le module qu'il a choisi, si tout répond à ce module, et dans les actions, et dans les discours, il a obtenu le degré de perfection que le genre de son ouvrage comportait, et vous n'avez rien de plus à lui demander. En entrant dans son poème, vous mettez le pied dans une terre inconnue, où rien ne se passe comme dans celle que vous habitez, mais où tout se fait en grand comme les choses se font autour de vous en petit (pp. 790–1).

Diderot does not here state that this kind of fiction does or can create an illusion. But the method of winning belief by a larger-than-life portrayal is described in the *Paradoxe sur le comédien*. What, he asks, is the key to the actor's success in convincing the audience that his borrowed character is 'real'? It is the talent

de bien connaître les symptômes extérieurs de l'âme d'emprunt, de

[1] *Œuvres romanesques*, p. 791.

s'adresser à la sensation de ceux qui nous entendent, qui nous voient, et de les tromper par l'imitation de ces symptômes, par une imitation qui agrandisse tout dans leurs têtes et qui devienne la règle de leur jugement.[1]

Here again he utilizes the notion of a new scale of magnitude which the work of art imposes, and which replaces our everyday standards of judgment. And in this case the effect is to 'deceive' the audience and win their belief.

The two kinds of fiction so far discussed, fantasy and the epic or heroic style, seemed to Diderot in some ways less interesting and important than the lifelike, realistic story which in *Les Deux Amis* he calls 'le conte historique'. This preference depends partly on the fact that in realistic fiction he saw a more effective vehicle for conveying moral lessons; fiction which seems to be true is more likely to convince us of moral truths.

His remarks on how the writer is to create this type of illusion constitute a recipe for, and a defence of, realism. We must however immediately limit the sense in which we can talk about 'realism' here. In his theoretical writings Diderot seems to attach relatively little importance to the inanimate objects of the visible world. He praises, in Richardson's novels, the effective use of 'de petits détails': 'C'est à cette multitude de petites choses que tient l'illusion' (p. 35). And in *Les Deux Amis* he likewise recommends the use of 'de petites circonstances'. But in both cases the context suggests that he is thinking in terms of behaviour, not objects. It is words, gestures, nuances of emotion, traits of conduct he has in mind, rather than details of clothes, furniture and buildings.

The purpose of these little touches is to create an atmosphere of everyday life and behaviour. The reader must be made to feel that this is the real world as he knows it, that the characters' thoughts and feelings correspond to his own experience. Diderot cites some of the kinds of fantasy and exaggeration which Richardson avoids, and goes on:

Le fond de son drame est vrai; ses personnages ont toute la réalité possible; . . . les passions qu'il peint sont telles que je les éprouve en moi; ce sont les mêmes objets qui les émeuvent, elles ont l'énergie que je leur connais; . . . il me montre le cours général des

[1] *Œuvres esthétiques*, p. 358.

choses qui m'environnent. Sans cet art, mon âme se pliant avec peine à des biais chimériques, l'illusion ne serait que momentanée et l'impression faible et passagère (p. 31).

Against this background of ordinariness the moments of high emotion will stand out, both forceful and convincing:

Ce sont toutes ces vérités de détail qui préparent l'âme aux impressions fortes des grands événements. Lorsque votre impatience aura été suspendue par ces délais momentanés qui lui servaient de digues, avec quelle impétuosité ne se répandra-t-elle pas au moment où il plaira au poète de les rompre! C'est alors qu'affaissé de douleur ou transporté de joie, vous n'aurez plus la force de retenir vos larmes prêtes à couler, et de vous dire à vous-même: Mais peut-être que cela n'est pas vrai. Cette pensée a été éloignée de vous peu à peu (pp. 35–6).

Diderot's realism is therefore largely a matter of emotional tone, of building up belief by touching in a background of everyday thoughts and feelings. The artist's skill lies in his selection of just those details which will impress the reader as being inevitable and 'true':

de petites circonstances si liées à la chose, de traits si simples, si naturels, et toutefois si difficiles à imaginer, que vous serez forcé de vous dire en vous-même: Ma foi, cela est vrai: on n'invente pas ces choses-là.[1]

As for the plot which is to be unfolded against this background, Diderot again has his theories, expressed in this case in the *Discours de la poésie dramatique*, where he points out the basic similarities between the novel and the *drame*.

The notion to which he seems to attach most importance here, since he repeats it several times in different guises, is that of causation; the audience or the reader must be able to see *why* the events of the plot take place as they do. In this respect the writer who invents the whole of his plot, instead of starting from known historical incidents, is the true poet, the 'maker' *par excellence*. (This idea is reminiscent of the Aristotelian view that 'poetry'—that is, imaginative writing—because it exhibits causation, is more philosophical than history.) Diderot anticipates Flaubert with his analogy between the writer and God:

---

[1] *Œuvres romanesques*, p. 791.

Il est, dans sa sphère, ce que l'Etre tout-puissant est dans la Nature. C'est lui qui crée, qui tire du néant; avec cette différence, que nous n'entrevoyons dans la nature qu'un enchaînement d'effets dont les causes nous sont inconnues; au lieu que la marche du drame n'est jamais obscure; et que, si le poète nous cache assez de ressorts pour nous piquer, il nous en laisse toujours apercevoir assez pour nous satisfaire.[1]

These causes must be not only perceptible but appropriate to the effects they produce. The standards of appropriateness, in this context, include importance and usualness: great actions should not be set in motion by trivialities, and the writer should avoid exceptional causes such as coincidence, 'la simultanéité des événements'. These 'rules', as Diderot admits, are not those of real life, in which minute causes can in fact lead to momentous events and coincidences do occur. In this matter, however, the 'imitation of nature' becomes subservient to the overall requirements of credibility.

When it comes to the kind of events and actions to be utilized, Diderot distinguishes between *le miraculeux*, which infringes the laws of nature, and *le merveilleux*, which here means simply the unusual: 'Les cas rares sont merveilleux: les cas naturellement impossibles sont miraculeux' (p. 213). The writer can and should use *le merveilleux*, in order to rise above 'la simple et froide uniformité des choses communes', but should avoid going to extremes which would strain belief. Without going into details about the kind of characters who are to enact the events of the plot, Diderot implies that they too may be unusual but not extravagantly so. His general requirements can be deduced from a passage in which he summarizes, in order to condemn them, the elements which constitute *le vernis romanesque*:

Un ouvrage sera romanesque, si le merveilleux naît de la simultanéité des événements; si l'on y voit les dieux ou les hommes trop méchants, ou trop bons; si les choses et les caractères y diffèrent trop de ce que l'expérience ou l'histoire nous les montre; et surtout si l'enchaînement des événements y est trop extraordinaire et trop compliqué (p. 214).

These recommendations seem to cover the ground pretty thoroughly, and show a clearer appreciation of the methods of realistic fiction than the comments of previous theorists.

[1] *Œuvres esthétiques*, p. 212.

If we now ask how far, in *La Religieuse*, Diderot carried out his own precepts, we can see that he observed them faithfully for much of the time. However unlikely we may find the sheer accumulation of Suzanne's misfortunes, the separate incidents are conveyed to us in practical everyday terms, often with those little details which Diderot sees as the secret of an effect of truth. Since he also held that 'truth to nature' should not be curtailed by conventional notions of *les bienséances*, these touches are sometimes of a kind which contemporary critics would have condemned as trivial, low or disgusting. There is the occasion, for instance, when Suzanne's nose bleeds as she is being taken home in the carriage with her mother. But, as always, this mundane detail has its bearing on character. In this case it leads up to a remark showing the mother's lack of tenderness for Suzanne: 'A quelques mots qu'elle dit, je conçus que sa robe et son linge en avaient été tachés, et que cela lui déplaisait' (pp. 247–8). In later stages of the book, where the events turn on physical suffering and sexual perversion, Diderot makes even more extensive use of small touches such as these. One has only to read the long interrogation-scene at Longchamp, or the account of the afternoon in the Mother Superior's room at Saint-Eutrope, to see Diderot utilizing the method which he so admired in Richardson. Gestures, glances, actions and of course dialogue are all part of the effect. Systematic descriptions are provided for some characters who seem important to the plot. Inanimate objects are mentioned, though rarely described, when they have some significance in the action. And there are set-pieces, the kind of *tableaux* Diderot advocated for the stage, groupings which please the eye and convey a situation or a mood:

> J'étais assise sur le bord de son lit, et je ne faisais rien; une autre dans un fauteuil, avec un petit métier à broder sur ses genoux; d'autres, vers les fenêtres, faisaient de la dentelle; il y en avait à terre assises sur les coussins qu'on avait ôtés des chaises, qui cousaient, qui brodaient, qui parfilaient, ou qui filaient au petit rouet. Les unes étaient blondes, d'autres brunes; aucune ne se ressemblait, quoiqu'elles fussent toutes belles (p. 359). [1]

[1] Page-numbers refer to the Garnier edition by H. Bénac, which I have kept for reference because it provides notes; but more recent student editions (e.g. Garnier-Flammarion) offer an improved version of the text of the novels.

But if Diderot makes effective use of circumstantial detail, there are other details which reveal a certain lack of care and attention. The text contains quite a number of inconsistencies concerning various practical aspects of Suzanne's story. To whom, for instance, is this story addressed? Suzanne was supposedly recounting her sufferings for the Marquis de Crois-mare alone, but occasionally, as in the very first paragraph, she is made to refer to a wider set of readers.[1]

We can also find several passages which are confused or contradictory about what the narrator knew by the time she began to write her memoirs. Sometimes these lapses are relatively unimportant or are quickly resolved: Suzanne's illegitimacy, for instance, which at first is merely a suspicion, but soon becomes certain; or the reference to Sœur Ursule as still alive, though her death is related shortly afterwards.[2] Such mistakes are due, I think, firstly to a lack of forward planning—Diderot simply had not decided in advance how things would develop; and secondly to the piecemeal nature of his revisions, which did not wholly eliminate the discrepancies.

Some critics have claimed that a further, more important inconsistency arises because of what Suzanne overhears Mme *** saying to Dom Morel in the convent parlour. This avowal, it is argued, makes clear to Suzanne the exact nature of the Superior's homosexual activities. When Suzanne assures the Marquis that she still does not understand what is so sinful about Mme ***'s behaviour, these protestations belie what she had discovered by eavesdropping, and what she thus knew when she came to write her memoirs. If this argument is valid, then the 'mistake' is a serious matter, since it affects the whole of a long episode and also throws doubt on the reliability of Suzanne as narrator. Georges May suggests that Diderot, living through each incident with his heroine as he composed the work, had forgotten the retrospective viewpoint of memoirs and was making the narrative into something more like a diary.

If we look more closely at the eavesdropping scene, however, we find that such excuses may not be necessary, since Suzanne did not, it seems, acquire a full knowledge of the facts:

[1] For Diderot's revisions concerning the putative reader(s), see J. Parrish's edition of the first version of *La Religieuse*, Geneva, 1963.

[2] For other examples, see G. May, *Diderot et 'La Religieuse'*, pp. 204–18.

Le premier mot que j'entendis après un assez long silence me fit frémir; ce fut:

'Mon père, je suis damnée . . .'

Je me rassurai. J'écoutais; le voile qui jusqu'alors m'avait dérobé le péril que j'avais couru se déchirait lorsqu'on m'appela; il fallut aller, j'allai donc; mais, hélas! je n'en avais que trop entendu. Quelle femme, monsieur le marquis, quelle abominable femme! (pp. 383-4).

In this passage the verb-tenses are crucial. After the isolated and completed actions ('entendis', 'fit', 'fut', 'rassurai'), we are told that the veil of ignorance which had protected Suzanne's virtue was just being torn apart ('se déchirait') when she was called away. That is, the process of her enlightenment had *not* been completed. We are to assume that Suzanne must have heard enough to shock her—conceivably some general remarks in which the Superior admitted to impure thoughts and unchaste actions—but no more. It is therefore quite justifiable for Suzanne to maintain, when writing her memoirs, that she still does not understand the precise nature of the sins which one woman can commit with another.[1]

A series of chronological slips which is less important, but not without some bearing on Diderot's methods, is the matter of Suzanne's age. At one point she is made to say 'Cependant je comptais mes années, je trouvais que j'avais à peine vingt ans...' (p. 301). If the reader too has been keeping count, since the time when she first entered the convent at the age of sixteen-and-a-half, he will know that she is at least twenty-three when this remark is made. What is more, after an interval which includes the hearing of her case, her own illness and long convalescence, the illness and death of Sainte-Ursule, and Suzanne's transfer to another convent, she tells her new Mother Superior, 'Je n'ai pas encore vingt ans' (p. 344). We have already seen how Marianne, in Marivaux's novel, 'ages' more rapidly than the chronology of the book should permit, because she undergoes a wide range of emotional experience in a very short period. Diderot handles the passing of time in the same impressionistic way, but in order to produce the opposite effect.

[1] For a fuller discussion of this problem, see my article, 'What Suzanne knew: Lesbianism in *La Religieuse*', *Studies on Voltaire and the Eighteenth Century*, Vol. CCVII, Oxford, 1981.

Suzanne remains unduly young because the qualities of innocence and ignorance are important attributes of her character,
and these are associated with youth and lack of experience.

The matter of her ignorance, in some of the scenes she relates, calls for special comment. May has shown, in his chapter
entitled 'Diderot sexologue', that the portrayal of Lesbianism
in the novel springs from a genuine and informed scientific interest, not from mere sensationalism. If however we consider
not the motive but the technique of that portrayal, we find
Diderot using a device which was widespread in eighteenth-
century fiction and served many different ends: the recounting
of scenes and incidents by a naïve witness who does not understand their full significance. In philosophic tales the simplicity
of an uncorrupted observer was used to make the reader see
familiar abuses and prejudices in a fresh light. In love-stories
the device acted, less creditably, as a source of *double-entendre* and
titillation. Innocent and ignorant characters, usually girls, relate other people's actions and remarks, and add comments of
their own, which have a special import for the knowing reader.
It is not so much dramatic as erotic irony. De Rozoi exploits
the device extensively in his *Lettres de Cécile à Julie*. His heroine
is fifteen when the novel begins, and fresh from the convent-
school. She is made to offer remarks like the following:

Ah, ma chère, la différence d'une cornette à un chapeau est donc
bien essentielle? Ce qui m'embarrasse encore, c'est que j'ai vu le
Marquis habillé en fille; je le trouvais aussi aimable sous la cornette.
Ou je me trompe, ou la différence n'est pas tout dans le chapeau
(Lettre I).

Later, when she is disguised as a young man, a lady is attracted
by 'his' charms. But as they are kissing,

mon jabot s'était entr'ouvert; je crus qu'il m'en coûterait deux yeux
au moins . . . Que prétendait donc cette femme? . . . Qu'espérait-
elle de moi? De quoi était-elle frustrée? . . . Il fallait que cette
femme se crût bien offensée, pour vouloir tant se venger; mais il faut
aussi que je n'eusse pas de quoi réparer l'offense (Lettre VIII).

Other writers went further in this use of naïveté as a source of
salacious implications.

Diderot's handling of certain scenes in *La Religieuse* clearly
depends on this kind of exploitation of innocence, and the irony

emerges in Suzanne's comments. After a page describing the ardours and embraces and *défaillance* of the Superior, Suzanne concludes: 'Cependant cette bonne supérieure, car il est impossible d'être si sensible et de n'être pas bonne, me parut revenir à elle' (p. 344). This kind of suggestive simplicity depends on the narrator being young and innocent and ignorant, so that some of Diderot's lapses in chronology and in the time-knowledge factor are bound up with his chosen manner of presentation.

In all this there is an element of sniggering over the unspeakable which may well seem distasteful. But Diderot's approach also possesses some artistic merits which should not be ignored. For most readers the character of Suzanne, seen in the book as a whole, arouses approval and sympathy. Part of this effect is due to her apparent candour and simplicity, and the fact that her judgment of others is for the most part charitable. It would be inappropriate to make such a character describe in detail scenes which she knew to be guilty or sinful. If he had observed the requirements of the memoir-form, Diderot would thus have been limited to discreetly colourless references to the Mother Superior's behaviour, which Suzanne would be obliged to condemn. Whatever the inconsistencies of the method Diderot did employ, it is obviously preferable, in its vividness and evocatory power, to the treatment which the logic of the form might seem to demand.

If we now turn to the question of plot, and ask how far Diderot made the events comprehensible in terms of cause and effect, the verdict is again largely favourable. The action goes back to Mme Simonin's lapse from virtue and the fact that Suzanne is not M. Simonin's child. Her mother's wish for Suzanne to become a nun has a double motive: the desire to make atonement for her own sin through the virtue of her daughter, and the practical consideration that Suzanne is not entitled to a share of M. Simonin's money for a dowry. Diderot has here created a situation which is all the more effective for being unusual, in the novel at least.[1] The commonest motive for a girl being forced to take the veil was the simple financial reason that her parents could not or would not give her the

---

[1] Cf. F. C. Green, *French Novelists, Manners and Ideas from the Renaissance to the Revolution*, London, 1928, p. 148.

dowry which would enable her to make a suitable marriage. If this had been Suzanne's case, her attitude towards her parents would have been resentment and condemnation of their cruelty. As things are, her feelings are complicated, and her actions are influenced, by the knowledge of her mother's dilemma. One may disagree with the solution which Mme Simonin adopts— and question the propriety of her *directeur de conscience* supporting it—but it does seem to be a decision which arises logically enough from the circumstances and from the character of Mme Simonin as we know it. This initial cause is serious enough for the events and emotions which are its consequence.

In the unfolding of the plot Diderot is fairly restrained in his use of chance and coincidence. The one glaring exception to this is the occasion when Suzanne eavesdrops on her Mother Superior's confession. We have already seen that such eaves-dropping was an accepted literary device for furthering the plot, especially in memoir-novels. But much of Diderot's criticism of contemporary novels was based on their use of literary conven-tions which were not true-to-life, and this opportune overhear-ing of a crucial revelation depends on just such a convention. Since the knowledge Suzanne acquires by eavesdropping is no news to the reader, and merely creates inconsistencies in the previous narrative, there are grounds for arguing that Diderot would have done better to excise this small incident entirely.

In the broader outline of events, chance may be said to play a part. Suzanne 'happens' to be sent to precisely those convents in which she will run the gamut of the evils of conventual life. In the first, the Mother Superior's hypocrisy and ignoring of Suzanne's own interests lead the girl almost to the point of tak-ing final vows. In the second, the emotional transports of Mme de Moni's mysticism are followed by the tyranny and per-secution of Mère Sainte-Christine. And in the third, Suzanne encounters the sexual aberration which ends in the Mother Superior's going mad. Considered in cold blood, such a sequence of emotional, physical and moral evils seems, at the very least, unlikely. Indeed, Diderot makes Suzanne recognize this im-probability:

Je vous entends, vous, monsieur le marquis, et la plupart de ceux qui liront ces mémoires: 'Des horreurs si multipliées, si variées, si continues! Une suite d'atrocités si recherchées dans les âmes religieuses! Cela n'est pas vraisemblable,' diront-ils, dites-vous (p. 309).

(The awkwardness of expression comes from Diderot's revision of this passage to suggest that the story will reach others besides the Marquis, an inconsistency already noticed.) Suzanne's only excuse is that, however improbable her story may seem, 'cela est vrai'. Here Diderot falls beneath his own standards; he knew, and should have remembered, that the reader's belief does not depend on explicit protestations of truth, but on a narrative so skilfully presented that it does not arouse doubts: 'Vous n'aurez plus la force . . . de vous dire à vous-même: Mais peut-être que cela n'est pas vrai.'

The apparent improbability of the plot can be excused, to some extent, by reasons more satisfactory than a plea of 'truth'. Suzanne's moves from convent to convent are all adequately motivated within the terms of the plot. And within the terms of Diderot's argument, she could be sure of finding *some* evils or abuses in any convent to which she might be sent. Then Suzanne herself is on more than one occasion the agent who brings out to their fullest extent the potential evils of conventual life. Her responsiveness to Mme de Moni's *élans de mysticisme*, her resistance to the domination of Mère Sainte-Christine, her physical attractions, all these act as catalysts in the appropriate circumstances. Since the reactions of others thus depend partly on her character, the rôle of chance is correspondingly reduced. Finally, and this is of course the most powerful point in Diderot's favour, he has managed to build up that atmosphere of reality which can make us accept the successive events, while reading, without pausing to doubt or query.

Artistically there is also considerable merit in the contrast of mood between the various main episodes. The religious ecstasies of Mme de Moni become all the more seductive, in retrospect, when we move into the subsequent period of persecution and physical cruelty; and this has a stark vigour beside the ambiguous sensual softness of the Lesbian scenes. Diderot has a notable gift for creating and sustaining the mood which runs through long sections of this kind. There are moments of failure, when a discordant note is sounded, and of these the most striking is the

much-quoted instance of M. Manouri's *plaidoyer*.[1] This rhetorical passage is so different in tone and approach from the rest of
Suzanne's narrative that one must surely see in it the product
of a moment when Diderot's personal convictions broke free
from the guiding hand of the artist in him. On the whole, however, he is successful in maintaining the moods which characterize the periods of rule of the respective Superiors.

This is not to say that the various stages of the plot are
sufficiently marked off from each other. On a first reading one
may indeed find that the structure of the story does not emerge
very clearly. Diderot lacks the ability, which we noticed in
Rousseau, to recognize the crucial moments of a plot and to
emphasize them by whatever devices the form of his novel per-
mits. As far as one can judge from his other writings, Diderot
had little or no gift—or inclination—for creating works whose
structure is systematic, regular and well defined. His favourite
form is the dialogue, which can wander freely and is not bound
by strict formal considerations.[2] His failure to stress the climac-
tic moments in *La Religieuse* is therefore characteristic of his
usual practice.

There is however one negative structural merit which deserves comment: the plot is free from interpolated stories. There
are at least two occasions in *La Religieuse* where earlier writers
would probably have succumbed to the temptation to branch
off into the life-story of a minor character: the death of Sœur
Ursule, when the heroine is left with a packet of documents
which presumably explain Ursule's continual melancholy
(p. 324); and the background of the young Benedictine, Morel,
who persuades Sœur Suzanne to escape from the convent:

A mesure que je m'ouvrais, sa confiance faisait les mêmes progrès;
si je me confessais à lui, il se confiait à moi; ce qu'il me disait de ses
peines avait la plus parfaite conformité avec les miennes; il était
entré en religion malgré lui; il supportait son état avec le même
dégoût, et il n'était guère moins à plaindre que moi (p. 378).

Lesage and Prévost, one feels, and Marivaux too, would have

[1] Concerning the confusion as to where M. Manouri's argument begins,
see R. J. Ellrich, 'The Rhetoric of "La Religieuse" ', pp. 138–40.
[2] Cf. R. Mortier, 'Diderot et le problème de l'expressivité', *Cahiers
de l'Association Internationale des Etudes Françaises*, Paris, 1961 (no. 13),
pp. 283–97.

seen these situations as the appropriate point of departure for another story. Diderot keeps strictly to the adventures of the heroine herself. He may have given this matter little conscious thought. It seems safe to say that by the 1760's the use of interpolated stories was a dying convention. (Rousseau's decision to withdraw Bomston's love-story from the body of his novel provides evidence to support this point.) But the question of interpolation was not wholly settled or out-moded: *Jacques le Fataliste* was to become a study in digression, and shows Diderot working—or playing—out the whole problem. Some commendation is therefore due for the way in which Sœur Suzanne is allowed to keep the narrative firmly in her own hands.

About Suzanne herself much has already been written by modern critics. Georges May's study of the novel provides many perceptive comments on the heroine's character. There are further valuable insights in the discussion by Robert Ellrich. In particular, he brings out the self-awareness of Suzanne, who is so often conscious not only of her own feelings but of the effect she produces upon other people. There is a parallel here with Marianne, who is similarly aware of other people's reactions to herself. For both Marivaux and Diderot the heroine they have created is something of an actress; she observes, and reacts to, her audience. People of this kind, in real life, may modify their behaviour according to the spectator's blame or approval; and in writing about themselves, they are influenced by the thought of the reader's possible reactions. Suzanne is just such a natural actress, and it was a subtle touch of 'sincerity' on Diderot's part to make her recognize the fact, overtly, in her postscript.

A discussion of atmosphere, of plot and character in *La Religieuse* should presumably lead up to an appreciation of its 'moral lesson', since Diderot repeatedly affirmed his belief that the function of literature was to raise moral standards. The most fervent passages of the *Eloge de Richardson* are those describing the force and effectiveness of the English novelist's teachings. Diderot claims that in many cases, including his own, the lessons of *Pamela*, and *Clarissa Harlowe* and *Sir Charles Grandison* have left their mark on the reader's behaviour and moral attitudes. These works, it would therefore seem, might be considered as models of the genre in respect of their moral instruction. Does *La Religieuse* follow their pattern?

Now Richardson's novels all deal with situations which, if not exactly commonplace, at least afford moral lessons of a broad and general character: that 'virtue', in the case of Pamela, can triumph over both vice and the prejudices of caste and fortune; that hypocrisy and corruption, in the person of Lovelace, may destroy purity but cannot bring happiness. As well as these general ideas which emerge from the plot as a whole, Richardson's virtuous characters also tend, as Julie and Saint-Preux were to do, to put the world right on minor matters of conduct and theory. Such characters are given opportunities to express the author's own beliefs on a multitude of subjects, with the result that the reader is often only too painfully aware of the sermonizing novelist behind the mask.

In *La Religieuse* the main lesson which emerges is of a much more specific nature than those of Richardson's novels. 'Girls should not be forced into convents against their will', or even, in still wider terms: 'The monastic life is socially and morally evil.' These are maxims directed against a single abuse which, however widespread in France at the time, cannot be thought to have such a general application as Richardson's pronouncements on human nature and sexual morality. Diderot has made a whole novel out of what might furnish a single discussion in Richardson. And having thus limited his field of action, Diderot remains strictly within the confines of this subject. Even if Suzanne is occasionally prolix, her remarks are always relevant to the theme of her sufferings and the evils of an enforced profession. The scope of Diderot's moral instruction is therefore considerably narrower than Richardson's.

What is even more striking and unlike Richardson is that Diderot seems, in this novel, to adopt and support certain views to which he was violently opposed in real life. In particular, the dogmas of Christianity and the authority of the Church are accepted by Suzanne without question; even if *La Religieuse* attacks a specific abuse in Catholic practice, it does not overtly attack Christianity or the Church. By 1760, Diderot had abandoned whatever faith in Christianity he may once have felt. The force of this rejection is expressed in passages such as that in the *Salon de 1763* where he argues that the mythology of Christianity is as rich in tragic subjects as that of the Ancients:

Peut-être la Fable offre-t-elle plus de sujets doux et agréables;
... mais le sang que l'abominable croix a fait couler de tous côtés
est bien d'une autre ressource pour le pinceau tragique.
Ce sont des crimes qu'il faut au talent des Racine, des Corneille
et des Voltaire. Jamais aucune religion ne fut aussi féconde en crimes
que le christianisme.[1]

Novelists like Richardson and Rousseau were capable of portraying characters who held views which their creators thought
false or reprehensible. But such authors would not allow a character of this kind to continue unrefuted to the end of the book:
Lovelace is confounded, Wolmar will be converted. Diderot not
only sets Suzanne in the centre of the stage, proclaiming
adherence to a faith he mistrusted and condemned, but apparently allows her ideas to stand uncorrected.

On the face of it this course of conduct seems so unlikely,
especially in one of the leading *philosophes*, that it should perhaps
make us look more closely at the implications of what Suzanne
says and does.

The initial outline of the nun's attitude towards religion was
to some extent forced upon Diderot and his friends. When they
began writing Suzanne's letters to Croismare, the latter was
living on his estates in Normandy where, if we can trust
Grimm's evidence on this point, 'il s'était tout à coup jeté dans
la plus grande dévotion' (p. 849). In these circumstances there
would have been little point in portraying a young woman who
was fleeing the convent because she was an agnostic or an
atheist; such views might have enlisted the sympathy of Grimm
or Diderot, but not of Croismare. Suzanne was therefore established as a nun who accepted the teachings of the Church but
lacked a sense of vocation. This attitude Diderot then carried
over into the memoirs where it is, in my view, extremely effective. Suzanne's desire to have her vows annulled becomes wholly
and uniquely a desperate cry for liberty, with no theological
debates to detract from its urgency. There is all the more pathos
in her situation, in that she is a faithful and obedient daughter
of the church which is holding her prisoner.

If this is true as a general outline of Suzanne's point of view,
we must not however suppose that Diderot could or would

---

[1] Written à propos of Deshays' *Mariage de la Vierge*; *Salons*, ed. J. Seznec
and J. Adhémar, Oxford, 1957, I, 214.

suppress every tendency of his own to criticize Christianity, its institutions and its practitioners. These criticisms may be slight, but they throw some light on Diderot's procedure, and should not be ignored. Sometimes they are explicit, if elliptical, as in Suzanne's suggestion that priests tend to become hard-hearted and unsympathetic. Of her *Directeur* she says, 'Ce prêtre était entré tard dans l'état religieux; il avait de l'humanité' (p. 248). And later, of M. Hébert's acolytes, 'Dieu veuille leur conserver ce caractère tendre et miséricordieux qui est si rare dans leur état' (p. 326). The idea that being a priest almost inevitably produces a bad effect on the character is scarcely what one expects from a fervent Catholic.

Also rather unexpected are the terms occasionally used by Suzanne about the cloistered life itself. She does recognize, more than once, that there are some good nuns with a true vocation; and when her appeal is being prepared by M. Manouri, she says, 'Je voulais qu'il ménageât l'état religieux.' Yet in a subsequent conversation with him she cries, 'Je ne saurais m'assujettir à toutes les misères qui remplissent la journée d'une recluse: c'est un tissu de puérilités que je méprise; . . . J'ai envié, j'ai demandé à Dieu l'heureuse imbécillité d'esprit de mes compagnes' (p. 316).

At other times it is not overt criticism by Suzanne so much as the implications of some action or situation she relates which may lead us to think twice about the religious views involved. What of the saintly Mme de Moni, for whom Suzanne has nothing but praise? There is surely something questionable, from a religious point of view, about the emotional transports she aroused with her prayers:

> Son dessein n'était pas de séduire; mais certainement c'est ce qu'elle faisait: on sortait de chez elle avec un cœur ardent, la joie et l'extase étaient peintes sur le visage; on versait des larmes si douces! . . . Quelques-unes [des religieuses] m'ont dit qu'elles sentaient naître en elles le besoin d'être consolées comme celui d'un très grand plaisir (p. 259).

Even more thought-provoking are the various incidents in which the question of 'the voice of God' is raised. When Suzanne decides to say that she will become a nun, her companions are delighted. According to them, 'Dieu avait parlé à mon cœur;

personne n'était plus faite pour l'état de perfection que moi'
(p. 244). Her previous doubts and reluctance are put down as
'des suggestions du mauvais esprit'. Suzanne herself comments
on this, clear-sightedly:

> Il me paraissait assez singulier que la même chose vînt de Dieu ou
> du diable, selon qu'il leur plaisait de l'envisager. Il y a beaucoup de
> circonstances pareilles dans la religion; et ceux qui m'ont consolée
> m'ont souvent dit de mes pensées, les uns que c'étaient autant
> d'instigations de Satan, et les autres autant d'inspirations de Dieu.
> Le même mal vient ou de Dieu qui nous éprouve, ou du diable qui
> nous tente.

Superficially, Suzanne's criticism is directed against those who
cite 'the voice of God' in support of their own desires and decisions. The sadistic Mother Superior at Longchamp was to
claim that her actions were divinely guided. However, to the
reader who is not *bien-pensant*, this passage satirizes the whole
notion of divine inspiration.

The problem is put into action when Suzanne herself, torn
between filial love and a natural desire for freedom, asks for
divine guidance. She does not receive the answer which, according to the import of the whole novel, we must think of as the
right one:

> On n'invoque presque jamais la voix du ciel que quand on ne
> sait à quoi se résoudre; et il est rare qu'alors elle ne nous conseille
> pas d'obéir. Ce fut le parti que je pris. 'On veut que je sois religieuse;
> peut-être est-ce aussi la volonté de Dieu. Eh bien! je le serai . . .'
> (p. 255).

This passage, in which Suzanne makes the fateful decision, is
obviously important. Failing an explicit sign from God—which
she, being honest, does not claim to have received—she follows
what she has been taught is usually the right course: obedience.
Such a course, as the rest of the novel proclaims, is wrong and
unnatural. Surely in this incident Diderot is inviting an unfavourable judgment on a religion, or an institution, which
makes a virtue of obedience even in situations where justice or
man's natural rights should call for resistance and opposition?

A similar interpretation can be given to Suzanne's lyrical
outburst beginning: 'Ce fut alors que je sentis la supériorité de

la religion chrétienne sur toutes les religions du monde' (p. 301). A religion of suffering, sacrifice and resignation is the only one which can comfort Suzanne when she is a victim of cruelty and hatred. But, the novel implies, she should never have been required to undergo such trials. Her resignation and forbearance in the face of such cruelties, carried out in the name of that very religion, may be superb and admirable but are also misguided.

The preceding interpretations are not put forward dogmatically as 'what Diderot meant' in these and similar passages. They are intended to suggest, first, that Diderot did not necessarily espouse Suzanne's views so completely as to forget his own. Secondly, they should remind us that what a given reader understands from a work, or from certain parts of it, may depend on the ideas and feelings he brings to it. To an agnostic or a Protestant, *La Religieuse* may offer certain implications that would not strike a Catholic. Similarly, the reader who is acquainted with Diderot's own ideas may be more apt to see concealed criticism than the person who takes up the novel without knowing much about the author. And thirdly, it must surely be admitted that Diderot's argument or moral lesson is in itself more complex, and in its presentation more subtle, than any of Richardson's. Some of the major issues concerning religion and the Church are raised for our consideration in *La Religieuse*, and if the answers are not spelt out for us, it is because Diderot usually effaces himself in favour of Suzanne, so that only momentarily do we glimpse the *philosophe* behind the nun.

If we go on from the end of the novel to read the *Préface-Annexe*, as Diderot would wish us to do, we find that the moral issues which run through the memoirs are scarcely touched upon here. Diderot had, it seems to me, two main reasons for wanting the *Préface-Annexe* to be linked to Suzanne's memoirs. One was the fact that in the letters supposedly written by Mme Madin we are shown Suzanne's last moments, so that her life-story is completed in a way which is obviously impossible in a straightforward memoir-novel. Various details of this apparent sequel are however still at odds with the main narrative, even after Diderot's revision of the *Préface-Annexe*.[1] For instance,

[1] For a discussion of this revision, together with a reproduction of Diderot's alterations and a fair copy of the amended text, see Herbert

Suzanne is younger than ever—'à peine dix-neuf ans accomplis'—and she is staying with Mme Madin, while at the end of the memoirs she writes to M. de Croismare from the house of a *blanchisseuse*. It seems therefore that Diderot did not devote much time or care to the business of making the *Préface-Annexe* combine coherently with Suzanne's memoirs.

Even more important to Diderot than the concluding of the main story was the question of how the character of Suzanne came to be created, as well as the nature of the aesthetic problems involved in its presentation. As Parrish puts it (p. 21): 'Il n'est pas exagéré de dire que l'intention de Diderot fut de laisser à sa *Préface-Annexe* le soin de fournir au lecteur une solution aux problèmes narratifs et esthétiques posés par le roman.'

The *Préface-Annexe* is a curious amalgam. The fictitious letters from Suzanne and Mme Madin, with their supposedly authentic answers from Croismare, are set in a narrative framework which was probably written by Grimm, with occasional comments inserted at a later stage by Diderot himself. In theory, this narrative lets the reader into the secret of how and why the fictitious personage of the nun was first invented.[1] Here Diderot seems deliberately to flout current ideas about illusion, and some of his first readers thought that the immediate effect of such an explanation would be to destroy the reader's belief. Diderot's editor Naigeon, for instance, objected to the publishing of the *Préface-Annexe* on these grounds. He says, in his long-winded way:

S'il est vrai, comme on n'en peut douter, que dans tous nos plaisirs, même les plus délicieux et les plus substantiels, si j'ose

Dieckmann, 'The Préface-Annexe of La Religieuse', *Diderot Studies II*, ed. O. E. Fellows and N. L. Torrey, Syracuse, 1952, pp. 21–147; see also the critical edition of *La Religieuse* prepared by J. Parrish, Geneva, 1963, p. 27 (Studies on Voltaire and the eighteenth century, Vol. XXII).

Most editions of *La Religieuse* follow the Assézat-Tourneux text of the *Préface-Annexe*, which retains the passages Diderot deleted, and thus creates additional inconsistencies. The 1961 *Bibliothèque de Cluny* edition is the only one, to my knowledge, which has so far given the *Préface-Annexe* as Diderot meant it to appear.

[1] For some queries as to the reliability of this account, see my article, 'Truth and illusion in the *Préface-Annexe* to Diderot's *La Religieuse*', *Modern Language Review*, LVII (1962), pp. 350–6.

m'exprimer ainsi, il entre toujours un peu d'illusion, s'ils se pro-
longent et s'accroissent même pour nous, en raison de la force et de
la durée de ce prestige enchanteur; en nous l'ôtant, on détruit en
nous une source féconde de jouissances diverses, et peut-être même
une des causes les plus actives de notre bonheur.

Je persiste à croire que, lues avant ou après le drame dont elles
sont la fable, [ces lettres] en affaiblissent également l'intérêt, et lui
font perdre ce caractère de vérité si difficile à saisir dans tous les arts
d'imitation, et qui distingue particulièrement cet ouvrage de
Diderot.[1]

By this verdict Naigeon shows that he held the over-simplified
view of literary illusion accepted by most of his contemporaries.
'Illusion' is seen as a kind of trap: the reader must be caught
and held in this, and if once he escapes, he is gone for ever. This
view also implicitly equates imaginative belief with literal belief; if once we discover that what we thought to be a 'fact' is
untrue, then we cease to trust our author.

As we have seen, however, Diderot was in this respect in
advance of the accepted ideas of his time. If, after telling us how
'Suzanne' came into being, he offers us a continuation of her
story, he must surely think that the illusion can be renewed,
and that in the *Préface-Annexe* the reader can still, or once more,
'believe in' this character. He has therefore realized the fluc-
tuating nature of imaginative belief, its possibilities of dis-
appearance and revival. By the juxtaposition of these various
elements of truth and fiction, authenticity and pretence, he
might even be setting himself, and us, a challenge: if I show you
on the one hand the real-life trick, and on the other hand the
story it produced, can you still be made to believe in Suzanne
and her touching end?

The girl we meet in this appendix is obviously only the first
sketch of the character which Diderot developed and enriched
in the life-story. To this extent the *Préface-Annexe* may weaken
the impression left on us by the novel. But if Diderot has successfully enlisted our belief in the Suzanne of the memoirs—and
with many readers he certainly achieves this success—then he
may still hold our interest in the fate of this weaker shadowier
first Suzanne. And we shall be able, in that case, to give the

[1] Quoted in the Assézat-Tourneux edition of Diderot's works, Vol. V,
pp. 206–7. (The complete text of Naigeon's preface is provided here.)

'right' answer to Diderot's concluding question: should the story-teller aim at beauty or seeming-truth? Should he arouse our admiration, or win belief?

Whatever the complications which *La Religieuse* and its *Préface-Annexe* may provide, this work is simplicity itself beside *Jacques le Fataliste et son Maître*. The latter can be seen as a combination of *roman, anti-roman* and *conte philosophique*. The nature and extent of Diderot's contribution to the *conte*, as a minor genre, is a subject which falls outside our discussion, and there will be no attempt here to evaluate the philosophical implications of *Jacques*. Instead we shall consider the work for the information it can provide about Diderot's literary theory and technique. And since the complexity of the book arises largely from an interweaving of several elements, our first task must be the teasing out of these various strands, so that we can distinguish the elements which Diderot chose to combine.

There is, first, a background situation which constitutes a kind of setting for the whole work. This is the dialogue between the fictional narrator and the reader, which is established in the first paragraph. The primary *Je* of the novel is the story-teller, who comments on the business of story-telling and addresses his reader on this and other topics. This was no innovation. Cervantes, Congreve, Marivaux and Sterne are only the most distinguished names in a long line of authors who made their narrators discuss the art of fiction in the intervals of relating the story.[1] For none of these writers, however, does the narrator-reader relationship play so vital a rôle as in *Jacques le Fataliste*.

Both the narrator and the fictional reader who questions and argues with him have certain well-defined traits of character. The narrator is, for the most part, domineering and intransigent, scornful of the reader and sure of his own rightness. He usually implies, and occasionally says outright, that the reader's questions are irrelevant and wrong-headed. He makes fun of what the reader expects to happen, and deliberately flouts these expectations. The reader is a more shadowy figure, although he does succeed once or twice, by sheer persistence, in obtaining what he wants, such as the tale of 'le poète de Pondichéry' (p. 527). Generally, however, the narrator insists on his own

[1] See Wayne C. Booth, 'The self-conscious narrator in comic fiction'.

right to mould the story as he pleases. The repeated use of remarks like: 'Il ne tiendrait qu'à moi de vous faire attendre . . .' emphasizes that it is he who chooses and shapes the events. Yet there is, apparently, one factor which supersedes the narrator's freedom of choice: truth itself.

Vous allez croire que cette petite armée tombera sur Jacques et son maître, qu'il y aura une action sanglante, des coups de bâton donnés, des coups de pistolet tirés; et il ne tiendrait qu'à moi que tout cela n'arrivât; mais adieu la vérité de l'histoire, adieu le récit des amours de Jacques (p. 505).

One might draw a neat parellel here with the fatalism which provides the philosophic theme of the book: the narrator thinks he is free to invent, but his liberty is limited by truth, by the unconquerable fact, so that he does not enjoy complete freedom of choice.[1] This however means taking the remarks about truth at their face-value, which may be an error. It seems to me much more likely that the narrator's frequent appeals to 'truth' are part of Diderot's attack on what the reader thinks a novel should be and do. Thus the repeated assurances that this is no mere novel are a mocking echo of the claims so widespread among novels of the time. Or else the narrator, after blaming *le mensonge*, slips in a clause which slyly restores his right to invent:

Vous voyez lecteur, combien je suis indulgent; il ne tiendrait qu'à moi . . . d'interrompre l'histoire du capitaine de Jacques et de vous impatienter à mon aise; mais pour cela il faudrait mentir, et je n'aime pas le mensonge, à moins qu'il ne soit utile et forcé (p. 551).

Elsewhere the status of 'truth' in story-telling is reduced by the 'fact' that the same adventure happened to two different people on different occasions, or that there are three possible endings to Jacques's own story. The narrator's claim that he respects the truth is therefore one aspect of Diderot's satire of the contemporary novel, with its pretensions to authenticity.

The plot of *Jacques le Fataliste*, which is a first element to be set against the narrator-reader background, is another aspect of

[1] For a further discussion of Diderot's remarks on truth in this work, see Alice G. Green, 'Diderot's fictional worlds', *Diderot Studies*, ed. O. E. Fellows and N. L. Torrey, Syracuse, 1949, pp. 20–2.

this satire. By 'plot', I here mean the account of the actions and adventures of Jacques and the Master, as distinct from their conversations. This narrative covers their travels and the events of the journey, and it is in this sequence of events that the narrator most often claims and exercises his right to tell the story as he wishes. He wilfully refuses, for instance, to provide realistic details in terms of place and time. The travellers spend their first night in the fields, and this is followed by another in 'la plus misérable des auberges'. Their next resting-place is apparently an allegorical château, but the narrator later 'remembers' that they really stayed with the Lieutenant-General of Conches. After Jacques's return to Conches to recover the purse and his master's watch, the two men meet and go on again together. At the end of the book they are separated again, and brought together by chance so that they can settle down for good.

This journey, with its slender motivation, its coincidences and final chance re-union, is a parody of a whole class of novels. The type goes back as far as the mid-seventeenth-century heroic novel and comes down to the time of Prévost. The plot of *Cleveland*, for instance, is built on journeys, separations and lovers' meetings. This kind of novel was no longer being written in 1773, when *Jacques le Fataliste* began to take shape; but Prévost was still being read, and some of the early heroic novels were re-published, even though in shortened form, during the eighteenth century. Diderot's target was therefore not wholly out of date.

Moreover in his use of this fantastic-journey framework Diderot was following, not attacking, another convention, that of the philosophic tale. Stories like *Zadig* and *Candide* were in the tradition of the *voyage imaginaire* and the Oriental travel-tale, as well as themselves being parodies of novels. Such a framework was therefore a familiar device for presenting a philosophic discussion in the form of fiction.

Apart from the narrator-reader dialogue, and the basic plot covering the events of the journey, we have a running debate between Jacques and his master on the question of fatalism.[1] 'Tout est écrit là-haut' develops into a catch-word comparable

---

[1] For a discussion of the distinctions to be drawn between fatalism and determinism, see O. E. Fellows and A. G. Green, 'Diderot and the Abbé Dulaurens', *Diderot Studies*, pp. 76–81.

to Candide's 'best of all possible worlds', and is shown to be equally questionable in its application to human behaviour. There is an entertaining touch of paradox in the way Diderot presents his case. It is the master, an 'automate' whose actions are predictable, who attacks fatalism; and Jacques, the quick-silver creature of initiative and impulse, is the one who maintains that all our actions and all their consequences are pre-determined.[1] In each character there is therefore a neat play of contrast between the beliefs he professes and the kind of be-haviour he usually displays.

As well as their discussion of fatalism, Jacques and his master also pursue, throughout the book, the story of Jacques's love-life. This is the narrative which Jacques undertakes to provide for his master, just as the primary narrator is telling the story of the journey for his fictional reader.

These then are the four elements which run through the whole book: two dialogues, between narrator and reader, be-tween Jacques and his master; two narratives, one about the journey and the other about Jacques's love-affairs. The narrator-reader-journey complex is largely concerned with literary prob-lems, while Jacques, his master and the love-story are used to work out the question of fatalism. But the one constant char-acteristic of this book is that no compartments are watertight; so the narratives mingle, the dialogues flow in and out of each other, Jacques criticizes the portrait as a literary device and the fictional narrator wonders whether we ever do decide for our-selves where we are going. No part of the book is neat, static, self-contained and predictable.

Into this four-fold tale comes, at intervals, a fifth type of in-terruption: the interpolated story. The narrator, the hostess of the inn, the Marquis des Arcis, the master himself, all break into the progress of the already complicated flow of narrative and dialogue. However, it may be misleading to speak of inter-ruptions or interpolations. The tales and anecdotes are not simply strewn along the book, as were the stories in *Gil Blas*, like so many beads on a string, distinct and detachable. Instead, these stories are woven into the stuff of the book. The longest of

[1] Cf. Georges May, 'Le Maître, la chaîne et le chien dans *Jacques le Fataliste*', *Cahiers de l'Association Internationale des Etudes Françaises*, no. 13, p. 280.

them, the tale of Mme de la Pommeraye, is broken up in its opening pages by all the distractions that go with life in a crowded hostelry. And even as it moves to its climax, the hostess never manages more than a few pages without some comment or discussion from her listeners. Diderot has shown, once for all, that a story by a subsidiary narrator *can* become an integral part of the larger work. Indeed, from the way these incidental stories are blended into the main narrative, we can see that Diderot means them to contribute, each in its own fashion, to the philosophical and ethical debate of the work as a whole.[1]

On the literary level he has also shown that the writer can blend the different kinds of fiction. If we follow his own classification, then a good deal of the plot of *Jacques le Fataliste* belongs to the *conte plaisant*. There are a number of passages where the narrator is 'gai, ingénieux, varié, original, même extravagant', and thus distracts our attention from 'l'invraisemblance du fond'. Certain episodes, however, like the majority of the interpolated tales and anecdotes, obey the rules of the *conte historique*; they are detailed, realistic, credible to a degree. And in the case of Mme de la Pommeraye, with her greatness in evil, one might even be tempted to see Diderot's third category, the 'larger-than-life' story.[2]

In his theoretical writings on drama, Diderot explicitly opposed the mixing of different genres. One might create new genres, filling the intervals along the scale of accepted forms, but these were not to come from a crossing or confusion of different kinds.[3] In fiction, however, he has taken this step by combining stories which use different methods and evoke a different type of response. He has moreover not merely juxtaposed them in contrasting blocks, as the writers of comic novels had done by inserting romantic *nouvelles*, but has shown the possibility of interweaving the farcical and the realistic, the light-hearted and sceptical with the moment of intense feeling. In

[1] See Lester G. Crocker, 'Jacques le Fataliste, an "expérience morale" ', *Diderot Studies III*, pp. 73–99; cf. also, on the unifying effect of recurrent images, Georges May, 'Le Maître, la chaîne et le chien dans *Jacques le Fataliste*'.

[2] Cf. the discussion of exceptional characters in R. Grimsley, 'L'Ambiguïté dans l'œuvre romanesque de Diderot', *Cahiers de l'Association Internationale des Etudes Françaises*, no. 13, pp. 223–38.

[3] *Œuvres esthétiques*, p. 138.

practice, therefore, he has gone beyond the constricting notion of genres as he had expounded it for drama in the *Entretiens sur le Fils Naturel*, for fiction in *Les Deux Amis*.

It is difficult to evaluate *Jacques le Fataliste*, because so many factors are involved in our judgment. One may be sure, to begin with, that this work will never attain the popularity of, say, *Manon Lescaut*. Diderot's work is not likely to win the reader's support by the universal appeal of its story. It requires a fair amount of knowledge in the field of literary history before one can see the point of, and be entertained by, its own literary form and the criticism of the novel which it expresses. It calls for a readiness to follow the debate, in dialogue and actions, over moral and philosophical problems. And it also requires a special kind of mental and emotional agility, a coloratura flexibility, as well as a fund of willingness to co-operate with the author and tolerate his waywardness. (One cannot doubt that, however serious the work may be in its fundamental conception, Diderot took some mischievous delight in creating a mixture which would tease and baffle his readers.) It is therefore the kind of book which acquires a small but enthusiastic following, while a larger public sees it as provoking, unmanageable and tedious. There will be some to say, like Saintsbury, that the story of Mme de la Pommeraye should be extracted and told on its own, as being a worthwhile tale spoilt by its setting. If one holds that stories of this kind are the only, or the chief, excellence of fiction, then such a view becomes defensible. If, on the other hand, one concurs with Diderot in thinking that fiction may have other ways of contributing to our pleasure or enlightenment, then one will be more ready to accept *Jacques le Fataliste* as a whole.

We need not, even then, set it up as a masterpiece without flaws. There are still debatable aspects of execution, including some practical inconsistencies in the realistic passages which not even the whim of the story-teller can excuse. But for originality it stands high, for variety of thought and emotion it deserves admiration, and for sheer verve, for the presentation of a work of art as creative play, it would be difficult to surpass.

There is yet another kind of problem for the critic who attempts a general evaluation of Diderot's fictional works. How can one produce a judgment that will cover a pornographic tale such as *Les Bijoux indiscrets*, a *roman à thèse* like *La Religieuse*, the unclassifiable mixture which is *Jacques*, the various dialogues with fictional frameworks like *Le Neveu de Rameau* and, finally, the late *contes*? Variety and experiment are the key-note. Freedom of form and tone, disregard for tradition, are the traits most likely to strike the reader who studies and compares them all. And yet the best of these works, considered as fiction, is the story in which Diderot accepted and put into practice, however imperfectly, the established narrative convention of his time. The memoirs of Suzanne remain, to my mind, Diderot's chief title to be considered as one of the major figures in eighteenth-century fiction.

XII

Restif de la Bretonne and Laclos

THE CULMINATION OF THE LETTER-NOVEL

THE increase in the vogue of the letter-novel in France was probably due, for the most part, to the popular success achieved by both Richardson and Rousseau in this form. It is scarcely possible to assess the relative importance of the two authors in this development, since they resemble each other in several respects, such as their sentimental tone and obvious didacticism, and since the generous use of realistic detail which was Richardson's most distinctive trait was greatly reduced in the early French translations of his works.[1] Whatever the immediate cause, in the years following the publication of *La Nouvelle Héloïse*, there was a marked rise in the use of letters as a narrative form in the novel. From Black's lists of epistolary novels, it appears that 1781–1790 was the decade when the fashion reached its height in England.[2] If one takes translations into account, as Black does, then much the same picture emerges for the production of new letter-novels in France.[3]

It should however be remembered that a considerable number of memoir-novels were still being written and published. Unfortunately there are hardly any works of real interest or merit among them. One or two, such as Louvet de Couvray's *Aventures du chevalier de Faublas* (1787–90), do occasionally achieve a mention in histories of literature, but usually for non-literary

[1] See F. H. Wilcox, *Prévost's translations of Richardson's Novels*.

[2] F. G. Black, *The Epistolary Novel in the late eighteenth century*, Oregon, 1940. The totals for the four decades 1761–1800 are: 112, 146, 191, 143.

[3] Using the figures in the Martin, Mylne and Frautschi *Bibliographie romanesque* (pp. xlvi-xlvii) we can calculate the numbers of new letter-novels as a percentage of the total output of fiction. If translations are included, the figures for the four decades are: 13·1, 17·6, 22·2, 11·2. Excluding translations however, the results show a slightly different pattern: 11·8, 19, 18, 10·5. Re-editions of letter-novels, expressed as a percentage of all re-editions, suggest a more rapid decline in popularity after 1790: 18, 16·8, 19·1, 7·2.

reasons—in this case for the novel's *succès de scandale* and its fortuitous likeness in many ways to the later *Mémoires* of Casanova.

The familiar memoir-form was therefore not abandoned, but one can see indications of the letter-novel's growing prestige in titles such as Mme de Saint-Aubin's *Mémoires en forme de lettres de deux jeunes personnes de qualité* (1765), or Mme d'Arconville's *L'Amour éprouvé par la mort* (1763), which was later re-issued as *Lettres de M. de Norville à Mme de Mirevaux* (1775). Authors and publishers were coming to consider the word *lettres* in a title as a potential attraction for readers.

As one might expect, a large proportion of letter-novels were cast in that form merely because of the current fashion, and not because their story could most effectively be unfolded by this method. Works of this kind seem affected as well as tedious, and impatience or annoyance may be the liveliest reaction they arouse in a modern reader.

There are a handful of exceptions. Of Mme Riccoboni's eight novels, six were in epistolary form and exploited the medium quite effectively. Her plots, if not always very plausible, do tend to avoid sensational events. The interest of the novel lies usually in the emotional vicissitudes of the introspective heroine: 'Le drame intérieur est infiniment plus important que les événements extérieurs.'[1] Mme Riccoboni's first novel, *Lettres de Mistriss Fanni Butlerd* (1757), had preceded Rousseau's success in this type of story, and her later works followed a similar pattern. For the modern reader there is a certain effect of monotony, but they won a good deal of favourable comment in their day. Stendhal recommended Mme Riccoboni's novels to his sister, with the admiring phrase: 'Cela remue l'âme.'

Another work which was widely admired, and swiftly ran into several editions, is *Les Lettres du marquis de Roselle* (1764) by Mme Elie de Beaumont.[2] The story concerns Léonor, a *fille d'Opéra*, who almost manages to get the twenty-year-old Marquis to marry her, but whose machinations are foiled at the last moment. The Marquis then meets and marries a virtuous young

[1] Emily A. Crosby, *Une Romancière oubliée, Mme Riccoboni*, Paris, 1924, p. 73. See also Joan H. Stewart, *The Novels of Mme Riccoboni*, Chapel Hill, 1974, pp. 120–21; and her edition of *Lettres de Mistriss Fanni Butlerd*, 1979.

[2] Not, as is sometimes stated, Mme Leprince de Beaumont.

woman who truly loves him, while Léonor, repenting of her sin, enters a convent.

Apart from the conventional ideas on virtue and morality which arise from this plot, Mme de Beaumont has a good deal to say on the habit of placing girls in convents to be educated and then arranging for them to be married almost as soon as they leave the convent. She maintains that this kind of schooling is no preparation for marriage, and illustrates her thesis by showing how bored the Marquis is in the company of various young ladies who have been educated in this way. Mlle de Ferval, whom he marries, is more lively, natural and virtuous because she has been brought up at home, with her two sisters, by their mother.

There is nothing particularly original about this argument, or indeed about the general outline of the plot. However, Mme de Beaumont has some skill as a story-teller, and does utilize the resources of her chosen form. Léonor, for instance, appears to us first through her letters to the Marquis, and seems to be more virtuous and charitable than her calling might lead one to expect. Valville, the unprincipled friend who is leading the Marquis into evil ways, does not trust Léonor and accuses her of hypocrisy. But since the reader does not trust Valville either, there is an element of uncertainty in the situation. Can it be that Léonor really deserves Roselle's devotion? She has, it appears, sold her diamonds to help 'une famille honnête et pauvre'. Surely such an *acte de bienfaisance* vouches for her fundamental goodness of heart? Our doubts are resolved in Letter 36, where we learn that Léonor arranged for a forged letter, containing a proposal of marriage, to arrive while the Marquis was with her, so as to provoke his jealousy and push him into making a proposal himself. However, the ambiguity up to this point stimulates the reader's interest.

Léonor's supposed act of charity reminds one, of course, of Valmont's similar artifice in *Les Liaisons dangereuses*. Léonor is a *fausse sensible*, pretending to have the ready sympathy and generosity that go with a tender heart. Since sensibility had for many people come to be a sign of virtue, it was inevitable that hypocrites and intriguers should put on a mask of sensibility to achieve their own ends. For the late eighteenth century this is the equivalent of the *faux dévot* of earlier generations, and illustrates the widespread divorce between religion and morality.

The second half of the book is overweighted by Mme de Beaumont's educational theory. This is worked into the letters without much finesse: a minor character simply reports two long conversations in which Mme de Ferval outlines the principles on which her daughters have been brought up. The style of these discussions is however pleasantly unpedantic. Here is Mme de Ferval explaining why she does not allow her daughters to read novels:

> Les romans sont les plus dangereuses des lectures pour les jeunes personnes. Elles se disent à chaque page: c'est moi, me voilà. Bientôt elles diront du premier jeune homme qu'elles verront: c'est lui, c'est Lindor, c'est Léandre (*Lettre* 97).

The only exceptions to this rule are a few English novels, chiefly, of course, those of Richardson. The eldest daughter is just reading *Clarisse* and acquiring from it 'ses premières idées de l'amour'.

One would not be justified in suggesting that *Les Lettres du marquis de Roselle* is a neglected masterpiece. It serves however to illustrate the fact that by the mid-sixties of the century even a writer of no formidable talent or originality could produce a novel which effectively utilized many of the resources of the letter-form. Judged by the sole criterion of narrative skill, indeed, this work might well be considered superior to *La Nouvelle Héloïse*. Mme de Beaumont's range of ideas is of course more limited than Rousseau's, but she deserved her contemporary popularity and might, I think, have been treated a shade more generously by later critics and literary historians.

Restif de la Bretonne, on the other hand, possessed a talent which has in some quarters been exaggerated. He was, admittedly, a man of wide-ranging interests and abilities, but in his novels he is often not at his best. What that best was, can be seen in the idealized biography, *La Vie de mon Père*, and in the vast series of anecdotes and character-sketches which appeared in collections like *Les Nuits de Paris*, *Les Contemporaines* and *L'Année des Dames Nationales*.[1] These provide a wealth of in-

---

[1] There have been several modern editions of selections from *Les Nuits*. The one prepared by Henri Bachelin (Livre Club du Libraire, 1960) con-

formation about contemporary life in Paris, particularly among
the lower classes. They have no parallel at the period and are
invaluable to the social historian. Most of them, moreover, are
written in the simple, vivid style which Restif brought to subject-
matter of this kind, and are consistently readable and entertaining. The same cannot be said for the score or so of long
narrative works he produced. He had many of the weaknesses
of his period, and some additional ones peculiar to himself.

Before we attempt to assess his merits as a novelist, it may be
as well to clarify Restif's ideas and practice concerning 'truth'.
Restif habitually insisted that his novels were true stories; *Le
Paysan perverti*, for instance, is described on the title-page as
'Histoire récente, mise au jour d'après les véritables lettres des
personnages'. Such claims, as we have seen, are so commonplace in eighteenth-century novels that they hardly seem to
require special comment. The case of Restif is different, however, in that there was some foundation for his assertions: the
majority of his *romans*, and all those which modern critics consider worth discussion, have some basis in the incidents of his
own life. But we cannot on this account accept them as mere
instalments of his autobiography. Restif's remarks on the incep-
tion of *Le Paysan perverti* show that he combined his own adventures with other factual anecdotes to produce an amalgam
which he still felt justified in calling *vrai*. In his autobiography, *Monsieur Nicolas* (1794–97), he describes this process:

> Je fis ces premières lettres avec un plaisir infini, parce qu'en
> parlant de mon héros, je racontai les aventures de ma jeunesse. . . .
> On a vu, par ces *Mémoires*, que ce sont les mêmes personnages qui
> agissent ici, et dans le *Paysan perverti*. Je ne me contentai pas de ces
> allusions: pour donner à mon livre ce fond de vérité dont je m'étais
> fait un devoir, . . . je donnai à mon *Paysan perverti* les aventures de
> Borne, le Procureur du Roi des Eaux-et-forêts, et je les amalgamai
> au revers des miennes et de celles de quelques autres jeunes gens que
> le séjour de la capitale avait perdus. Une histoire terrible d'un jeune
> homme qui, s'étant déshonoré, n'osa plus se montrer et n'errait que
> la nuit, vint à mon secours pour achever celle du malheureux
> Edmond. Ainsi ce personnage romantique est un composé de

---

tains a reliable bibliography of Restif's works, and a discussion on the alternative spellings: *Rétif* or *Restif* (p. 11). I follow M. Bachelin in adopting
the form which the novelist used from 1791 onwards.

vérités, dont ma propre vie a fourni la moitié des détails, et le reste, non moins vrai, je l'ai pris à d'autres. Je me disais, en écrivant, Il ne faut pas mentir! Qui n'écrit que des mensonges, s'avilit soi-même.[1]

This method is somewhat reminiscent of Courtilz de Sandras's pseudo-memoirs, in which the account of a real person's adventures was embellished with anecdotes from other sources. To this extent Restif's procedure could be called old-fashioned. His originality lies in the use of his own experience as basic material. One could cite Hélisenne de Crenne and Tristan l'Hermite as predecessors. But it would still be true to say that no writer before Restif had so fully and systematically exploited the events of his own life as a starting-point for his novels.

Yet there is at least one work in which Restif's romancing of his facts is less creditable, and throws fresh light on his procedure in the novels. *Monsieur Nicolas* begins with a grandiloquent assurance of good faith:

Ami de la vérité, ne crains pas de lire! Tu ne seras ni séduit par du clinquant, ni trompé par les faits. J'ai assez composé de romans dont les bases vraies n'excluaient pas l'imagination: j'ai soif de la vérité pure, et c'est elle que je te donne, parce qu'elle seule peut être utile dans cet ouvrage.

Unfortunately his promise of 'truth' here is no more reliable than in the prefaces of his novels. In a number of cases where verification is possible from other sources, it has been shown that Restif adapted and embroidered his life-story with a novelist's disregard for mere factual veracity.[2] Generally speaking these changes and inventions show him in a flattering light, whether they concern the company he kept, his sexual prowess, or the nobility of his character. Indeed, he evinced such an aptitude for twisting the facts to suit his fancy that one may well become sceptical about his ability to record the literal truth concerning any event which touched him personally.

To the modern reader, however, what matters is obviously not the fidelity to fact of Restif's stories, but their power to carry conviction. With this in mind we shall examine the novel which Restif preferred among his own works, and which he described

---

[1] 'Mes Ouvrages', in *Monsieur Nicolas*, VIII, 4578–9.
[2] See Marc Chadourne, *Restif de la Bretonne ou le siècle prophétique*, Paris, 1958, pp. 124–32.

as 'peut-être la plus utile production qu'on ait mise au jour depuis le commencement du siècle'. (Excessive modesty was not one of Restif's failings.)

Le Paysan perverti, ou les Dangers de la ville was begun in 1769 and published in 1775. It tells the story of the gradual corruption of Edmond and of his sister Ursule. In 1784 Restif published a separate, expanded version of Ursule's adventures, *La Paysanne pervertie*. And three years later he brought out a conflation of the two works, *Le Paysan et la paysanne pervertis*. Since the careers of Edmond and Ursule are often interwoven, it was a logical enough step to combine them. (Indeed, *La Paysanne* is not wholly satisfactory if read in isolation, as it frequently refers back to *Le Paysan*.)[1] The process was not difficult; Restif had only to insert the letters constituting Ursule's story at the appropriate moments in the course of *Le Paysan*. He did however revise the complete work, making some alterations in the rôle of the corruptor, Gaudet d'Arras, and adding about forty fresh letters. The final version comprises 462 letters, as well as a ballad of 56 stanzas, *Complainte du Paysan et de la Paysanne*, and the Statutes for the setting up and maintenance of an ideal village, to be run on communal lines.

It is not easy to convey an adequate impression of so large and uneven a work as *Le Paysan et la paysanne pervertis*. For the obvious first step, an outline of the plot, we can scarcely do better than consider the summary which Restif himself provided in the 1776 edition of *Le Paysan*.[2] The chief incidents of the eight parts are outlined as follows:

I: Edmond, ou le Paysan, arrive à la ville et il y éprouve des

---

[1] Restif followed this procedure elsewhere. In *Ingénue Saxencour*, for instance, which describes the marital sufferings of one of his daughters, he discusses a letter for whose text the reader is referred to *La Femme infidèle*, an account of his own wife's misdeeds. These links between separate works, and the way that characters appear in more than one *roman*, can be seen as a foreshadowing of Balzac's *retour des personnages*, though Restif's reasons for, and handling of, the device are of course quite different.

[2] I quote from the authentic 1776 edition, 'Imprimé à La Haye, et se trouve à Paris, Chez la Veuve Duchesne . . .' Another edition, also dated 1776, 'Imprimé à La Haie, et se trouve à Paris, Chés Esprit . . .', dates in reality from 1784, and contains references, in footnotes, to *La Paysanne*. The later edition contains some passages which were previously censored, so that the mis-dating may cover an attempt to assimilate the two editions.

désagréments qui ne tardent pas à cesser. Les corrupteurs commencent à s'emparer de lui, et ses passions les secondent à merveilles.

II: Le peintre, maître d'Edmond, lui fait épouser une fille qu'il avait séduite. Les corrupteurs tâchent de détruire dans le jeune paysan toute idée d'honnêteté, qu'ils nomment 'préjugés de village'. Edmond, déjà corrompu, séduit une jeune fille nommée Laurette. Sa femme en meurt de jalousie.

III: Les corrupteurs, et surtout un M. Gaudet, endoctrinent Edmond, en abusant des vérités de la physique. Edmond est amoureux de la femme de son maître, qui est vertueuse, et il ose abuser de la bonté de cette dame pour lui déclarer sa passion. Il a une aventure avec une coquette, et donne à son frère une fille qu'il a aimée. Il fait violence à la femme de son maître.

IV: Edmond va à Paris, pour secourir sa sœur qu'un marquis a enlevée. Il se bat avec le ravisseur. Il se corrompt au point de consentir que ce seigneur, dont il aime la femme, entretienne sa sœur.

V: Edmond et sa sœur donnent dans la plus crapuleuse débauche.

VI: Edmond veut se faire comédien, auteur, et cet. Sa sœur change. Il épouse une vieille par intérêt, et il est accusé de l'avoir empoisonnée: étrange catastrophe.

VII: Edmond est condamné aux galères; ses parents meurent de douleur. Il en sort et se punit de ses crimes en désespéré. Il tue sa sœur.

VIII: Mort d'Edmond. Moyens pris dans sa famille pour éviter de pareils malheurs.

This summary gives a fair idea of the general progress of the plot though it omits, inevitably, a number of the more sensational incidents. We must now ask how this plot is handled, whether the events are plausibly linked and convincingly presented.

Judged by the standards of causation and internal logic which we saw Diderot advocating, Restif's plot-structure is weak. He has obviously tried to make events depend upon personality rather than outside causes, but this means, among other things, that the wicked characters engage in intrigues and machinations which render the story-line more complicated and less plausible. And in these intrigues, as elsewhere, there is a lavish use of coincidence, eavesdropping, disguises, chance meetings and the like.

As for the narrative method chosen to convey these events,

Restif often handles the letter-form in a clumsy and implausible fashion. The motivation of the letters may be inadequate; here is Gaudet supplying a typical pretext for sending to Ursule some disquisitions on religion and morals:

> Je suis en commerce de lettres avec votre frère, mademoiselle; et quoique nous soyons dans la même ville, nous traitons par écrit. Comme votre situation présente vous prive de tous les divertisse-ments et de tous les plaisirs, je pense que la lecture de notre corre-spondance vous distraira et pourra vous instruire (*Paysan et paysanne, Lettre* 151).

Sometimes it is the way that letters are preserved and passed on which strains belief. Mme Parangon discovers her husband's liaison and his plot to trick Edmond into marriage when she reads two *billets* which were used, 'par hasard', in the packing of some baskets of fruit and game sent to her in Paris. From all this it is not unfair to conclude that Restif's choice and handling of events is often crude and unrealistic.

There are however some ways in which the story is made more convincing. Chief among these is the range of styles in the letters of the various correspondents. Restif himself asserts that the different styles are so distinctive that 'si on n'avait pas mis aux lettres le nom des personnages, on les reconnaîtrait dès le premier mot' (*M. Nicolas*, p. 4977). As usual, his self-praise is exaggerated but has some foundation. The letters of Edmond and Ursule, in particular, show an interesting development from an initial naïve 'peasant' style to a more sophisticated and literary mode of expression. Of the two styles, the latter is generally less attractive. Edmond, one feels, has altered for the worse in taste as well as morals when, after only ten months of town-life, he can begin a letter to his brother as follows: 'Dans un violent orage, mon cher aîné, les branches des noyers plantés sur la cime d'un tertre sont moins agitées que mon esprit et mon cœur' (*Lettre* 29).

One of Restif's principal contributions to the novel as a genre is the importance he gives to simple uneducated characters whose language effectively suggests their status and background. In this he goes far beyond Marivaux, whose vulgar characters fill only minor rôles, and whose realism of speech is limited. Restif devotes considerable space to his peasants: many of

Edmond's letters are addressed to, and answered by, his brother Pierre, who has remained on the farm. And he takes pains to convey not merely the naïve tone but also the regional accents of such personages. Ursule, describing the ways of village wooing, cites a typical snatch of dialogue:

> — Où qu'vou alez donc, Jeanne?
> — Donner de la paille à nos vaches.
> — J'vas donc vou ainder?
> — Ça n'est pas de refus, Jaquot (*Lettre* 36).

This was a vein in which Restif delighted. In *Les Contemporaines*, for instance, one finds long passages of narrative or conversation in which he has tried to suggest different types of dialect. There was little precedent for such an interest in regional or uneducated modes of speech.[1] The theatre occasionally exploited a stylized 'peasant' language, as in Collé's *La Partie de chasse de Henri IV*; but this type of dialogue probably owed as much to the tradition of Molière's stage peasants as to first-hand observation. In the novel, likewise, there had appeared a few works utilizing Poissard or other 'vulgar' forms of speech. These however have a self-conscious air, and were generally written by authors whose own idiom from childhood had been that of the educated Parisian. Restif's more intimate acquaintance with the usage of country-folk in his native Yonne valley, combined with an obvious sensitivity to nuances of pronunciation and grammar, give to his rendering of various dialects an effect of far greater authenticity.[2]

The other quality which lifts Restif above the ruck of eighteenth-century novelists is the sheer force and vigour of his work. With this strength goes a lack of subtlety and a tendency to melodrama which may irk the modern reader. Yet in certain scenes and with some characters he achieves a memorable intensity. As an example of this mixture of failings and merits one may cite a passage from a letter which Restif himself thought one of his best. Pierre's wife, Fanchon, describes how the news

[1] See my article, 'Social realism in the dialogue of eighteenth-century French fiction', *Studies in Eighteenth-Century Culture*, Vol. 6, 1977, pp. 265–84.

[2] For later developments in realistic lower-class dialogue, see the sections on Sand and Balzac in S. Ullmann, *Style in the French Novel*, Cambridge, 1957, pp. 73–93.

of Edmond's condemnation to the galleys is brought to the farm:

Le digne homme allait monter à cheval, quand une chaise a paru à la porte. Le conducteur en a tiré Ursule, mourante, qui est venue s'évanouir aux pieds de ses père et mère. On l'a fait revenir, mais elle était en délire.
— Mon frère! s'écriait-elle, mon frère, mon pauvre frère! . . . Ne voyez-vous pas ses chaînes? . . . Il traîne ses chaînes!
Notre bonne mère lui a dit: O ma pauvre fille, où est-il, ton frère?
— Aux galères.
A ce mot notre père a frémi: Monsieur Loiseau? . . . Il n'a pas achevé. Le bon M. Loiseau a baissé la vue. Notre père a regardé tous ses enfants, l'œil sec, mais pâle, défiguré. Il a tendu la main à notre bonne mère sans parler. Hélas, sa langue était liée pour jamais! Saisi, frappé, comme s'il eût reçu le coup mortel, il n'a plus ouvert la bouche. Il est tombé sur une chaise; il a couvert son front de sa main; il a poussé un seul et douloureux soupir; il est devenu froid, raide; son cœur battait encore. Mon mari l'a voulu soulever. Il était mort (*Lettre* 375).

Once the interest has shifted from Ursule to the reactions of Edmond's father, the narrative develops a speed and simplicity which are both effective and in keeping with the supposed narrator's character and station.

As for force of personality, it is undoubtedly the corruptor, Gaudet d'Arras, who takes pride of place. This is one of the few characters which Restif altered in the successive stages of the novel. In 1775 we have two characters, M. Gaudet and Le Père d'Arras. Gaudet is the principal agent of Edmond's corruption, and the monk acts chiefly as an assistant and messenger when help is required. After some intermediate changes in *La Paysanne*, the two figures are finally blended into one in the combined version. Le Père Gaudet d'Arras is both a skilled engraver, like the earlier Gaudet, and a Cordelier as was Le Père d'Arras. He gets his vows annulled, having been forced to take them against his will, and joins Edmond in Paris. He shares in and guides the activities of the brother and sister, rescues them more than once from difficulties, and is tried, with Edmond, on a charge of murder. Rather than face execution, he commits suicide. Restif, in his long discussion of the final version of the work, never admits or refers to any change in his conception of the personage.[1] One may gather, however, from some of his comments, that the shifting of the responsibility for Edmond's corruption on to the shoulders of an ex-religious was merely a manifestation of his anti-clerical sentiments:

> C'est dans le cloître, ou dans l'état ecclésiastique seulement, qu'on acquiert, par l'inoccupation, cette profondeur de réflexion et de raisonnement qui produit une logique habituelle qui fait qu'on sent tout, et que rien n'échappe. C'est ce qui rend les moines et les prêtres si dangereux dans la société (*M. Nicolas*, p. 4677).

The character who assumed the rôle of an agent of corruption was a relatively familiar figure in the eighteenth-century novel. Crébillon's Versac and Mme de Beaumont's Valville are two earlier instances of the roué who seeks to convert an innocent young man to his own cynical view of society and its conventions. What Restif particularly stresses is that Gaudet d'Arras acts on principle, and out of affection for Edmond:

> Gaudet d'Arras, pour être un personnage profitable, ne devait être ni un libertin sans principes, ni un ennemi d'Edmond et d'Ursule. Aussi voit-on en lui un homme sans frein, mais par principes; car il admet un frein quand il le croit nécessaire, celui que donnait Epicure à ses disciples. Sa morale est donc celle d'un athée honnête-homme, qui ne connaît dans la nature aucun pouvoir moral supérieur à l'homme (*M. Nicolas*, p. 4677).

We have here a relationship closely resembling that of Vautrin and Eugène in *Le Père Goriot*. Gaudet believes that Edmond will be happier and more prosperous if he can shed his conventional notions about 'virtue', and some of the most tedious letters in the novel are those in which the two discuss Gaudet's 'philosophy'. Gaudet is at his best, however, not when preaching but when planning or executing an intrigue, when acting swiftly to rescue Edmond, or defying their captors when

---

[1] Gaudet d'Arras figures, as a person who influenced Restif's youth, in the body of his memoirs. It seems highly probable that this is another episode which Restif has romanced. Among other suspicious elements we may note that in *Monsieur Nicolas* Restif provides the true names of the real-life people whom he had brought into *Le Paysan*. No such alternative is given for Gaudet d'Arras, and this implies that for this character there was no single model whose real name Restif could supply in his memoirs.

the two are arrested. He is scarcely 'realistic', but like Balzac's great *monomanes* he compels our interest by his single-minded drive and sense of purpose.

Critics have been fascinated by this disturbing figure, and a good deal has been written on Restif's possible models or sources of inspiration for Gaudet.[1] What may be more important than the literary or real-life origins of the character is this very interest he inspires. He overshadows the whole work, and lends his own aura of disinterested villainy to many of the major events. We shall return, with *Les Liaisons dangereuses*, to the problem of using such vivid characters as ostensible warnings against vice. As for *Le Paysan et la paysanne pervertis*, one may conclude that the dominating force of Gaudet d'Arras is one of the book's chief attractions. Without him there would be little enough to redeem the exaggerations, implausibilities, shortcomings of form and style, and the tedious theorizing to which Restif is all too prone.

To turn from Restif's peasants to *Les Liaisons dangereuses* is like moving from chaos to order. This applies particularly to the structure and organization of Laclos's work, which from a technical point of view is undoubtedly the best novel of the eighteenth century. The mechanics of the plot and the effective ordering of the letters show that Laclos, unlike most contemporary novelists, was a literary craftsman of the first order. This practical ability may well be one of the reasons why the book has survived; the modern reader is used to the well-made novel, and Laclos comes up to these standards.

Les Liaisons dangereuses is indeed one of the few novels of the period which have so far attracted close consideration from a technical point of view. Several critics have analysed the structure of the work and Laclos's handling of the epistolary form.[2] There have also been numerous studies which deal with more conventional topics such as characterization, the implications of the plot, etc. Because the technical aspects of

---

[1] See F. C. Green, *Minuet*, pp. 443–6; Armand Bégué, *Etat présent des études sur Rétif de la Bretonne*, Paris, 1948, p. 54, n. 4; M. Chadourne, *Restif de la Bretonne*, p. 87.

[2] The best of these is still, in my view, Jean-Luc Seylaz, *Les Liaisons dangereuses et la création romanesque chez Laclos*, Paris, 1958.

Les Liaisons dangereuses have already been accorded so much attention in critical works, I am here providing only a brief discussion of some of the major issues involved, although the importance of this book in terms of skill and workmanship would warrant our devoting far more space to its varied and manifold merits.[1]

Laclos's practical approach can be seen in several aspects of the novel's construction. Useful, for instance, and making its own small contribution to the story, is his handling of time. The letters are dated and arranged so that the narrative is held within the precise bounds of the passing days and weeks. One may pay only slight attention to these dates (in fact, as Dr Thelander shows, they involve some minor inconsistencies), but they do play their part in fixing the speed of events for us. And occasionally the crossing of two letters in the post, or the specific moment at which a letter is delivered, becomes an element in the plot. Rousseau had not helped the reader with dates; one has to work out the passage of time from remarks in the letters. Both Mme de Beaumont and Restif de la Bretonne did provide this information, so that Laclos's practice had precedents, though it was by no means universal among letter-novelists.

Another, and a more specifically literary, kind of skill is involved in the motivation of the letters. Far too many people in previous letter-novels seem to have composed their missives for no other reason than that supplied by De Rozoi's Cécile: 'Je suis née communicative.' Laclos's letters, by contrast, are always written because circumstances require them. This may be simply a question of good manners: the first letter from Mme de Tourvel is a formal congratulation on the marriage arranged for Cécile. Or it may be some more personal and private affair which prompts the letter, like Mme de Merteuil's request or invitation to Valmont to seduce Cécile.

For the letters which lack pretexts of this kind there are equally plausible reasons, depending on personality as well as circumstance. It is 'natural', for instance, that a young girl like Cécile, transplanted from her convent-school intō adult society, should feel the need to share her impressions. At first, when she has no friends in this new world, Sophie is the only person in

---

[1] See below, Chapter XV, for a discussion of recent trends in the type of criticism which this novel has attracted.

whom she can confide. Once Cécile has learnt to trust Mme de Merteuil, her letters to Sophie become less frequent and finally stop—or are stopped for us by the 'editor'. One might assume that it is also 'natural' for Mme de Merteuil and Valmont, old friends and ex-lovers, to keep in touch by post. But Laclos has supplied more cogent reasons than this. At the practical level there is the question of Cécile's seduction as a means of revenge on Gercourt. Valmont's initial refusal to undertake this project introduces the subject of Mme de Tourvel. From then on, the two of them have a sufficient motive for writing in their debate about the worth of these two possible conquests, but it is plain that deeper interests are also at work. Mme de Merteuil is driven throughout by a desire for power. In all her relationships she seeks to control and manœuvre others. Her letters to Valmont are an expression of this desire, for she is constantly trying to influence him and re-assert her control over his actions. She has to keep writing to him, since it would be an intolerable injury to her pride to accept the fact that she has no say in his decisions. Valmont, the weaker of the two characters, accepts to some extent the view of their 'friendship' which she imposes on him. While frequently asserting his independence, he continues to justify himself in ways that show his reliance on her opinion. He has to write, to try and win her approval. And behind all this, there is a more general reason motivating their exchanges. The chief interest of these two characters is in activities which society will not allow them to boast about in public. Therefore they both need an audience to applaud their finesse, to give their successes the full savour which comes from appreciation by a connoisseur. In every respect, then, the writing of these letters is necessary.

If considerations of character explain how many of the letters come into being, the letters in their turn reveal the personalities of their writers. And Laclos manages this not merely by differences of thought and feeling in their subject-matter, but by differences of style. We have already noticed that Restif de la Bretonne was proud of his skill in differentiating his characters by their individual modes of expression. His effects, however, are not particularly subtle, and lie chiefly in the contrast between 'peasant' language and more conventional educated usage. Laclos is clearly superior in this field.

M. Le Hir, after a detailed analysis of the various characters' linguistic habits, concludes that 'chaque personnage dans le Roman a une langue et un style bien personnels'.[1]

Among these stylistic effects, I would rate the creation of Cécile's individual style as Laclos's most interesting achievement. Several previous writers had tried to suggest the simplicity of the *jeune fille*, or more specifically of the girl straight from a convent education. Generally speaking, however, this naïveté was couched in fluent and appreciably literary language. Laclos's merit lies not only in the vocabulary he attributes to Cécile, but in the syntax and constructions she is made to use. She is, for instance, addicted to the loosely-built sentence made up of statements linked by *et*. This gives her prose a distinctive rhythm which, it seems to me, is one of the most important factors marking off her letters from the more disciplined and formal writing of the mature characters.

The differentiation and portrayal of the characters is carried further, in a way more common among letter-novelists, by the contents of the letters, supplying details of their thoughts and feelings and actions. Mme de Merteuil even provides a long passage of autobiography and self-analysis which helps to explain her present outlook and behaviour, if not the initial causes of her exceptional development (*Lettre* 81).

Laclos thus illustrates the wide variety of uses which letters can serve in a narrative. Their individual style is a vital factor in characterization; they convey the intimate thoughts and feelings of all the actors; they can be used, in memoir-style or like a messenger speech, to relate past events; they can constitute events themselves and take the plot a stage further; they can predict events and thus build up suspense about future developments. Laclos exploits all these possibilities, and the mere fact that he utilizes the correspondence for different purposes in this way introduces a variety of approach which is itself an asset.

Further touches of interest arise from the interplay between the contents of successive letters. There is no need to underline the effects of dramatic irony which run through the whole work. From the second letter onwards, we know that Mme de Merteuil and Valmont are unscrupulous schemers, and we can

[1] Laclos, *Les Liaisons dangereuses*, p. xlviii.

see how the more innocent characters unknowingly play into their hands. Laclos has carried this situation to the further extreme of making Valmont pretend to be an ally of Danceny, just as Mme de Merteuil appears to be the friend of Cécile and her mother. When Cécile wants consolation and advice, it is to Mme de Merteuil that she turns, the woman whom we, the readers, know to be her worst enemy.

On another level, the unprincipled characters themselves sometimes play on their superior knowledge and make their letters ironic by telling the truth in terms which the person receiving the letter is unable to interpret correctly. Mme de Merteuil answers Mme de Volanges's appeal for advice with a two-edged discussion of virtue and expediency, of Danceny's qualities as compared with Gercourt's (*Lettre* 104). Valmont writes to Mme de Tourvel describing in ambiguous terms the night he has spent with Emilie (*Lettre* 48). Apart from their cynical or salacious implications, these letters may be criticized on literary grounds. They seem to degenerate into mere cleverness. The kind of reading they call for, and the interests they satisfy, are not on a par with the wider effects of dramatic irony running through the book as a whole.

More interesting, and again often ironic, are the effects obtained by portraying similar reactions in the letters of different correspondents. Mme de Tourvel's rejection of Valmont's first declaration of love (*Lettre* 26) is followed immediately by Cécile's account of her reactions on receiving Danceny's first note. Cécile does not disguise the fact that she was pleased to learn of his feelings: 'Mais je savais bien que je ne devais pas le lui dire, et je peux bien vous assurer même que je lui ai dit que j'en étais fâchée.' This provides a childish echo to Mme de Tourvel's protest, only a page earlier: 'Je m'en tiens, Monsieur, à vous déclarer que vos sentiments m'offensent, que leur aveu m'outrage . . .', and points to a parallel between the two characters which subsequent events will carry much further. The novel is rich in echoes of this kind, whose value is often not apparent on a first reading, but which take on a fresh significance when one comes back to the work.

Another kind of echo is apparent in the device of making more than one character describe the same event. Valmont's account of the seduction of Cécile is followed by her own version of the incident, so that we see it from both points of view. Laclos does not utilize this process in order to present us with more factual information about what happened; instead we obtain further insight into the thoughts and feelings of the respective narrators. Indeed, as Seylaz has pointed out, there is a continual 'jeu de miroirs' by means of which we see the various characters and incidents from different aspects and in different lights:

Ainsi la réalité de Mme de Tourvel se compose de ce qu'elle dit à ses correspondants, de la façon dont elle le dit, et aussi de ce qu'elle ne dit pas et que nous apprenons par ailleurs, de ce qu'elle fait et de ce que les autres disent d'elle.[1]

This variety of points of view about individual characters and events is something which few other ways of story-telling can accomplish so effectively. In first-person narrative the writer is supposedly confined to his single vision. The third-person narrator likewise gives us, usually, no more than a single account of each event. He may vary this viewpoint by shifting his 'centre of consciousness', giving us one incident as seen and felt by A, the next as it affects B, and so on. But this device still leaves us with only one impression of each stage of events. (Whether this is a 'correct' version, or whether the reader should infer a different interpretation, depends in each case upon what Booth calls the 'reliability' of the narrator.)[2]

The only method comparable to the letter-novel's multiple viewpoint is to have whole sections of the story told twice over, by different narrators, as Crébillon did in *Les Heureux Orphelins*. There is something to be said for this way of taking a second look, from a fresh standpoint, at events already portrayed, but the great advantage of the letter-novel, in this respect, is that the relative shortness of the letters allows the separate versions of an event, or the fresh view of a character, to emerge as the plot is unfolding. There is no need to end the action, or halt it, and then go back to begin again.

If we now turn to the ideas and beliefs on which the charac-

[1] Seylaz, *Les Liaisons dangereuses*, p. 73.

[2] Wayne C. Booth, *The Rhetoric of Fiction*, Chicago, 1961, pp. 158–9 and Ch. VII.

ters base their behaviour, we find that Laclos is again generally
superior to his contemporaries in his method of conveying
them. Instead of the long conversations or dissertations which
all too many letter-novelists used to express their theories,
Laclos tends for the most part to let such ideas remain implicit
or only briefly stated. He shows their scope and influence by
the characters' behaviour and by what they take for granted.
Cécile, for instance, pays lip-service to the moral standards of
her mother and of the convent-school she has just left, but as
soon as there is a choice to be made, she shows that these
principles are not really binding on her. From the moment that
she receives Danceny's first note and keeps it to herself, she
demonstrates a readiness for deceit which is the first step
towards her seduction. And this extends to self-deception,
since she is unwilling to face the implications of her own
behaviour: Mme de Merteuil talks of her 'fausseté naturelle'. In
his portrait of Cécile, Laclos doubtless intended to suggest,
among other things, that a convent education is no guarantee
of Christian principles or of the ability to resist temptation: we
are told of Gercourt's 'ridicule prévention pour les éducations
cloîtrées'. But how vividly and economically this is conveyed
by Cécile's actions, as compared with Mme de Beaumont's
lectures on the same subject.

The more articulate characters, especially Valmont and
Mme de Merteuil, do discuss their ideas on life more fully, but
even they are not allowed to descend, as does Gaudet d'Arras,
for instance, to writing long letters which merely state or
explain their creed. They too reveal their beliefs largely in
actions and reactions.

These beliefs are reflected, moreover, in the metaphors and
images which both of them use freely, images to do with the
theatre and acting, and more especially with war. Laclos's
imagery is perhaps not as striking or poetic as Rousseau's, but
the theme of warfare is carried through *Les Liaisons dangereuses*
by recurrent metaphors which are no less effective for being
relatively inconspicuous. Martin Turnell, discussing the implications of these images, has pointed out that Valmont and
the Marquise devote their energies and their lively talents to
sexual intrigue largely because there is no other outlet, in the
society of their day, for these gifts of aggression, manœuvre

and command.[1] Laclos illustrates, with force and clarity, the situation already outlined by Crébillon's Meilcour: 'La paix qui régnait alors me laissait dans un loisir dangereux.' If the rich nobles are left with no serious social tasks to challenge their capabilities, then the stronger minds among them will seek for mastery in more trivial domains, such as sex.

The desire for domination, in Laclos's chief characters, is combined with a strong sense of superiority and *amour-propre*. The Marquise cannot allow that anyone should have the right to criticize her; and Valmont abandons the Présidente in order to refute the suggestion that he loves her and cannot leave her. It is excessive pride which blinds them to the dangers of quarrelling with each other, and which therefore brings about the dénouement. At this stage, anger and resentment take over, and the two characters cease to be able to control events.

Up to this point the strength of both has lain in their lucidity, about others and about themselves. Seylaz says: 'Laclos nous a donné ce qu'on pourrait appeler le roman hyperbolique de l'intelligence.'[2] Their creator, indeed, endows Valmont and the Marquise with great skill in penetrating the feelings and motives of others. Each of them is an observer, noting the phenomena of the heart and mind. Valmont in particular, as well as catching the slightest reactions of others, analyses his own reactions with a dispassionate eye. He notices that a mere simulation of feeling may generate real tears: 'je m'étais livré à tel point que je pleurais aussi' (*Lettre* 23). And his involuntary emotion at the gratitude of the poor family makes him reflect on the possible motives for acts of charity (*Lettre* 21). Observations of this kind, which recur throughout the book, are a continual reminder that behaviour is rarely as simple as it may appear, and that there may be no direct correlation between actions and motives, either in emotional or in ethical terms.

It is also Valmont, more than any other single character, who observes the physical world and evokes it for us, by visual

---

[1] Martin Turnell, *The Novel in France*, London, 1950, pp. 69–75. His generalizations about 'the battle of the sexes' are however unjustified, as Dr Thelander has pointed out (*Laclos and the Epistolary Novel*, p. 93).

[2] Seylaz, *Les Liaisons dangereuses*, p. 129; see also André Malraux, 'Laclos', *Tableau de la littérature française, XVIIe–XVIIIe siècles*, Paris, Gallimard, 1939, p. 420.

details, by the mention of a gesture or a tone of voice. The reason why he is more lavish with these descriptive touches than the other correspondents can again be shown to accord with plot and character: for much of the novel he is the one who is in action, carrying out the two projects of seduction. He makes his reports to the Marquise as full and lively as possible partly because he is the kind of person to enjoy dwelling on every detail of the manœuvres, and partly because he is always trying to impress her. As a consequence, his letters contain a number of 'scenes' which are described with enough concrete detail for them to be easily visualized. Laclos is both skilful and discreet. He avoids the prolixity of a Richardson; a word or two of scene-setting is enough. Valmont returns unannounced to the château, and times his arrival so that he can enter while dinner is in progress:

Ma belle, par la place qu'elle occupait, tournait le dos à la porte, et, occupée dans ce moment à couper quelque chose, elle ne tourna pas seulement la tête: mais j'adressai la parole à Mme de Rosemonde; et au premier mot, la sensible dévote ayant reconnu ma voix, il lui échappa un cri . . . (*Lettre* 76).

Similarly, there are no lengthy descriptions of appearance, bearing and facial expressions, but these are touched in often enough to help us imagine the world of the novel in visual terms. This economy has its place in making the letters seem to be more like real-life letters. The writer appears to be telling the correspondent only what is necessary for a full understanding of the situation being related. And when his characters report a conversation, Laclos usually saves appearances by limiting the length of the dialogue and not drawing attention to it overtly.

So far we have been concentrating chiefly on the artistic merits of the work, which are manifold. But it has its imperfections. There are occasions, for instance, when Laclos adopts some of the less admirable habits of letter-novelists of the day. The first letter, from Cécile, offers a case in point. The trick of breaking off a letter and then resuming it to report what has happened in the interval, reminds one of, for instance, Clarissa's continual to-and-fro between her desk and the happenings in the parlour. One might forgive Laclos even this jaded device if he had not made Cécile continue for a full paragraph after being summoned to her mother's room: such perseverance is not even consistent with Cécile's character.

In the same way, there is something patently contrived about the beginning of Cécile's first letter of confidences to Mme de Merteuil: 'Mon Dieu, que vous êtes bonne, Madame! comme vous avez bien senti qu'il me serait plus facile de vous écrire que de vous parler!' (*Lettre* 27). This is palpably an excuse to explain why Cécile is writing to the Marquise, whom she sees almost daily, instead of explaining the situation by word of mouth.

There is also the unfortunate occasion when Laclos makes Valmont vouch for the accuracy of a reported conversation. In the letter describing the scene where Mme de Tourvel finally yields, Valmont is made to remark: 'J'étudiais si attentivement mes discours et les réponses que j'obtenais, que j'espère vous rendre les uns et les autres avec une exactitude dont vous serez contente' (*Lettre* 125). Lapses of this kind show that Laclos's technique is weakest when he utilizes the tricks of presentation current among earlier letter-novelists.

One could argue that his plot too becomes unsatisfactory when he follows the standard practice of the time, in his dénouement. The punishment of the wicked was of course obligatory in any novel which claimed to convey a moral lesson. And most readers are quite content to see a story rounded off with some retribution for the unrighteous. But the writer needs to exercise tact and judgment concerning the nature of that punishment. Valmont is killed by the young man he had most offended. This is swift and simple, and develops logically from the events of the plot. But with Mme de Merteuil, Laclos surely committed an error of judgment in adding to her public disgrace both the loss of her lawsuit and her disfigurement by smallpox. These incidents, and particularly the smallpox, introduce an idea of a punitive Providence which upsets the purely human motivation of the rest of the book. Such interventions of God or Fate are hard to handle convincingly. We have seen the problems they raise in, for instance, *La Nouvelle Héloïse*. But Rousseau did at least make religion an integral part of the second half of his story. Laclos's utilization of smallpox is unheralded, and suggests that Fate is not only vindictive but rather slow in the uptake. However, the intention is plain: Mme de Merteuil's offences are great, and she must be punished greatly. Reputation, wealth and beauty are all taken from her, and she is left to drag out her life without any of the attributes that once gave her satisfaction. We do not hear from her own pen how she reacted to these catastrophes, and here at least one feels that the author has made the right choice. Mme de Merteuil without her power would be either grotesque or pitiful, and would introduce a jarring note into the subdued atmosphere of the last pages.

There is a still larger issue connected with Mme de Merteuil and Valmont, an issue which also concerns Restif's Gaudet d'Arras, that of the effect such characters produce upon the reader. If Restif and Laclos sincerely did intend to make the ideas and actions of their villains obnoxious, one may doubt if they were, or are, consistently successful with all their readers. Restif made great play with the notion of Gaudet as a fearful warning:

Cet ami du paysan perverti est l'homme le plus extraordinaire, par ses vues pour Edmond, qui soit dans aucun de nos romans. Il est un véritable ami, et il perd le frère et la sœur! Mais c'est par là même qu'il est le personnage le plus moral qui ait jamais existé! Il montre que l'amitié la plus vraie, témoignée par des moyens vicieux en eux-mêmes, peut conduire à leur perte celui qui la ressent et ceux qui en sont l'objet. Par le personnage de Gaudet d'Arras, on peut inspirer aux jeunes gens une salutaire défiance, qui les fasse tenir ferme à leurs principes, malgré les sophismes brillants des séducteurs, si communs à la capitale (*M. Nicolas*, pp. 4585–6).

Laclos's asseverations of his moral aims are equally high-minded, if less picturesque. And yet . . .

There is always some appeal to our admiration in the portrayal of a great rebel or outlaw—or in the portrayal of the rebel and outlaw as great. Like Gaudet, towering above his peasant disciples, Mme de Merteuil and Valmont are the most clear-sighted and capable people in their world. Because Laclos makes them assume that they are supreme in the domain of sexual conquest, we are led to accept them as being in some sense 'superior'. Their plans are conceived and executed without any weakness or hesitation. On these counts alone they claim our interest, if not our sympathy.

There is a further aspect of Laclos's plot which may engage the reader even more actively on the side of these two characters. This is the fact that the story begins with the formulation of two challenging projects, and proceeds to show the difficulties which are faced and overcome before the projects are carried out. The notions of seducing Cécile and 'winning' Mme de Tourvel are put before us as aims, and for a good many readers the inherent interest of seeing whether, and how, the aims can be achieved may tend to overshadow the moral judgments which might otherwise come into play. A parallel may be drawn from a work such as the film *Rififi*. Here the most exciting sequence showed a group of burglars who had to break through a floor and the ceiling below it without making any sound which would betray their presence to other people in the building. Played in silence, the scene gripped cinema-audiences with suspense as to whether the task could be managed, and there can be little doubt that a good many respectable and virtuous members of those audiences were temporarily on the side of the safe-breakers. Similarly, some of Laclos's readers may well find themselves involved in the seducer's plans to the extent of wanting, momentarily at least, to see Valmont succeed.

This can scarcely have been the conscious and avowed intention of Laclos when he planned his novel, though some deeper level of his personality doubtless helped to enhance and magnify the apostles of evil as he wrote. Whenever Valmont and Mme de Merteuil monopolize our interest and enlist, however fleetingly, our sympathy, then Laclos the moralist has failed. At the same moments, on the other hand, Laclos the artist is succeeding. He has taken us into the compact and complex world of his own creating, and taught us to share for a while the vision of the characters who people it.

XIII

Bernardin de Saint-Pierre

TRANSITIONAL FORMS

LE BRETON is thankful that the study of the eighteenth-century novel closes with *Paul et Virginie*: 'Après avoir feuilleté tant d'œuvres inquiétantes ou même malsaines, il fait bon rencontrer cette fleur fraîche et s'y reposer les yeux.'[1] Tastes have changed, and the twentieth-century reader probably takes a less favourable view. To deal with *Paul et Virginie* as the last novel of note before the Revolution may suggest that we are finishing 'not with a bang but a whimper'. Yet whatever its intrinsic merits or defects, this work must be included in any history of the French novel, since it constitutes a necessary link in more than one chain of development.

In mood and tone it prolongs the sensibility of which Prévost was the first notable exponent, which Rousseau intensified, and which was to continue after the Revolution in Chateaubriand and Mme de Staël. In its stylistic qualities it looks back to Fénelon's *Télémaque*, has some affinities, again, with *La Nouvelle Héloïse*, and foreshadows the increased importance of metaphor and symbol in the nineteenth-century novel. As for the stress on its setting, the unfamiliar natural world of Mauritius, here again it is a stepping-stone between Rousseau and Chateaubriand. And in its narrative method it leads from Prévost, via Crébillon *fils*, to the nineteenth-century masters of the genre. Even if all these traits were to exist in another novel of the period, which is not as far as I know the case, there is a final, historical reason for studying *Paul et Virginie*: its extreme popularity. It had a wide following, including admirers as varied as Napoleon, Lamartine, Sainte-Beuve and the Goncourt brothers. Even if it no longer appeals to us, this novel therefore serves to illustrate the taste and temper of another age.

If we start by looking at the narrative-form of the book, we

[1] André Le Breton, *Le Roman français au XVIIIe siècle*, p. 375.

245

find that in some respects it approximates very closely to the methods of *Manon Lescaut*. The first 'I' whom we meet is not the true narrator, but someone who has merely recorded the tale for us. In *Manon Lescaut* this recorder is the Man of Quality himself. Scarcely anyone nowadays has come to know the Man of Quality by reading the previous six volumes of his memoirs, but he still assumes some kind of personality in *Manon Lescaut*, largely because we see him in action, helping Des Grieux at Passy. Bernardin's recorder is far more vague and insubstantial: he likes going to sit and meditate in solitary places; he is prepared to benefit from the instruction of 'les images du malheur'; and he sheds tears as he listens to the sad story. This is all we know about him. Since he apparently adds so little to the work by his character or comments, we may wonder why the author wrote him in at all. Why did he not start with the *Vieillard* sitting looking at the ruins of the two huts, and taking them as the pretext for telling us the story? One way at least in which the first 'I' is useful is that he takes us with him to the island, tells us about the situation of the little valley, and sets the scene for the whole narrative. And his meeting the Old Man and eliciting the story from him means that the valley is present as a background for the whole work. The tale is not being written at a desk, withindoors, but unfolded in the very place where most of it happened. The Old Man can point to signs and landmarks as the events proceed. By this device, therefore, we are continually reminded of the tropical landscape which becomes the setting of the narration itself, as well as of the story it conveys.

The Old Man is the true narrator, as was the Chevalier des Grieux in *Manon Lescaut*. But he is slightly more aware of his fictional listener. As well as breaking off once to ask whether it is worth pursuing the unhappy tale, he occasionally brings the listener into the picture by phrases such as: 'l'église des Pample-mousses dont vous voyez le clocher là-bas dans la plaine' (p. 122).[1]

The parallel between the Chevalier and the Old Man as narrators breaks down, however, when we come to consider the rôle each plays in the story he tells. The Chevalier is concerned

[1] Page-numbers refer to the 1958 Garnier edition prepared by Pierre Trahard; they are unchanged in the re-edition of 1964.

with his own adventures and with Manon as their primary cause. The Old Man talks more as a witness than an actor. He is inside the story to the extent of being a friend of the two Frenchwomen and their children. He helps them in their work and shares their amusements. He is even consulted about important decisions. In the event, however, his actions and his advice never make any difference to the plot. For instance, he supports the plan for Paul to make a trading trip to the East Indies, but Paul decides of his own accord not to go. Similarly, the Old Man is against Virginie's being sent to Europe, but she is nevertheless compelled to leave Mauritius. The narrator's personal contribution to the story lies therefore not in any crucial share of the action, but in the expression of his opinions. His long dialogue with Paul is the most obvious instance, but there are a number of shorter passages, such as his praise of inscriptions or his sermon of consolation after Virginie's death, which illustrate the narrator's didactic rôle. While these reflections do help to build up the character of the Old Man for us, they contribute little to the plot, and they break the flow of a narrative which has in any case all too little movement.

This method of narration, in which the first-person narrator is a witness and a commentator rather than an actor, is not common in eighteenth-century fiction. We have seen Prévost resorting to something of the kind in Le Doyen de Killerine, where the Dean relates the adventures of his sister and his two brothers. He is however quite active in his pursuit of their affairs. If we are seeking an example of the truly passive observer, we shall find it in Crébillon's Le Sopha. The hero of this work, Amanzéi, is condemned by Brahma, as a punishment for his dérèglements, to become a sofa—or rather, to inhabit several sofas in turn. Naturally enough, this means that he can narrate what went on in the various houses in which he found himself, but except in the last episode where he himself falls in love, his story consists entirely of accounts of, and comments on, the actions of other people. This technique, in Prévost and Crébillon, does shift the centre of interest in the first-person story, but Bernardin de Saint-Pierre goes a stage further, moving towards the omniscience of the nineteenth-century third-person narrator. The Old Man does not in fact confine himself to what he has actually seen or heard, nor even to what we might, by stretching a point, suppose him to have been told. He repeatedly gives details of thoughts and actions which he could not, in the framework of the novel, be expected to know. Often these are only minor matters. One would scarcely query, for instance, how the Old Man knew the thoughts of the sick people whom Virginie and her mother visited: 'Madame de la Tour parlait avec tant de confiance de la Divinité que le malade en l'écoutant la croyait présente' (p. 123). One has however a right to wonder how the Old Man knew the details of Virginie's midnight bathe and her thoughts on that occasion:

> Elle se plonge dans son bassin. D'abord la fraîcheur ranime ses sens, et mille souvenirs agréables se présentent à son esprit. Elle se rappelle que dans son enfance sa mère et Marguerite s'amusaient à la baigner avec Paul dans ce même lieu; que Paul ensuite, réservant ce bain pour elle seule, en avait creusé le lit, couvert le fond de sable, et semé sur ses bords des herbes aromatiques. Elle entrevoit dans l'eau sur ses bras nus et sur son sein, les reflets des deux palmiers plantés à la naissance de son frère et à la sienne, qui entrelaçaient au-dessus de sa tête leurs rameaux verts et leurs jeunes cocos. Elle pense à l'amitié de Paul, plus douce que les parfums, plus pure que l'eau des fontaines, plus forte que les palmiers unis; et elle soupire. Elle songe à la nuit, à la solitude, et un feu dévorant la saisit. Aussitôt elle sort, effrayée de ces dangereux ombrages et de ces eaux plus brûlantes que les soleils de la zone torride (p. 134).

What Virginie did next was to seek the comfort of her mother's company, but once there she could not find words for her feelings: 'son cœur oppressé laissa sa langue sans expression'. Even if Mme de la Tour had discussed Virginie's behaviour with the Old Man, she could scarcely have passed on the thoughts which the girl had not been able to communicate.

Here, obviously, the novelist has cheated by breaking the rules of his own game. It may be remembered that Crébillon took the same kind of liberty in *Les Egarements du cœur et de l'esprit*. These cases are a presage of what was to come: if the exploitation of first-person narrative is the major formal innovation of the eighteenth-century novel, then the omniscient third-person narrator is the nineteenth century's equivalent procedure. Crébillon's M. de Meilcour is still an active first-person narrator, telling his own adventures, and penetrating other people's motives only in so far as they concern himself.

The Old Man stands outside much of the action in *Paul et Virginie*, and is already more of a passive observer than most first-person narrators. To this extent, Saint-Pierre has drawn all the nearer to the methods of Balzac and Stendhal, whose narrators are external to the action and do not attempt to account for their knowledge either of events or of the characters' inmost thoughts and feelings.[1]

It should be noticed that Saint-Pierre has done this so successfully that his 'cheating' has become a positive merit. The scene of Virginie's awakening to love is effective in its context, and so effective that one is not disposed to question the Old Man's narration of it. This example should remind us once and for all that the rules and conventions of a given art-form are not sacred. If the artist can circumvent them skilfully enough to avoid detection by the ordinary reader or spectator, then his success is all the justification he needs. (Nor need this infringement be a conscious or deliberate affair; it seems to me highly unlikely that Saint-Pierre thought about the limits of first-person narration and then made the Old Man overstep them.) The narrative form of *Paul et Virginie*, therefore, while doing no more than extend certain practices found in previous novels, is undoubtedly moving towards the characteristic nineteenth-century method of presentation.

By contrast, the subject-matter of this narrative is of a kind which would seem to have passed away with the eighteenth century. This is the 'pastoral', a type of fiction which traced its ancestry back to the Latin eclogue and beyond, and which was practised by such distinguished writers as Boccaccio, Sir Philip Sidney and Honoré d'Urfé.[2] Bernardin himself refers repeatedly

---

[1] Each of these authors does in fact make an omniscient narrator suggest, at an early stage in one novel, that he is inside the story and knows one of the characters involved. In *Le Père Goriot*, the narrator says of Eugène: 'Sans ses observations curieuses et l'adresse avec laquelle il sut se produire dans les salons de Paris, ce récit n'eût pas été coloré des tons vrais qu'il devra sans doute à son esprit sagace . . .' (Garnier, p. 10). Similarly, in *Le Rouge et le Noir*, the narrator remarks, à propos an action of the Mayor: 'Quoiqu'il soit ultra et moi libéral, je l'en loue' (Garnier, p. 8). Neither of these curious hints is ever developed in the remainder of the work. Cf. the opening pages of *Madame Bovary*, discussed above, p. 88, n. 1.

[2] See J. Fabre, 'Une question de terminologie littéraire: *Paul et Virginie*, pastorale', *Etudes de littérature moderne*, II (1953), pp. 168–200 (Faculté de Lettres de Toulouse).

to *Paul et Virginie* as a *pastorale* and it fulfils in nearly every respect the requirements laid down by Florian in his *Essai sur la pastorale*. Works of this kind are essentially pictures of simple country life, in contrast to the life of the city or the court; and the convention demands that the shepherds who people the countryside should be virtuous.

Il faut que l'amour des pasteurs soit aussi pur que le cristal de leurs fontaines; et comme le premier attrait de la plus belle des bergères consiste dans sa pudeur, de même le principal charme d'une pastorale doit être d'inspirer la vertu.[1]

Vertu and *pudeur* are the keynotes of Bernardin's story, and all he has done is to transfer his virtuous souls to an island where he could 'réunir à la beauté de la nature entre les tropiques la beauté morale d'une petite société' (clxv).

Florian thinks of the *pastorale* as a prose narrative interspersed with poems, and his own works contain songs for the shepherds and shepherdesses. Mercifully, Bernardin did not follow his example in this.[2] His prose style, however, does conform to Florian's recommendations:

Quant au style de la prose, il doit tenir du roman, de l'églogue et du poème. Il faut qu'il soit simple, car l'auteur raconte; il faut qu'il soit naïf, puisque les personnages dont il parle et qu'il fait parler n'ont d'autre éloquence que celle du cœur; il faut aussi qu'il soit noble, car partout il doit être question de la vertu et la vertu s'exprime toujours avec noblesse.[3]

Bernardin's language does not in fact satisfy the strict requirements of *style noble*, as used in tragedy, since he introduces both the names of humble everyday objects and also specialized technical terms. But in its general tone and grammatical constructions his style is elevated rather than familiar. The dialogue, in particular, is stylized and formal, with

---

[1] Florian, *Essai sur la pastorale* (1787), Paris, 1798, p. 10.

[2] One of Saint-Pierre's first English translators, Helen Maria Williams, did intersperse the text with sonnets of her own composition, on subjects such as 'Disappointment', 'The Curlew', 'The Torrid Zone', etc. These poems are attributed to Mme de la Tour.

[3] Florian, *Essai sur la pastorale*, p. 17.

apostrophes—'O Paul! O Paul! tu m'es beaucoup plus cher qu'un frère!'—and with balanced rhetorical sentences:

> Non, mon amie; non mes enfants, reprit Madame de la Tour; je ne vous quitterai point. J'ai vécu avec vous, et c'est avec vous que je veux mourir. Je n'ai connu le bonheur que dans votre amitié. Si ma santé est dérangée, d'anciens chagrins en sont cause. J'ai été blessée au cœur par la dureté de mes parents et par la perte de mon cher époux. Mais depuis, j'ai goûté plus de consolation et de félicité avec vous, sous ces pauvres cabanes, que jamais les richesses de ma famille ne m'en ont fait même espérer dans ma patrie (p. 140).

Here and throughout the book the naïve feelings are couched in language which, if relatively simple, is also consciously literary.

In one respect at least, Bernardin creates linguistic effects which his readers would think of as poetic. This is his liberal use of metaphor and more especially of simile. His favourite sources for these comparisons are the natural world and classical mythology. In some cases they are extended and quite elaborate:

> Comme deux bourgeons qui restent sur deux arbres de la même espèce, dont la tempête a brisé toutes les branches, viennent à produire des fruits plus doux, si chaçun d'eux, détaché du tronc maternel, est greffé sur le tronc voisin; ainsi ces deux petits enfants, privés de tous leurs parents, se remplissaient de sentiments plus tendres que ceux de fils et de fille, de frère et de sœur, quand ils venaient à être changés de mamelles par les deux amies qui leur avaient donné le jour (p. 88).

There are similes of dawn and sunset and of the stars; of flowers, trees and rivers; of Leda's children and Niobe's; and of the primal innocence of Eden:

> Au matin de la vie, ils en avaient toute la fraîcheur; tels dans le jardin d'Eden parurent nos premiers parents, lorsque, sortant des mains de Dieu, ils se virent, s'approchèrent, et conversèrent d'abord comme frère et sœur. Virginie, douce, modeste, confiante comme Eve; et Paul, semblable à Adam, ayant la taille d'un homme avec la simplicité d'un enfant (p. 130).

Occasionally the comparison is made briefly, in passing, but more often, as in the examples above, it stands as a separate statement and thus becomes more noticeable as an element of the writing.

One may assume that Saint-Pierre's generous use of simile arose from his conception of the *pastorale* as a quasi-poetic form. But whatever his theories may have been, his practice provides an historical link between the figurative style of Prévost and Rousseau and the use of imagery in novelists like Balzac and Flaubert. (We have already noticed how Laclos too makes a fairly wide, if unobtrusive, use of metaphors on themes such as acting and fighting.) Bernardin's range is of course more limited, and his effects more simple, than those of the nineteenth-century masters. Nevertheless, his similes make a significant contribution to the atmosphere and mood of *Paul et Virginie*, as well as reflecting its ideological basis, and to this extent they foreshadow the importance which imagery was to assume in the subsequent development of the novel.

Apart from using the world of nature as a source for figures of speech, Saint-Pierre is lavish in his descriptions of the out-door world of Mauritius. Trahard points out in his introduction that Saint-Pierre showed considerable tact in limiting his use of the material at his disposal. Even so, the passages of description take up a good many pages, and play an important part in the overall effect of the novel. There is no need to emphasize the attraction of the exotic local colour, which was a relatively new sensation for the eighteenth-century public.[1] The effect may not be quite so potent on modern readers, but there is still a lingering charm, for 'nous autres Européens', about the strange names which, even if we have met them before, are not a part of our everyday life. The calabash and the coconut-palm, latanias and lianas possess some touch of far-away glamour which does not hang about the oak and the ivy.

What is less frequently pointed out is that Bernardin's descriptions are rich with colour. In Virginie's pool the plants are allowed to grow freely on the rock-walls:

Sur ses flancs bruns et humides rayonnaient en étoiles vertes et noires de larges capillaires, et flottaient au gré des vents des touffes de scolopendre suspendues comme de longs rubans d'un vert pourpré. Près de là croissaient des lisières de pervenche, dont les

---

[1] See J. W. Hovenkamp, *Mérimée et la couleur locale*, Paris, 1928, pp. 11–32.

fleurs sont presque semblables à celles de la girofleé rouge, et des piments, dont les gousses couleur de sang sont plus éclatantes que le corail (p. 117).

Sunset among the trees is equally vivid:

Le feuillage des arbres, éclairés en dessous de ses rayons safranés, brillait des feux de la topaze et de l'émeraude; leurs troncs mousseux et bruns paraissaient changés en colonnes de bronze antique (p. 127).

These colours may now seem rather blatant, laid on too thick. But how they suddenly illuminate the novel, after so many decades of writers who are barely interested in the look of things, and who might, for all we know, be colour-blind. Even Rousseau would seem to have had little eye for colour, which is surprising in so keen a botanizer. In Saint-Pierre's case the vividness of the tropical world left a lasting impression, and some of this intensity comes through to us in these passages glowing with jewel-colours.

The descriptions of natural scenery have a certain vigour of their own, and in some cases seem more lively than the narrative they embellish. For by its very nature, a good deal of the book is the reverse of dramatic. Saint-Pierre means us to see every aspect of the delights of the simple life. This means that the first third of the book is given up to presenting these delights, and is almost devoid of events. The period when Virginie is away from the island is likewise empty of action, and is devoted to the discussion between the Old Man and Paul. There is a general paucity of specific incidents and scenes in proportion to the descriptions of rustic pursuits and pastimes, and the discursive comments which supply the 'philosophy' of that life. There are several disadvantages to this construction. We become aware, for instance, looking back, that the first episode to be fully portrayed, that of the runaway slave-woman, has no relevance to the main plot whatever. It is all too patently an illustration of Virginie's repeated remark: 'Oh qu'il est difficile de faire le bien!' (For many readers Virginie's action, considering its consequences, is not a good deed at all; one is reminded of Renard's dictum: 'Il faut avoir le courage de préférer l'homme intelligent à l'homme très gentil.') Moreover, Saint-Pierre devotes far more space to the journey back than to the slave-incident itself. Although one is given ample opportunity to admire Paul's fire-making and Fidèle's tracking capacities, one cannot help feeling that the author has here strayed away into the Robinson Crusoe—or Swiss Family Robinson—territory of adventure-in-the-wilds for its own sake.

Apart from this episode, the incidents are usually brief scenes such as the reception of the letter from Mme de la Tour's Aunt, the visit from M. de la Bourdonnais, and the conversation on the eve of Virginie's departure. The only other long scene is of course the storm, which is partly a set-piece of natural description, and Virginie's death. It may seem carping to complain that too little happens, since we have criticized some earlier authors such as Prévost for their reliance on a plethora of extraordinary events. But if a plot is sparing of incident, then we need some compensation, in the form, for instance, of detail about what *does* happen. This Bernardin does not usually supply. He is far more ready to tell us what vegetables Paul planted, or how Mme de la Tour's birthday was habitually celebrated, than to enlarge on the scene where Virginie is made to leave her home and embark for Europe.

Part of the weakness of the plot also lies in the fact that the behaviour and reactions of most of the characters are predictable. Practically everyone who appears is portrayed as consistently good or irremediably bad, and this simple point of view eliminates the possibility of any unexpected quirk of character coming out in words or action. This clear-cut picture was a part of Bernardin's intention, since he deliberately set out to create an impression of 'beauté morale'. Early readers of the book would seem to have been charmed by the peaceful perfection of the little colony, but if this appeal to the emotions does not work, then there is little in the way of varied behaviour or subtlety of motive to hold our interest.

The way in which the characters are simplified and idealized is one reason, no doubt, why the book became children's reading. It has much in common with fairy-tales: its atmosphere of far-away enchanted climes; its perfect little heroine; and its bad fairy or wicked stepmother in the shape of Mme de la Tour's Aunt. Fabre makes the further point that Providence itself assumes the rôle of a good fairy when the children are lost in the forest, answering their wishes as soon as they are expressed.[1] And just as one would scarcely expect to analyse the characterization of *Cinderella* or *The Sleeping Beauty*, so it seems almost pointless to elucidate the motives and behaviour of Virginie and Paul and their mothers. It may however be worth while to consider the assumptions on which Bernardin bases the creation of his characters. There are two fundamental concepts, sensibility and the influence of civilization. Thus, to take the extreme of badness, the Aunt is repeatedly referred to as 'hard'. She had not married because 'il ne s'était trouvé personne qui eût voulu s'allier à une fille aussi laide, et à un cœur aussi dur' (p. 94). And the other element of her badness is her acceptance of European standards: the importance of rank and wealth, the founding of marriages upon these two attributes rather than on love, the teaching of futile 'accomplishments' to girls, and so on. Throughout the book Europe and things European are taken to represent all that is evil and vicious in human behaviour. (The only exception, an amusing sidelight on Saint-Pierre's tastes, is the wine from Europe which the Old Man supplies for picnics.) Part of the virtue of Marguerite and Mme de la Tour is that in leaving Europe they have also managed to cast off the misguided standards of civilization and come to rely on the voice of nature. The other characteristic which shows that they and their children are good is their soft-heartedness, manifested above all in their easy tears. Bernardin de Saint-Pierre carries the fondness for weeping even beyond Prévost and Rousseau, and the process is infectious:

Et voyant madame de la Tour pleurer, elle se jeta à son cou, et la serrant dans ses bras: 'Chère amie, s'écria-t-elle, chère amie!' mais ses propres sanglots étouffèrent sa voix. A ce spectacle Virginie, fondant en larmes, pressait alternativement les mains de sa mère et celles de Marguerite contre sa bouche et contre son cœur (p. 95).

(Chill common-sense asks how Virginie could hold the hands of both women if her mother was in Marguerite's arms . . .) In his 1789 preface, the author shows that he also wanted the reader to weep:

Lorsque j'eus formé, il y a quelques années, une esquisse fort imparfaite de cette espèce de pastorale, je priai une belle dame qui fréquentait le grand monde, et des hommes graves qui en vivaient

---

[1] J. Fabre, 'Une question de terminologie littéraire', p. 177.

loin, d'en entendre la lecture, afin de pressentir l'effet qu'elle produirait sur des lecteurs de caractères si différents: j'eus la satisfaction de leur voir verser à tous des larmes. Ce fut le seul jugement que j'en pus tirer, et c'était aussi tout ce que j'en voulais savoir (p. cxlvi).

A ready flow of tears both sets the seal of approval on a literary work, and demonstrates the essential good-heartedness of the reader or listener.

In this simple world of good people and bad people there are two slightly equivocal characters. One, who makes only the briefest of appearances, is the missionary priest. Now Mme de la Tour and her companions are ostensibly Christians. Their attendance at Mass is frequently mentioned, and the priest is also their confessor. In reality, their religion is a watered-down version of Rousseau's deism, but as good citizens, they follow the forms and observances of the Church. The priest, it would seem, is not on the side of natural virtue, since he supports the plan for Virginie to go to France. And his first remarks, when he visits the hut, appear to place him among those who accept the evil standards of civilization: 'Dieu soit loué! Vous voilà riches' (p. 144). But he goes on to express an idea which agrees with the continual praise of *bienfaisance* in the novel: 'Vous pourrez écouter votre bon cœur, faire du bien aux pauvres.' From this and his subsequent remarks it looks as though he is merely misguided; he is advocating the wrong thing for the right reasons. One may therefore conclude that he represents the sincerely religious person whose judgment has been warped by too much contact with civilized society.

M. de la Bourdonnais falls into much the same category. He is good-hearted, but misled. His first view of Mme de la Tour is biased by the Aunt's malicious comments. However, when he visits the little community in the valley he is impressed by the simplicity and virtue he finds there. This impression is not strong enough to make him abandon his European ideas about what will be good for Virginie—and indeed if he did, there would be no story to speak of—but he does pay homage to Virginie's virtue after her death. His function in the book is all too clearly that of an agent who keeps the plot moving, but he does introduce a mixture of attitudes which provides some slight variety.

The dénouement of the story, and in particular Virginie's death, is difficult for many modern readers to accept. Bathing-suits and bikinis have accustomed us to a wholesale exposure of the human body, and pictures of life in the tropics can only strengthen the assumption that it may be 'natural' not to wear clothes. Virginie's modesty therefore seems not only out of date but inconsistent with Bernardin's defence of the 'natural' life. One must simply accept another of his ideas, so much taken for granted that he does not explain or defend it, that modesty about letting one's body be seen is instinctive in the virtuous female.

We may still wonder why, in terms of the 'lesson' of the novel, Virginie should have to die. She has not, of her own intention, committed any fault, and her death cannot be con-sidered as a punishment. Nor does it even, as did Julie's death, serve to avert a greater evil. The clearest explanation from Saint-Pierre himself comes in the *Avis* of the 1789 edition, where he discusses a proposal to dramatize *Paul et Virginie* and give it a happy ending. Bernardin disapproves of this plan because, by altering the end, the adapter

retrancherait de ce sujet ce que son but moral a de plus intéressant, parce qu'il est dangereux de n'offrir à la vertu d'autre perspective sur la terre que le bonheur, et qu'il faut apprendre aux hommes, non seulement à vivre, mais encore à mourir (p. clviii).

Thus the main portion of the book demonstrates the truth that 'notre bonheur consiste à vivre suivant la nature et la vertu', and the final catastrophe teaches us how to die with virtue too.

However, we may well be wasting our time if we try to reconcile Saint-Pierre's ideology with his plot. Firstly, it seems very probable that the idea of using the shipwreck as the climax of his story was present from the beginning, and the literary attractions of this scene may well have outweighed its possible significance in the overall moral lesson of the book. In that case the moral aim expressed in the passage above was merely a justification, not the true reason for the turn taken by the story.

Secondly, there is not much to gain from looking closely at Saint-Pierre's ideas for he is, it must be acknowledged, a poor and muddle-headed theorist. He has not, for instance, really resolved the problem of how Europeans were to lead a simple rustic life outside Europe, since Marguerite and Mme de la Tour and their children depend on slave-labour. Trahard talks of Saint-Pierre as an 'ardent anti-esclavagiste' and mentions his arguments for the abolition of slavery in *Empsaël* (p. 97, n. 2). In the 1789 *Avis* he does show that he holds such views. But I doubt whether anyone could deduce this from the novel itself. The episode of the *négresse marronne* is obviously a plea against cruelty to slaves, but Mme de la Tour and Marguerite never contemplate freeing Marie and Domingue; the aim of Paul's projected journey to the East Indies is to get enough money to buy another slave; and his dream of a happy life when Virginie comes back rich includes the phrase, 'Nous aurons beaucoup de noirs.' That is, in order to make this Arcadian life seem acceptable to his readers, Bernardin had to condone the use of slavery, which he elsewhere condemned. And to provide a plausible motive for Mme de la Tour's acceptance of the offer from Europe, he even has to make her afraid that Virginie should be reduced to manual labour like a slave or a peasant.

These questions of work and money illustrate the conflict which is the greatest weakness of the novel. On the one hand it is presented as an idyllic dream, a vision of happiness remote in setting and poetic in expression. In this aspect it lies beyond the bounds of reality—or of realism—and has no bearing on our everyday lives. On the other hand it is a programme for living, a prototype of Utopia, a 'real' world where factors like the need for food and the necessity of working for it come into play. If it were only an idyll, one would not be tempted to make practical criticisms. But if it was intended to be practical, and Bernardin more than once expresses this view, then he should have worked out more carefully the economic and ethical basis of his ideal society. Rousseau could have taught him a lesson in this: the community at Clarens is presented as both idyllic and viable. We may nowadays disagree with the principles of its organization, but Rousseau has portrayed an effective working community which satisfies its members' physical needs and brings them peace of mind, while complying with the author's own ethical standards. Saint-Pierre had none of Rousseau's coherence of approach in this matter, and *Paul et Virginie* shifts unhappily between the idyllic-impossible and the practical-desirable.

Bernardin confuses the literary and moral issues still further by his assurances that the story was a true one. Though his social and political views were in some ways advanced, his aesthetic assumptions are as old as Prévost's; he clearly considers it both justifiable and advisable to try and convince the reader of the literal truth of his tale. Indeed, he was more consistent than Prévost. He may refer to *Paul et Virginie* as a *roman*—but only in a private letter; he may admire the fictions of Homer and of modern novelists, but he does not admit, in print, to having resorted to invention or fancy himself.

Il ne m'a point fallu imaginer de roman pour peindre des familles heureuses. Je puis assurer que celles dont je vais parler ont vraiment existé, et que leur histoire est vraie dans ses principaux événements. Ils m'ont été certifiés par plusieurs habitants que j'ai connus à l'Ile de France. Je n'y ai ajouté que quelques circonstances indifférentes, mais qui, m'étant personnelles, ont encore en cela même de la réalité (pp. cxlv–cxlvi).

The characters and the main events of the plot are 'certified' as true; the author has added only some slight touches of his own. The suspicious vagueness of these 'circonstances indifférentes' would probably arouse doubts if a preface of this kind were to be written nowadays. If an author adds his own experiences to an account of events which happened in his absence, how far is the resulting compound 'true'?

A year later he is more explicit and by modern standards more honest, though the carefully accurate statements are made with intent to deceive:

Je le répète, j'ai décrit des sites réels, des mœurs dont on trouverait peut-être encore aujourd'hui des modèles dans quelques parties solitaires de l'Ile-de-France ou de l'Ile de Bourbon qui en est voisine, et une catastrophe bien certaine, dont je peux produire, même à Paris, des témoignages irrécusables (p. clvii).

All this, with the inclusion of that admirably cautious 'peut-être', we can accept at its face-value. But there follows the account of his chance meeting with a relative of Virginie, who could vouch for the death of 'cette sublime victime de la pudeur'.

In 1806 there is fresh circumstantial evidence from the young man who has seen Paul's coconut tree, talked to Domingue about Paul and Virginie, and verified 'les principaux événements de leur histoire' (p. 5). Pure invention on Bernardin's part? Or had some credulous traveller really swallowed the legend and found the 'proofs' he was expecting to find? It looks, in any case, almost as if Saint-Pierre had begun to believe his own story.

According to Legras, people in Mauritius were coming to believe it too:

> Il y avait encore, à cette époque, tant de bonne foi et de simplicité dans ces îles sans commerce, qu'on ne comprendrait pas que là, où s'était accompli le fait qui avait inspiré à l'auteur l'épisode le plus touchant de son livre, on eût pu se soustraire à l'émotion qu'il produisit en paraissant, et se défendre des larmes qu'il avait fait verser dans la vieille Europe. La fiction avait un tel charme de grâce et de naturel qu'elle séduisit tout le monde et que pour tout le monde elle devint aussitôt la réalité. L'auteur aurait-il osé affirmer que ses personnages avaient vécu, s'il n'avait affirmé la vérité elle-même?[1]

Legras suggests that the 'reality' of the setting and descriptions would also convince the Mauritians of the story's truth, and he concludes: 'Tout se réunissait donc pour les entraîner invinciblement dans une illusion à laquelle leurs souvenirs mêmes se prêtaient naturellement.' Thus the accuracy of description of scenery, and the fact that there had been a shipwreck in 1744, apparently combined to authenticate the whole narrative.

The shipwreck itself has provided numerous investigators with material for detective-work and discussion. Their conclusions show, not surprisingly, that Bernardin did not abide by the historical facts of the disaster. Articles dealing with 'la partie historique du roman' or 'la véritable Virginie' are interesting not so much for the information they offer as for the assumptions they conceal.

The first of these is that Saint-Pierre's protestations of truth should be taken seriously. The critic who 'refutes' Bernardin by showing up his departure from the facts seems to forget, or not to know, how much these claims to truth were a matter of

---

[1] Pierre Legras, 'Le Naufrage du Saint-Géran: histoire et légende', *Album de l'Ile de la Réunion*, ed. A. Roussin, Saint-Denis, 1863, Vol. III, pp. 177–92.

convention. Admittedly the development of memoir- and letter-novels had led some authors to be less emphatic, or even occasionally ironic, about the 'proofs' which certified their books as true. But a good many novelists of the 1770's and 1780's—with Restif de la Bretonne as an outstanding example—still persist in their elaborate assurances of authenticity. Saint-Pierre was therefore doing no more than comply with a declining fashion. The complicating factor, that he did utilize an historic incident, should not be given undue importance. Lesage, Prévost, and many lesser authors like Mme de Tencin, had done the same, without attracting critics to challenge the 'truth' of their works.

A second assumption would seem to be that the unearthing of the historical truth about the wreck of the Saint-Géran is in some sense a contribution to the study of literature. This is of course nonsense. It is not the 'real' facts of the event which matter to literature, but what Bernardin thought to be the facts. And this information is relevant to literature only if it is used to show how the author moulded and presented his knowledge in the novel.

Thirdly, it is noticeable that discussions about the 'facts' of *Paul et Virginie* are confined to the question of the shipwreck.[1] No one seems to have tried to verify the story of Mme de la Tour or the existence of Marguerite. It is tacitly accepted that while the shipwreck bears some relation to historical truth, the idyllic episodes which precede it are not 'real' enough to warrant investigation. This both illustrates the futility of any general discussion of the factual truth of the novel, and also provides an implicit criticism of the work as a whole: the shipwreck is striking and attracts attention; the life of the ideal society is pale and negligible.

Can we, perhaps, formulate some clearer verdict on the book? As I suggested earlier in this chapter, *Paul et Virginie* undoubtedly deserves a place in the history of the novel; it is proper material for study. Its capacity for giving real pleasure to the modern reader, as a work of art, is more debatable. The greatest weakness of the book, in modern eyes, is that it offers such a limited range of simple emotional responses. The frame

---

[1] One might conceivably add to this the matter of Virginie's tomb. See the passages cited by Trahard, p. 210, n. 2, and p. 227, n. 1.

of mind required to enjoy it is probably the one in which we approach narrative poetry at its most naïve. This is a field of imaginative experience as well worth exploring as any other, but developments in the novel have trained us to expect more depth and complexity from works in that genre. We have grown used to fiction which asks more of us, as readers, and also satisfies us in more varied ways. Overshadowed by the more ample growth of its successors, *Paul et Virginie* seems a slight and ephemeral creation. We may endorse Le Breton's description of it as 'une fraîche fleur', but it is a flower which, in Bernardin's own image, does not capture our full attention: 'Ainsi des violettes, sous des buissons épineux, exhalent au loin leurs doux parfums, quoiqu'on ne les voie pas.'

XIV

Conclusion

In the opening chapter of this study the suggestion was put forward that the eighteenth-century novel introduced techniques and practices which enriched the resources of later novelists for the representation of real life and the creation of literary illusion. Now that we have considered in some detail a number of the major eighteenth-century novels, it should be possible to decide whether this suggestion is justified, and if so in what respects.

One element in this formulation of the problem may appear to be unjustified: when we speak of 'resources' available to later novelists, this may seem to imply that, for instance, writers such as Balzac and Stendhal had read all the novels we have discussed, and took from them the devices and procedures which suited their own designs. The true state of affairs is of course more vague and complex. First of all, it should be remembered that the score of novels we have dealt with is only a minute fraction of the eighteenth-century output. About 2,900 new works of fiction written in French were published during the period, while another 600 or so foreign works were translated into French. Among this stream, a large proportion were derivative, merely weak exercises in the methods established by more talented and original writers. That is, the novels chosen for discussion here led to the writing, in their own day, of works showing similar trends and techniques. When we speak, therefore, of nineteenth-century novelists benefiting from earlier fiction, we do not need to suppose that a Balzac or a Stendhal had read precisely those works which we now think worth studying. We are merely implying that such writers would have a sufficient acquaintance with a fair number of eighteenth-century novels, good and bad, to give them some idea of what the genre had been like and the lines it had followed.

The great nineteenth-century novelists in France—Balzac,

Stendhal, Flaubert, Zola—shared the common aim of portraying 'life as it is', 'the truth' or 'reality'. They differed in the
theories which justified that aim, and in the aspects of 'reality'
which they chose to stress. Nevertheless, they all aspired to
offer their readers a faithful picture of the real world.

Occasionally, as in *Salammbô*, such writers sought to give
a realistic impression of a period long past. It can be stated at
once that in the specifically historic aspect of works like these,
eighteenth-century precedents could have had little or no
effect. There had been a fair amount of treatment of supposedly
historical material in eighteenth-century fiction, especially in
the *nouvelle*, but the historical novel, as we now understand the
term, is a creation of the early nineteenth century, with Sir
Walter Scott as its pioneer.[1] Our problem is therefore limited
to the representation of life and conditions in the author's own
times.

Let us summarize, for the sake of clarity, the various aspects
of real life which may come within the province of the novelist's
work. There is first the whole of the external world, taken as
visible phenomena: the realm of nature, either in its original
state or shaped by man's activities; and the appearance of
people, their clothes, furniture and buildings, the objects they
make and use. There is, next, the human society in which the
individual lives; the novelist may choose to expound its structure, and to describe the manners of all or some of the groups
which compose it. Thirdly, moving among these various
elements of his milieu, is the individual man or woman whose
actions, thoughts and feelings are subjects for portrayal as well
as helping to constitute the plot of the novel. And a final aspect
of reality which the novelist may try to convey is the factor of
time, whether in the importance of a particular moment
caught and held, or in the way that individuals and groups
develop through time.

It would be tedious, and should be unnecessary, to re-
capitulate all the examples we have noticed of realistic treatment in one or another of the categories listed above. To choose
only some outstanding cases: *Manon Lescaut* supplies details
about the Paris of Prévost's time, its streets and gaming-houses
and prisons; Marivaux dwells on the details of the clothes worn

[1] See Louis Maigron, *Le Roman historique à l'époque romantique*, Paris, 1912.

by Marianne and Jacob; Rousseau and Bernardin de Saint-Pierre describe both the natural world untouched by man and the ways in which land can be cultivated for usefulness or beauty. Not all these details and descriptions are innovations, but many eighteenth-century novels can be called 'visual' in a sense which would scarcely apply to the earlier heroic novels. And concrete objects are introduced for purposes other than the grotesque and sordid effects which chiefly characterize the *roman réaliste* of the seventeenth century.

The portrayal of social factors like class and rank comes out most clearly in *Gil Blas* and in the works of Marivaux. As for the detailed description of the individual's ideas and feelings, we have had occasion to notice this repeatedly, from Prévost through to Laclos. And some authors, such as Crébillon, were aware of the relevance of the historic moment to their stories, while others—Prévost, Marivaux, Laclos—consciously utilize the experience that comes with time as an important factor in their narrative.

These examples, however, as presented here, can for the most part be classified under the heading of subject-matter. To say that nineteenth-century novelists benefited from such material would seem to suggest merely that they wrote about the same aspects of 'reality' as did earlier authors. Such a conclusion hardly warrants much interest or attention.

To penetrate more deeply into the nature of the eighteenth-century legacy we must consider not only the 'realism' of the subject-matter but the forms and techniques of its presentation.

We have seen that, with the ostensible aim of giving the effect of a true story, the vast majority of eighteenth-century novels were cast as memoirs or as collections of letters, with first-person narrators. At the turn of the century both these forms declined rapidly in popularity, and it might appear at first sight as though the nineteenth century had come to reject the methods of the previous age. The characteristic narrative form of the nineteenth-century novel is a story told by an omniscient third-person narrator.

As we have already observed, however, the prevalence of the first-person approach in the serious eighteenth-century novel did not mean that third-person narrative had vanished. It was kept alive in the numerous *contes* and *nouvelles* of the period. There was therefore a continuing tradition of third-person stories which might offer models to the nineteenth-century writer who no longer saw in memoirs or letters the ideal form for a novel. But Balzac and Stendhal do not merely take over the quasi-historical methods of eighteenth-century *conteurs*; nor do they confine themselves to occasional infringements of the historical approach. They become completely omniscient, moving into the minds of any or all of their characters as they choose.

How are we to explain this change? One way of describing the narrative techniques of such authors is to say that their works revert to the procedures of the seventeenth-century comic novelist, who was by convention allowed such omniscience. But this is the kind of description which, while true in general terms, is also profoundly misleading. There is, firstly, little or no direct continuity between these early comic novels and the writings of, say, Balzac and Stendhal; and secondly, the quality and scope of the device itself are markedly different by the time we meet it again in the nineteenth century.

In French criticism before 1700 there is a clear-cut distinction between the heroic novel and the novel which is referred to as *comique* or *satirique*. Among the eighteenth-century works we have discussed there are no obvious examples of the latter type apart from *Gil Blas*, and even this has picaresque and historic elements which distinguish it from earlier French novels in the comic vein. However, we do find in many eighteenth-century novels certain traits which, in the previous century, would have been considered permissible only in the comic novel: bourgeois or lower-class 'heroes', naturalistic dialogue, a disregard for the spirit if not the letter of *les bienséances*, and, above all, situations in which the reader is invited to laugh with or at a hero or heroine.[1] While some of its characteristic elements thus survive by being transplanted into serious or sentimental works, the comic novel in its pure form seems, in France at least, to have suffered an eclipse. It is therefore unsound to assume that its distinctive technique of third-person omniscient narrative, a

---

[1] This development supports the general thesis illustrated in Auerbach's *Mimesis*, that modern realism depends initially on the breakdown of the Classical concept of the separation of literary genres and styles.

device *not* taken up by the serious eighteenth-century novelist, was carried over to the beginning of the nineteenth century.

But 'omniscience' itself, to come to our second point, is a blanket term which calls for closer consideration. There are many ways of exploiting a narrator's omniscience, and those used by the great nineteenth-century novelists seem to me to differ radically from the practice in early comic novels. In particular, the device of telling successive episodes in relation to the feelings and reactions of this or that character is *necessary* to the nineteenth-century writer, while in the old comic novel it was often merely a trimming or a flourish. *Francion* would still be largely comprehensible and coherent were one to delete the author's excursions into his characters' motives and emotions. But to excise from *Le Rouge et le Noir* all the passages which discuss the inner life of Julien and Mme de Rênal and Mathilde would leave us with something unreadable. Balzac and Stendhal and their successors used their omniscience to create the very basis of action, to explore motivation, to register significant nuances of feeling and thought. But this approach is obviously akin to the methods of Marivaux and Crébillon, Rousseau and Laclos. Once several generations of writers had shown how thoroughly one could analyse and convey the inner life of a character by stepping into his shoes and viewing the world through his eyes, later novelists were not likely to forgo this gain. The omniscient point of view of the nineteenth-century French novelist is therefore, in my opinion, less a development of previous third-person techniques than an extension of the methods of character-revelation practised in memoir-novels and letter-novels.

So far in this chapter I have left unaltered the arguments which were put forward when I first wrote this study. Now, some fifteen years later, it seems necessary to bring in a new element at this stage. I would still contend that it was chiefly first-person forms which prepared the way for omniscient narrators, but I am convinced that we need to recognize the beginnings of this omniscience during the years when letter-novels and fictional memoirs were still flourishing, well before the Revolution. This conviction has been forced upon me by the bibliographical data for the period. In the second half of the century the sheer quantity of works with a third-person narrator was often equal to, and in many years greater than, the number of new memoir-novels or letter-novels. Some of these third-person fictions were labelled *conte*, and had the traditional characteristics of being both fairly short and not at all realistic. But an increasing proportion of the short tales set out to portray contemporary manners and morals; these constitute a sub-genre, the *conte moral*, with Marmontel as its best-known exponent. There were also some long works, up to two or three volumes, with the word *conte* in their titles; and finally, a number of long, serious third-person narratives, some of which even bore the label of *roman*. This last group includes certain works in which the narrator describes quite extensively the innermost thoughts and emotions of the characters. Examples of such treatment are the anonymous *Apolline et Dancourt, histoire véritable* (1769), and Mme Benoist's *Folie de la prudence humaine* (1771). In such cases, clearly, the novelist no longer feels limited to relating only what an observer might see of, or deduce from, people's behaviour; he or she is starting to exploit the resources of narrative omniscience. In the absence of any systematic research on this point, we cannot tell how widespread the development was among French writers. Nor, as far as I know, has the emergence of the omniscient narrator in serious English novels been adequately explored. It may well be that novelists in England, who paid less regard to notions of genre and the strict observance of conventions, began the process and —through translations—influenced their French counterparts. Or perhaps it is more a matter of certain trends which were developing simultaneously throughout western Europe. In any case, while we can justifiably talk of the nineteenth century as the great age of omniscient narrative, it now seems that we should look back over several decades for the beginnings of this technique in serious novels.

The adoption of this kind of omniscience in the narrator must surely be envisaged as an advance in the art of fiction.[1]

---

[1] Jean-Paul Sartre objects, theoretically, to omniscience in the novelist (see 'M. François Mauriac et la liberté', *Situations I*, Paris, 1947, pp. 36–57). He does, however, utilize the method in practice: we are allowed to 'enter the mind' of successive characters in *Les Chemins de la liberté*. What Sartre really dislikes, it would appear, is explicit judgment and comment by the author-narrator.

Should the novelist desire it, he is now freed from the pretence of obtaining his information by real-life methods. In practice, any novelist has always 'known' as much about a given character as he chose to 'know'; further knowledge, in this sphere, is only a matter of exercising imagination and invention. The omniscient-narrator technique recognizes this fact, and obviates the sometimes hampering necessity for the writer to observe real-life standards about his sources of knowledge. At the same time, of course, the novel becomes unmistakably a fiction, since in everyday life no one can be sure of knowing exactly what other people have thought and felt. It is something of a paradox, which critics of the novel generally fail to notice, that nineteenth-century 'realism' in fiction goes hand-in-hand with a narrative technique which abandons real-life criteria concerning the novelist's sources of knowledge and thus situates the business of story-telling overtly in the domain of art. This recognition that the novel belongs to art, this casting-off of the claim that it is a 'true' story, brings a new dignity to the genre. An element of masquerade is removed; fiction can be treated for what it is worth.

The eighteenth century had contributed to this development in another way, by producing novels which could be taken seriously as works of art. If the public and critics of the nineteenth century were prepared to discuss novels as literature, it is because a succession of eighteenth-century writers had shown that the novel could rise to the standards used for judging the literary merits of plays or poetry: beauty or fitness of style, coherence of structure, the effective working-out of a theme. The eighteenth-century novels we have analysed are all superior, in one of these respects at least, to practically all French novels before them. (*La Princesse de Clèves* is, as always, an honourable exception.) These criteria are purely literary, and concern style and presentation rather than subject-matter. In general terms, one can say that eighteenth-century novelists had found better methods of shaping and conveying a story than those used by their predecessors. At the level of plot-structure there is an ever-increasing number of writers who do not simply propel their characters from one adventure to the next, but can build up events to create a climax. Another obvious and important discovery is the standard of relevance, which finally banished the extraneous interpolated story. Beside this we can set other literary skills: the growing capacity for recognizing which incidents are proper material for a fully developed 'scene'; the effective use of dialogue to illuminate character as well as to advance the action; the willingness to depart from a neutral style if the story calls for a more poetic or a more colloquial mode of expression. These and similar developments are new skills in the handling of the story, regardless of its 'truth'. But a consequence of their exploitation is that as the novel becomes more artistic, a more effectively organized construct, it also becomes more attractive to the reader, more satisfying in its coherence and balance, and even, in a sense, more credible.

The simple view of artistic illusion held by many eighteenth-century writers no longer satisfies the modern theorist. It has been realized, for instance, that imaginative belief can vary in quality and intensity, depending on the various factors which appeal to the reader's interest and on the strength of that appeal.[1] We may—and this is the commonest form of 'belief'—become absorbed and emotionally involved in the characters themselves and their reactions. But in reading a work like *Candide*, this emotional response to the characters may be lacking. Instead it is the movement of ideas, shaped into a form which creates suspense and tension and resolutions, which provides an attraction and an excitement of its own. And since such philosophic or allegorical tales can lead us to accept, while reading, certain points of view we might reject in real life, there is some justification for concluding that these stories too, however unrealistic they may appear, can create an effect which merits the name of 'illusion'. Similarly, not only the content of a narrative but also its formal qualities can arouse expectations, appeal to our interests and desires, and help to hold us under the spell of the work. It is in this sense that we can see eighteenth-century improvements in the art of story-building as a factor contributing to the reader's belief.

In eighteenth-century theories of illusion, the onus of winning and maintaining belief is laid largely on the artist. If he has 'imitated nature' well, it is implied, then the observer or

[1] For an illuminating discussion of various types of appeal to the reader's interest, see Booth, *The Rhetoric of Fiction*, pp. 125–33.

reader will inevitably respond by believing. Here again modern theories have exposed fresh complications. The rôle of the observer, we can now see, is neither as passive nor as predictable as many early writers on the subject supposed. His response is, or should be, an active participation; and it is conditioned by his expectations, including his ideas concerning the kind of thing a picture, play or novel may be.

If we now ask ourselves not why certain eighteenth-century novels can still afford us some pleasure, but why practically all seventeenth-century novels are so irksome to read, the answer can be found in our expectations about both the subject-matter and the form of the novel as a genre. Over the last three centuries there has been an increasing emphasis on the exploration of the complexities of human life and on the working out of narrative methods which could effectively convey these complexities. The seventeenth-century novel, set against these later developments, presents a limited and implausible view of human nature, relayed in forms which appear both long-winded and clumsy. A student may, by faithful application to such works, come to familiarize himself with their norms and understand to some extent how and why they were enjoyed by contemporary readers. Without such efforts, the modern reader is generally cut off from the appreciation of works so foreign to his accepted standards.

The eighteenth-century novels we have discussed are, in the main, less remote and rebarbative. They already possess in varying degrees the qualities a modern reader expects from the novel. But to enjoy them fully, one may still need actively to co-operate and to make allowances—without disdain—for the writing habits of the age. It may be that through frequenting these and other eighteenth-century works, I have developed more sympathy and admiration for them than some of my readers will feel. This is a hazard inseparable from specialized studies. All I can hope is that the friendly reader, after this excursion through eighteenth-century fiction, has become aware of some merits which might otherwise have gone unperceived. There is no call to admire blindly, but we can at least try to extend our powers of appreciation, and learn to measure such works against the standards of their distant day as well as against those, no less relative, of our own. In the process we may well find that we have increased our willingness to accept and believe in such works of another age.

The willingness will not suffice, of course, unless the writer too has done his share in creating a fiction which can appeal in some way to our belief. And this is doubtless the moment to remind ourselves that however much the novelist may insist on his function as an historian, a recorder of reality or a purveyor of truth, he is ultimately a 'maker', one who creates fictitious life. The world of his books is not, and cannot be, the same as what we call the 'real world', if only because he has selected his matter and shaped it, while the reality is unsifted and not to be contained in a single literary form. What he creates is a structure embodying a partial version of human experience. That creation we can enjoy only if it stirs our interest and wins, by whatever means the use of language can afford, our imaginative belief. In this essential task of the novel, it was the writers of the eighteenth century who laid the foundations on which future generations were to build.

XV

Post-script:
Developments and Perspectives

W HAT has been going on in studies of the eighteenth-century French novel over the last two decades? And what may we look forward to in this field?

The most obvious change is in the sheer quantity of published work: the annual output of books and articles on the subject is nowadays at least three times as large as it used to be in the early 1960s. This phenomenon is not of course peculiar to our subject. It has affected all branches of learning, and can be attributed largely to the expansion of the universities—more teachers and research students mean more work submitted for publication.

If we take the amount that appears in print as a criterion of interest, we can establish a fairly clear ranking among the individual authors who have been discussed in this book. Diderot is the front-runner, followed by Prévost, Laclos and Marivaux; then comes Rousseau, with Crébillon and Rétif de la Bretonne on equal terms some way behind him; and trailing along as last in the popularity stakes are Lesage and Bernardin de Saint-Pierre.[1] This ordering, I imagine, reflects fairly accurately the tastes and interests of those who nowadays write about eighteenth-century French novels. The modern predilection for what is experimental, complex and rich in ambiguities would account for the stress on *Jacques le fataliste* and the relative neglect of *Paul et Virginie*. We should however keep in mind that the preferences of those who read but do not aspire to publish might well show a different pattern.

---

[1] This ranking is based on publications listed in *The Year's Work in Modern Languages* and the *Revue d'Histoire Littéraire de la France*. I took into account only each author's works of narrative fiction; so *Le Neveu de Rameau*, for instance, which is often placed in the 'fiction' category, was not included because it has no main story-line or plot.

273

The field of study itself is in a certain sense being broadened. Partly as a consequence of the amount of work being brought out on the well-known authors, some researchers in quest of fresh subjects have been turning their attention to novels which were previously neglected or forgotten. Thus there have been editions and/or studies of novels and tales by writers such as Duclos, Mme Riccoboni, Baculard d'Arnaud and Mme de Charrière. None of these, in my view, is as important as the work previously rediscovered by Frédéric Deloffre, Challe's *Les Illustres Françaises*. However, the novels of Mme de Charrière are of considerable interest. Though still embodying eighteenth-century narrative techniques, her novels bear comparison, if only to a limited extent, with those of Jane Austen. Mme de Charrière can be ironic, has discovered how to make small everyday incidents into 'events' in the plot, and has a critical awareness of the social hierarchy. The new edition of her works, together with editions of other neglected novels of the period, should make a wider range of fiction generally available.

The scope of the subject has been enlarged in other ways, by developments in kindred subjects. The history of printing and printers, and of various aspects of book-production— economic, legal, sociological— has made notable advances. Some of these explorations are not as remote from the study of literary forms and values as might at first appear. Matters of apparently insignificant detail, such as the history of punctuation practice, may throw light on the articulation and rhythm of a given author's prose, or illustrate the increasing importance of dialogue.[1] At another level, historical information about the effects of censorship has a bearing on what writers felt they could safely say in officially authorized books, and what they chose to publish by clandestine methods. It is worth recalling, for instance, that *Les Liaisons dangereuses* went through the official procedures: it was submitted in manuscript to be read by one of the royal censors, and the printer received a *permission tacite* for its publication—so neither Laclos nor the authori-

---

[1] See, for example, J. Proust, 'La Ponctuation des textes de Diderot', *Romanische Forschungen*, 90 (1978), pp. 369–87; and my article on 'The Punctuation of dialogue in eighteenth-century French and English fiction', *The Library*, Sixth series, 1 (1979), pp. 43–61.

ties considered the book to be flagrantly immoral.[1] New bibliographies, too, can contribute directly or indirectly to our understanding of what was going on in the domain of fiction. Statistics of re-editions, for instance, if used with due caution, can serve as a criterion of the relative popularity of various works, and this in turn may help to explain certain fashions or trends among writers. Just as the success of *La Nouvelle Héloïse* encouraged some novelists to opt for the letter-form, so the comparable success of Marmontel's *Contes moraux* (1761) doubtless led various other authors to produce third-person tales, or even novels, about manners-and-morals. The rise in the literary status of the novel is likewise reflected in statistics: by the late 1790s the number of new novels carrying the author's name on the title-page was at last regularly exceeding the number of works published anonymously or under a pseudonym.[2] The study of different aspects of book-production has thus proved fruitful for our subject in a surprisingly varied range of ways.

As for literary history and criticism, a number of important works have appeared. (A selection of these is listed below, in the Supplement to the Bibliography.) Of particular relevance to this study are the books which offer a general view of the period. Henri Coulet's historical account, for instance, includes discussion of romances and tales, as well as dealing with novels which aspire to portray the real world.[3] English Showalter, on the other hand, has concentrated on some of the specific ways in which 'realism' gradually gained ground between 1640 and 1782.[4] Works of this kind have provided some new perspectives on eighteenth-century fiction.

Many of the recent publications follow a fairly traditional pattern—and I use the word 'traditional' in no derogatory sense. However, the most striking development during the last twenty years or so has undoubtedly been the flowering of the New Criticism. The phrase is something of a misnomer, since it

[1] The *permission tacite* was usually accorded to books which, while not qualifying for the official *approbation*, were not thought to be dangerously subversive or corrupting.

[2] A. Martin, V. Mylne, R. Frautschi, *Bibliographie du genre romanesque*, pp. xlii-xliv.

[3] Henri Coulet, *Le Roman jusqu'à la Révolution*, Paris, 1967.

[4] English Showalter, *The Evolution of the French novel*, Princeton, 1972.

may suggest a certain homogeneity of theory and method which does not in fact exist, and since some of the 'new' approaches were being exploited well before 1960 and have their roots in systems such as Russian formalism or Saussurian linguistics, which go back to the early years of the century. For the purpose of this discussion we need to distinguish between two kinds of theory which have emerged from the New Criticism: general theories about the nature of the literary work and how it should be read and studied; and one specific branch of literary research, the theory of the novel.

This is not the place for an exposition or evaluation of the various fresh ideas about literature and literary criticism which have gained a following not only in France but elsewhere in Europe and also in North America.[1] The effect of these ideas, as regards our particular subject, can be seen both in a tendency to question or reject some long-established critical practices, and in a widespread (but by no means unanimous) willingness to try out new approaches. The factor which is common to the majority of such studies is the application to literature of concepts or methods which were initially evolved in some other field of learning: linguistics, semiotics, philosophy, sociology, etc. I shall discuss some examples shortly.

Work on the theory of the novel has developed in a variety of ways. This subject comes into the purview of what is nowadays referred to in France as 'la poétique', taking the word in the sense of Aristotle's *Poetics*, as the study of the nature and potentialities of a given kind of literary work. Certain scholars, notably Gérard Genette, have analysed procedures such as the novelist's handling of different planes of time, the possible types of narrative voice, etc.[2] Some academics object to the 'poétique' approach because they find it 'arid' or 'sterile' or 'pseudo-scientific', and because some of its exponents use a terminology which involves a variety of 'pretentious' neologisms. Such objections, in my view, show a certain failure to understand the purpose of these discussions of theory. Narrative

---

[1] There is now a small but steady trickle of books which explain and compare and evaluate the writings of the New Critics, e.g. Josué V. Harari (editor), *Textual strategies. Perspectives in Post-structuralist Criticism*, New York, 1979, and London, 1980.

[2] G. Genette, *Figures III*, Paris, 1972. A bibliography of the most important theoretical studies can be found in Mieke Bal, *Narratologie*, Paris, 1977. For a good general introduction to the subject, see R. Bourneuf and R. Ouellet, *L'Univers du roman*, Paris, 1972.

fiction has for far too long been written about in ways which do not adequately distinguish it from drama. The attempt to clarify those procedures which are peculiar to the novel is therefore justifiable, and the creation of a technical vocabulary, to avoid the use of ambiguous and overworked terms, is equally defensible. This does not mean, of course, that all scholars can be expected to find 'la poétique du roman' an interesting subject; nor even that those of us who do enjoy it will necessarily relish all the new terms which have been coined for our benefit.

The investigation of narrative methods is obviously important to eighteenth-century fiction, in which the evolution of memoir-novels and letter-novels is a central issue. First-person narrative as found in our memoir-novels has been the subject of several studies, of which I shall cite just three. In *Narcisse romancier* Jean Rousset divides his treatment into two parts: first a section which is largely theoretical, and secondly the 'applied' section, discussing how the narrative 'je' is handled by specific novelists such as Challe, Prévost and Marivaux.[1] René Démoris, taking a different line, is concerned with historical trends in the development of the memoir-novel, which he relates not only to the parallel literary phenomenon of authentic autobiography, but also to the social attitudes of the period.[2] As for Philip Stewart's discussion of 'the art of makebelieve', this concentrates on the devices and techniques of the first-person novelist as they are to be found in a wide range of memoir-novels.[3] Here, as in the book by Démoris, general notions about the resources of first-person narrative emerge as conclusions from the detailed study of a large body of texts.

The letter-novel, more closely linked to a specifically eighteenth-century context, has also inspired a certain amount of research, both as to theory and practice.[4] *Les Liaisons dan-*

[1] Jean Rousset, *Narcisse romancier*, Paris, 1973.

[2] René Démoris, *Le Roman à la première personne*, Paris, 1975. Démoris provides a basic bibliography of first-person narrative, to which one can now add: P. Lejeune, *Je est un autre: l'autobiographie, de la littérature aux médias*, Paris, 1980.

[3] Philip Stewart, *Imitation and illusion in the French memoir-novel, 1700–1750*, New Haven and London, 1969.

[4] See François Jost, 'Le roman épistolaire et la technique narrative au XVIIIe siècle', *Comparative Literature Studies*, 3 (1966), pp. 397–427; and 'L'évolution d'un genre: le roman épistolaire dans les lettres occidentales',

gereuses in particular has prompted a number of books and articles since the mid-1960s. As a way of illustrating the variety of current approaches to eighteenth-century fiction, I shall therefore give a brief outline of a selection of these studies. (The titles which follow have been chosen chiefly because they represent certain types of criticism, not necessarily for their intrinsic merit; some very worthwhile studies have in fact been omitted.)

Two works which appeared in 1967 and 1968 respectively might be taken to epitomize the extremes of the new and the traditional.[1] Tzvetan Todorov is one of the few writers amongst the recognized early practitioners of 'la Nouvelle Critique' who has dealt with eighteenth-century fiction. (Admittedly Roland Barthes did write an essay on Sade; but as Sade's novels offer a dream—or nightmare—world which has little to do with the representation of reality, neither the novels nor Barthes' essay need concern us here.) In *Littérature et signification* Todorov looks at *Les Liaisons dangereuses* 'dans la perspective de la poétique'. He uses the conceptual framework of structuralism and semiology, considering the letters, for instance, as objects with a social significance over and above their meaning as texts made up of words; he also raises the theoretical problems involved in analysing plot-structure. His brief compact book is in striking contrast to the massive volume produced by Laurent Versini as the published form of the traditional scholarly thesis prepared for a doctorate. Though he does devote some space to questions of technique, Versini demonstrates above all his detailed knowledge of the historical and literary context in which Laclos wrote the novel. Both these works would seem to be addressed to the specialist rather than to the general reader.

One may also note that they provoked an echo, in eighteenth-century studies, of the more widely publicized polemics over

---

Essais de littérature comparée, Urbana, 1969, pp. 89–179; also René Ouellet, 'La théorie du roman épistolaire en France au XVIIIe siècle', *Studies on Voltaire and the eighteenth century*, Banbury, 1972, Vol. LXXXIX, pp. 1209–27; and Janet Altman, *Epistolarity: approaches to a form* (Unpublished Ph.D. thesis, Yale University), 1973.

[1] Tzvetan Todorov, *Littérature et signification*, Paris 1967; Laurent Versini, *Laclos et la tradition. Essai sur les sources et la technique des Liaisons dangereuses*, Paris, 1968.

'la Nouvelle Critique'. Maurice Roelens criticized Versini for suggesting that the form and the content of the novel could be envisaged separately; and Versini responded with a defence of Laclos's conscious choice of a form, and an ironic attack on 'La Nouvelle Scolastique', including works such as Todorov's.[1]

By 1972, one could apparently assume that undergraduates, in France at least, were familiar with the concepts and the vocabulary of some of the new approaches to the literary work. In his monograph on *Les Liaisons dangereuses* in the 'Poche critique' series, Henri Blanc takes it for granted that the student can deal with terms such as 'discours métalinguistique' or 'fonction référentielle', which would never have been employed in this type of context ten or twenty years previously.[2] The study of Laclos by René Pomeau, in another series destined primarily for university students, shows a more thorough blending of new and traditional resources, and his bibliography covers a wide spectrum of possible approaches.[3]

During the 1970s, various critics have chosen one particular aspect of the novel as the focus of their examination. Christine Belcikowski looks at the elements she finds poetic (but not in the Aristotelian sense), such as myth and revery, with Bachelard and Foucault among her sources of reference. The title of another study, in which Freud comes into his own, is self-explanatory: *Eros and Power in Les Liaisons dangereuses, a Study in Evil*. And Laclos figures in several thematic and comparative studies: Peter Brooks treats the novel as an important example of *mondanité*; Alexandrian sets Laclos between Sade and Fourier in a series of essays on precursors of the current struggle for freedom of sexual behaviour, while Nancy Miller deals with the work as one of a group of 'feminocentric' novels.[4]

[1] M. Roelens, 'Le texte et ses "conditions d'existence": l'exemple des "Liaisons dangereuses"', *Littérature*, 1 (1971), pp. 73–81; L. Versini 'Laclos épistolier ou la préméditation', *Cahiers de l'Association Internationale d'études françaises*, 29 (1977), pp. 187–203.

[2] Henri Blanc, *Les Liaisons dangereuses de Choderlos de Laclos*, Paris, 1972.

[3] René Pomeau, *Laclos*, Paris, 1975.

[4] Christine Belcikowksi, *Poétique des Liaisons dangereuses*, Paris, 1972; Suellen Diaconoff, *Eros and Power in Les Liaisons dangereuses*, Geneva and Paris, 1979; Peter Brooks, *The Novel of Worldliness*, Princeton, 1969; Alexandrian, *Les Libérateurs de l'amour*, Paris, 1977; Nancy K. Miller, *The Heroine's text*, New York, 1980.

To close with, we may consider three widely disparate pieces of work. Laurent Versini has produced a new critical edition of the novel in a volume of *Œuvres complètes* which includes some fresh writings by Laclos and a meticulously thorough annotation of the whole corpus. Irving Wohlforth looks at a range of critical arguments about Laclos and subjects them in turn to critical apprasial, at a level of discourse which invokes Hegel and Kierkegaard on the knotty problem of irony.[1] And finally we have an anthology called, appropriately, *Critical approaches to Les Liaisons dangereuses*, which ranges from the simple and out-dated to the sophisticated, innovatory and esoteric.[2] A list of key-phrases from the titles of some of the articles in this collection is enough to convey an impression of their variety: 'Profile of the writer', 'The status of evil', 'Authors and actors: the characters', 'Balancing a closed ecological system', 'Suspense structures', 'A communicational approach'.

There are obvious gaps in this summary account of recent work on *Les Liaisons dangereuses*; I have barely touched, for instance, on the forty to fifty articles in learned journals. One might argue, moreover, that this particular novel attracts certain types of approach—the structural, the feminist— which other novels in our canon are less likely to invite. In spite of these reservations, the quantity and variety of these Laclos studies do serve to illustrate a general state of affairs: interest in the eighteenth-century French novel shows no signs of flagging; and critics see it as fit material for fresh experimental methods of analysis as well as for more conventional approaches.

Before concluding, I ought perhaps to make plain my own views on the matter of method. In principle I am for allowing the critic or theorist complete freedom to choose his own approach. My only proviso, made necessary by the exploiting of methods drawn from other disciplines, is that a critic who uses extra-literary concepts and terms in a discussion intended for the non-specialist should adequately explain those concepts and terms. But faced with any type of criticism or theory, it

---

[1] Irving Wohlforth, 'The irony of criticism and the criticism of irony: a study of Laclos criticism', *Studies on Voltaire and the eighteenth century*, Banbury 1974, Vol. CXX, pp. 269–317.

[2] Lloyd R. Free (editor), *Critical approaches to Les Liaisons dangereuses*, Madrid, 1978.

is eventually up to the reader, who must himself be critically alert, to decide whether a given study does contribute in some way to a better understanding of the literary text, or whether it is confused, illogical, irrelevant, pretentious, simplistic or bombastic—failings which one may come across in 'new' and traditional critics alike.

As for future developments, my own interest in aspects of form and technique leads me to hope for further investigations into the theory of the novel, with eighteenth-century texts being used as source-material or illustrations. There is still scope for investigation of the whole business of characterization, for instance, or the ways in which the novelist uses dialogue. The evolution of third-person narrative in both *conte* and *roman* throughout the period also calls for attention, as do the conventions of plot-building. For those of us who are caught up in the fascination of the 'Siècle des Lumières', there is still a challenge in the prospect of dispersing some of the shadows and uncertainties in the unexplored regions of its worlds of fiction.

Select Bibliography

(The place of publication is Paris unless otherwise stated)

NOVELS

Editions referred to in this study

BEAUMONT, MME ELIE DE, *Lettres du marquis de Roselle*, 1764.

CRÉBILLON *fils*, *Les Egarements du cœur et de l'esprit* (1736–8), ed. Etiemble, Bibliothèque de Cluny, 1961.

— *Les Heureux Orphelins* (1754), in *Œuvres complètes*, London, 1772, Vol. V.

— *Lettres de la marquise de M**** (1732), in *Œuvres*, ed. Pierre Lièvre, 1930, Vol. IV.

DIDEROT, DENIS, *Jacques le Fataliste*, in *Œuvres romanesques*, ed. H. Bénac, Garnier, 1951.

— *La Religieuse*, ibid.

LACLOS, CHODERLOS DE, *Les Liaisons dangereuses* (1782), ed. Y. Le Hir, Garnier, 1952.

LESAGE, ALAIN RENÉ, *Histoire de Gil Blas de Santillane* (1715–34), ed. M. Bardon, Garnier, 1955.

MARIVAUX, CHAMBLAIN DE, *Le Paysan parvenu* (1734–5), ed. F. Deloffre, Garnier, 1959.

— *La Vie de Marianne* (1731–42), ed. F. Deloffre, Garnier, 1957.

PRÉVOST, ABBÉ ANTOINE-FRANÇOIS, *Le Doyen de Killerine* (1735–40), 1784.

— *Histoire du chevalier des Grieux et de Manon Lescaut* (1731), ed. F. Deloffre and R. Picard, Garnier, 1969.

— *Mémoires et aventures d'un Homme de Qualité*, Amsterdam, 1728–31.

— *Le Philosophe anglois, ou Histoire de Monsieur Cleveland*, 1731–9.

RESTIF DE LA BRETONNE, *Le Paysan perverti*, 1775.

— *Le Paysan et la paysanne pervertis*, 1787.

— *La Paysanne pervertie*, 1784.

ROUSSEAU, JEAN-JACQUES, *Julie, ou la Nouvelle Héloïse* (1761), ed. R. Pomeau, Garnier, 1960.

SAINT-PIERRE, BERNARDIN DE, *Paul et Virginie* (1787), ed. P. Trahard, Garnier, 1958.

CRITICISM AND THEORY

Works written before 1800

ARGENS, JEAN BAPTISTE D', 'Discours sur les nouvelles', *Lectures amusantes*, La Haye, 1739.

ARNAUD, F. T. A. DE BACULARD D', *Nouvelles historiques*, 1774, *Préface*.

BAYLE, PIERRE, *Dictionnaire historique et critique*, La Haye, 1697, Article: *Jardins*.

BELLEGARDE, ABBÉ J.-B. MORVAN DE, *Lettres curieuses de littérature et de morale*, 1702.

BENOIST, MME FRANÇOISE-ALBIN PUZIN DE LA MARTINIÈRE, *Agathe et Isidore*, 1768, *Préface*.

CHAPELAIN, JEAN, *Opuscules critiques*, ed. A. C. Hunter, 1936.

DEFOE, DANIEL, *A New Family Instructor*, London, 1727.

DESFONTAINES, ABBÉ PIERRE FRANÇOIS GUYOT, *Histoire de Dom Juan de Portugal*, 1724, *Préface*.

— *Observations sur les écrits modernes*, 1735, Vol. III.

DESMARETS DE SAINT-SORLIN, *Rosanne*, 1639, *Préface*.

DIDEROT, DENIS, *Œuvres esthétiques*, ed. P. Vernière, Garnier, 1959.

DRYDEN, JOHN, *Of Dramatic Poesy and Other Critical Essays*, ed. G. Watson, London, 1962, 2 vols.

DUCLOS, CHARLES PINOT, *Lettre à l'auteur de 'Madame de Luz'*, La Haye, 1741.

FLORIAN, J. P. C. DE, 'Essai sur la pastorale', pre-fixed to *Estelle*, 1787.

FRÉRON, ELIE, *L'Année littéraire* (1754–90), 1760, Vol. III.

HUET, DANIEL, *Traité de l'origine des romans* (1670), ed. A. Kok, Amsterdam, 1942.

JACQUIN, ABBÉ ARMAND PIERRE, *Entretiens sur les romans*, 1755.

Journal de Trévoux (1701–67), 1703.

LA CALPRENÈDE, GAUTIER DE COSTE DE, *Faramond*, 1661–70, *Avis au lecteur*.

LA PORTE, ABBÉ JOSEPH DE, *Observations sur la littérature moderne* (1749–52), 1751, Vol. V.

LENGLET DU FRESNOY, NICOLAS-ALEXANDRE (pseud. 'Gordon de Percel'), *De l'Usage des romans*, Amsterdam, 1734, 2 vols.

SCUDÉRY, MADELEINE DE, *Ibrahim*, 1641, *Préface*.

SEGRAIS, JEAN REGNAULT DE, *Les Nouvelles françoises*, 1656–7, 2 vols.

SOREL, CHARLES, *De la Connoissance des bons livres*, 1671.

SUBLIGNY, ADRIEN-THOMAS PERDOU DE, *La Fausse Clélie*, Amsterdam, 1671, *Préface*.

Since 1800

ADAM, ANTOINE, *Histoire de la littérature française au XVIIe siècle*, 1949–56, 5 vols.

ALDRIDGE, A. O., *Essai sur les personnages des Liaisons dangereuses en tant que types littéraires*, 1960 (Archives des lettres modernes, no. 31).

ALLOTT, M., *Novelists on the Novel*, London, 1959.

ARLAND, MARCEL, *Marivaux*, 1950.

ATKINSON, G., *The Extraordinary Voyage in French Literature before 1700*, New York, 1920.

AUERBACH, ERICH, *Mimesis*, Berne, 1946.

BÉGUÉ, ARMAND, *Etat présent des études sur Rétif de la Bretonne*, 1948.

BELLENOT, JEAN-LOUIS, 'Les formes de l'amour dans la Nouvelle Héloïse, et la signification des personnages de Julie et de Saint-Preux', *Annales Jean-Jacques Rousseau*, Geneva, XXXIII (1953–5).

BERNARDIN, N.-M., *Un Précurseur de Racine, Tristan l'Hermite*, 1895.

BLACK, FRANK G., *The Epistolary Novel in the Late Eighteenth Century*, Univ. of Oregon, 1940.

BOOTH, WAYNE C., *The Rhetoric of Fiction*, Chicago, 1961.

— 'The self-conscious narrator in comic fiction before *Tristram Shandy*', *Publications of the Modern Language Association*, 67 (1952), pp. 163–85.

BRUNEAU, CHARLES, 'L'Image dans notre langue littéraire', *Mélanges de linguistique offerts à Albert Dauzat*, 1951.

CHADOURNE, Marc, *Restif de la Bretonne ou le siècle prophétique*, 1958.

CHANDLER, F. W., *Romances of Roguery*, London, 1899.

CHASSANG, A., *L'Histoire du roman et de ses rapports avec l'histoire dans l'antiquité grecque et latine*, 1862.

CHERPACK, CLIFTON, *An Essay on Crébillon fils*, Duke University Press, N. Carolina, 1962.

CLARETIE, LÉO, *Essai sur Lesage romancier*, 1890.

CROCKER, LESTER G., '*Jacques le Fataliste*, an "expérience morale" ', *Diderot Studies III*, ed. O. E. Fellows and G. May, Geneva, 1961.

CROSBY, EMILY A., *Une Romancière oubliée, Mme Riccoboni*, 1924.

DALLAS, D. F., *Le Roman français de 1660 à 1680*, 1932.

DELOFFRE, FRÉDÉRIC, 'Une Mode préstendhalien d'expression de la sensibilité à la fin du XVIIe siècle', *Cahiers de l'Association Internationale des études françaises*, no. 11, 1959, pp. 9–32.

— 'Le problème de l'illusion romanesque et le renouvellement des techniques narratives entre 1700 et 1715', *La Littérature narrative d'imagination*, Presses Universitaires, 1961 (Colloque de Strasbourg), pp. 115–29.

DIECKMANN, HERBERT, 'The Préface-Annexe of La Religieuse', *Diderot Studies II*, ed. O. E. Fellows and N. L. Torrey, Syracuse, 1952.

DULONG, GUSTAVE, *L'Abbé de Saint-Réal. Etude sur les rapports de l'histoire et du roman au XVIIe siècle*, 1921, 2 vols.

ELLIS, M. B., *Julie: or, La Nouvelle Héloïse: a synthesis of Rousseau's thought (1749–1759)*, Toronto, 1949.

ELLRICH, R. J., 'The Rhetoric of "La Religieuse" ', *Diderot Studies III*, ed. O. E. Fellows and G. May, Geneva, 1961.

ENGEL, CLAIRE-ELIANE, 'L'Abbé Prévost et Jean-Jacques Rousseau', *Annales Jean-Jacques Rousseau*, Geneva, XXVIII (1939–40).

ETIENNE, E., *Le Genre romanesque en France depuis l'apparition de la 'Nouvelle Héloïse' jusqu'aux approches de la Révolution*, Brussels, 1922 (Mémoires de l'Académie de Belgique, 2e série, Vol. XVII).

FABRE, J., 'Une question de terminologie littéraire: *Paul et Virginie*, pastorale', *Etudes de littérature moderne*, II (1953), Faculté de Lettres de Toulouse.

FELLOWS, O. E., AND GREEN, ALICE G., 'Diderot and the Abbé Dulaurens', *Diderot Studies*, ed. O. E. Fellows and N. L. Torrey, Syracuse, 1949.

GOVE, P. B., *The Imaginary Voyage in Prose Fiction*, 2nd edition, London, 1961.

GREEN, ALICE G., 'Diderot's fictional worlds', *Diderot Studies*, ed. O. E. Fellows and N. L. Torrey, Syracuse, 1949.

GREEN, F. C., *French Novelists, Manners and Ideas from the Renaissance to the Revolution*, London, 1928.

— *Jean-Jacques Rousseau*, Cambridge, 1955.

GREEN, F. C., *Minuet*, London, 1935.

— 'The eighteenth-century French critic and the contemporary novel', *Modern Language Review*, XXIII (1928), pp. 174–87.

— 'Some observations on technique and form in the French seventeenth-and eighteenth-century novel', *Stil- und Formprobleme in der Literatur*, Heidelberg, 1959, pp. 208–15 (International Federation for Modern Language and Literature, 7th Congress).

GRIMSLEY, R., 'L'Ambiguité dans l'œuvre romanesque de Diderot', *Cahiers de l'Association Internationale des Etudes Françaises* (no. 13), Paris, 1961, pp. 223–38.

— *Jean-Jacques Rousseau*, Cardiff, 1961.

GUYON, BERNARD, (editor), *La Nouvelle Héloïse*, in Rousseau, *Œuvres complètes*, Vol. II, Bibliothèque de la Pléiade, 1961.

GUYON, BERNARD, 'Un chef-d'œuvre méconnu: "Julie" ', *Cahiers du Sud*, 49 (1962).

HAINSWORTH, GEORGE, *Les 'Novelas exemplares' de Cervantes en France au XVIIe siècle*, 1933 (Bibliothèque de la Revue de littérature comparée, no. 95).

HAZARD, PAUL, *La Crise de la conscience européenne (1680–1815)*, 1935, 3 vols.

— *Etudes critiques sur Manon Lescaut*, Chicago, 1929.

HOVENKAMP, J. W., *Mérimée et la couleur locale*, 1928.

IKNAYAN, M., *The Idea of the Novel in France: the critical reaction, 1815–1848*, 1961.

JONES, S. PAUL, *A List of French Prose Fiction from 1700 to 1750*, New York, 1939.

KANY, CHARLES E., *The Beginnings of the Epistolary Novel in France, Italy and Spain*, Berkeley, California, 1937.

LASSERRE, EUGÈNE, *Manon Lescaut de l'Abbé Prévost*, 1930.

LE BRETON, ANDRÉ, *Le Roman français au XVIIIe siècle*, 1898.

LEGRAS, PIERRE, 'Le Naufrage du Saint-Géran, histoire et légende', *Album de l'Ile de la Réunion*, ed. A. Roussin, Saint-Denis, 1863, III, 177–92.

McKILLOP, A. D. *The Early Masters of English Fiction*, Lawrence, 1956.

MAGENDIE, M., *Le Roman français au XVIIe siècle*, 1932.

MAIGRON, LOUIS, *Le Roman historique à l'époque romantique*, 1912.

MAJOR, JOHN C., *The Role of Personal Memoirs in English Biography and Novel*, Philadelphia, 1935.

MALRAUX, ANDRÉ, 'Laclos', *Tableau de la littérature française, XVIIe–XVIIIe siècles*, Gallimard, 1937.

MASSON, PIERRE-MAURICE, 'Contribution à l'étude de la prose métrique dans la *Nouvelle Héloïse*', *Annales Jean-Jacques Rousseau*, Geneva, V (1909).

MAY, GEORGES, *Diderot et 'La Religieuse'*, 1954.

— *Le Dilemme du roman au XVIIIe siècle. Etude sur les rapports du roman et de la critique (1715–1761)*, 1963.

— 'L'Histoire a-t-elle engendré le roman?', *Revue d'histoire littéraire de la France*, LV (1955), pp. 155–76.

— 'Le Maître, la chaîne et le chien dans *Jacques le Fataliste*', *Cahiers de l'Association Internationale des Etudes Françaises* (no. 13), Paris, 1961, pp. 269–82.

MERLANT, JOACHIM, *Le Roman personnel de Rousseau à Fromentin*, 1905.

MORNET, DANIEL, (editor), Rousseau, *La Nouvelle Héloïse*, 1925, 4 vols., Vol. I, Introduction.

— 'Les Enseignements des bibliothèques privées, 1750–1780', *Revue d'histoire littéraire de la France*, XVII, 1910, pp. 449–96.

MORRISSETTE, B. A., *The Life and Works of Marie-Catherine Desjardins (Mme de Villedieu)*, Saint Louis, 1947.

MYLNE, VIVIENNE, 'Structure and symbolism in *Gil Blas*', *French Studies*, XV (1961), pp. 134–45.

— 'Truth and illusion in the Préface-Annexe to Diderot's *La Religieuse*', *Modern Language Review*, LVII (1962), pp. 350–6.

OSMONT, R., 'Remarques sur la genèse et la composition de la *Nouvelle Héloïse*', *Annales Jean-Jacques Rousseau*, Geneva, XXXIII (1953–5).

PARRISH, J. (editor), Diderot, *La Religieuse*, édition critique, Geneva, 1963 (Studies on Voltaire and the Eighteenth Century, Vol. XXII).

PICARD, RAYMOND, 'L'Univers de "Manon Lescaut"', *Mercure de France*, 1961. avril, pp. 606–22; mai, pp. 87–105.

POULET, GEORGES, *Etudes sur le temps humain*, 1952, 2 vols.

RATNER, MOSES, *Theory and Criticism of the Novel in France from L'Astrée to 1750*, New York, 1938.

REYNIER, GUSTAVE, *Le Roman sentimental avant l'Astrée*, 1908.

RODDIER, HENRI, *L'Abbé Prévost, l'homme et l'œuvre*, 1955.

ROUSSET, JEAN, *Forme et Signification*, 1964.

SARTRE, JEAN-PAUL, *Situations I*, 1947.

SCHINZ, A., *La pensée de Jean-Jacques Rousseau*, 1929.

SEYLAZ, JEAN-LUC, *Les Liaisons dangereuses et la création romanesque chez Laclos*, 1958.

SINGER, G. F., *The Epistolary Novel*, Philadelphia, 1933.

SPITZER, LEO, 'A Propos de la *Vie de Marianne*', *Romanic Review*, XLIV (1953), pp. 102–26.

THELANDER, DOROTHY R., *Laclos and the Epistolary Novel*, Geneva, 1963.

TIEJE, A. J., 'A peculiar phase of the theory of realism in pre-Richardsonian fiction', *Publications of the Modern Language Association*, 28 (1913), pp. 213–52.

ULLMANN, S., *Style in the French Novel*, Cambridge, 1957.

WAGNER, N., 'Quelques cadres d'études pour "Gil Blas"', *L'Information Littéraire*, VIII (1956), pp. 29–38.

WATT, IAN, *The Rise of the Novel*, London, 1957.

WILCOX, F. H., *Prévost's Translations of Richardson's Novels*, Berkeley, California, 1927.

WOODBRIDGE, B. M., *Gatien de Courtilz, Sieur du Verger*, 1925.

SUPPLEMENT

BLANC, HENRI, *Les Liaisons dangereuses de Choderlos de Laclos*, Hachette, Collection Poche critique, 1972.

BOURNEUF, ROLAND, and RENÉ OUELLET, *L'Univers du roman*, Presses Universitaires de France, Collection SUP, 1972.

BROOKS, PETER, *The Novel of Worldliness: Crébillon, Marivaux, Laclos, Stendhal*, Princeton, 1969.

COULET, HENRI, *Marivaux romancier. Essai sur l'esprit et le coeur dans les romans de Marivaux*, 1975.

—*Le Roman jusqu'à la Révolution*, Armand Colin, Collection U, 1967.

DÉMORIS, RENÉ, *Le Roman à la première personne, du classicisme aux Lumières*, 1975.

FORT, BERNADETTE, *Le Langage de l'ambiguïté dans l'œuvre de Crébillon fils*, 1978.

FREE, LLOYD R. (editor), *Critical approaches to Les Liaisons dangereuses*, Madrid, 1978.

FUNKE, HANS-GÜNTER, *Crébillon fils als Moralist und Gesellschaftskritiker*, Heidelberg, 1972.

GIRAUD, YVES, *Bibliographie du roman épistolaire en France des origines à 1842*, Fribourg, 1977.

GODENNE, RENÉ, *Histoire de la nouvelle française aux XVIIe et XVIIIe siècles*, Geneva, 1970.

LAUFER, ROGER (editor), Lesage, *Histoire de Gil Blas de Santillane*, Garnier-Flammarion, 1977.

LECERCLE, JEAN-LOUIS, *Rousseau et l'art du roman*, 1969.

LECOINTRE, SIMONE and JEAN LE GALLIOT (editors), Diderot, *Jacques le fataliste et son maître*, Paris and Geneva, 1976.

LEVER, MAURICE, *La Fiction narrative en prose au XVIIe siècle. Répertoire bibliographique du genre romanesque en France*, 1976.

MARTIN, ANGUS, VIVIENNE MYLNE and RICHARD FRAUTSCHI, *Bibliographie du genre romanesque français, 1751–1800*, London, 1977.

MAY, GEORGES, H. DIECKMANN et al. (editors). *La Religieuse*, in Diderot, *Œuvres complètes*, Vol. V, 1975.

MEAD, W., *Jean-Jacques Rousseau ou le romancier enchaîné*, New Jersey and Paris, 1966.

MYLNE, VIVIENNE, *Diderot: La Religieuse*, London, 1981.

PARKER, ALEXANDER A., *Literature and the Delinquent. The picaresque novel in Spain and Europe, 1599–1753*, Edinburgh, 1967.

PICARD, L. (editor), Crébillon fils, *Lettres de la marquise de M****, 1970.

POMEAU, RENÉ, *Laclos*, Hatier, Collection Connaissance des lettres, 1975.

PORTER, CHARLES A., *Restif's novels, or an Autobiography in search of an author*, New Haven and London, 1967.

Roman et lumières au XVIIIe siècle, Centre d'Etudes et de recherches marxistes, 1970.

ROSBOTTOM, RONALD C., *Marivaux's novels. Theme and function in early eighteenth-century narrative,* New Jersey and London, 1974.

ROUSSET, JEAN, *Narcisse romancier,* 1973.

SGARD, JEAN (General editor), Prévost, *Œuvres,* 1978–.

—*Prévost romancier,* 1968.

SHOWALTER, ENGLISH, *The Evolution of the French novel, 1641–1782,* Princeton, 1972.

STEWART, PHILIP R., *Imitation and illusion in the French memoir-novel, 1700–1750. The art of makebelieve,* New Haven and London, 1969.

—*Le masque et la parole. Le langage de l'amour au XVIIIe siècle,* 1973.

TESTUD, PIERRE, *Rétif de la Bretonne et la création littéraire,* Geneva and Paris, 1977.

TODOROV, TZVETAN, *Littérature et signification,* 1967.

VERSINI, LAURENT (editor), Laclos, *Œuvres complètes,* Gallimard, Bibliothèque de la Pléiade, 1979.

—*Laclos et la tradition. Essai sur les sources et la technique des Liaisons dangereuses,* 1968.

WALTER, ERIC, *Jacques le fataliste de Diderot,* Hachette, Collection Poche critique, 1975.

Index

(The titles of novels are indexed under authors)